COOK IT IN CAST IRON

Kitchen-Tested Recipes for the One Pan That Does It All

THE EDITORS AT AMERICA'S TEST KITCHEN

CONTENTS

Cinnamon Buns

WELCOME TO AMERICA'S TEST KITCHEN

This book has been tested, written, and edited by the folks at America's Test Kitchen. Located in Boston's Seaport District in the historic Innovation and Design Building, it features 15,000 square feet of kitchen space including multiple photography and video studios. It is the home of *Cook's Illustrated* magazine and *Cook's Country* magazine and is the workday destination for more than 60 test cooks, editors, and cookware specialists. Our mission is to test recipes over and over again until we understand how and why they work and until we arrive at the best version.

We start the process of testing a recipe with a complete lack of preconceptions, which means that we accept no claim, no technique, and no recipe at face value. We simply assemble as many variations as possible, test a half-dozen of the most promising, and taste the results blind. We then construct our own recipe and continue to test it, varying ingredients, techniques, and cooking times until we reach a consensus. As we like to say in the test kitchen, "We make the mistakes so you don't have to." The result, we hope, is the best version of a particular recipe, but we realize that only you can be the final judge of our success (or failure). We use the same rigorous approach when we test equipment and taste ingredients.

All of this would not be possible without a belief that good cooking, much like good music, is based on a foundation of objective technique. Some people like spicy foods and others don't, but there is a right way to sauté, there is a best way to cook a pot roast, and there are measurable scientific principles involved in producing perfectly beaten, stable egg whites. Our ultimate goal is to investigate the fundamental principles of cooking to give you the techniques, tools, and ingredients you need to become a better cook. It is as simple as that.

To see what goes on behind the scenes at America's Test Kitchen, check out our social media channels for kitchen snapshots, exclusive content, video tips, and much more. You can watch us work (in our actual test kitchen) by tuning in to *America's Test Kitchen* or *Cook's Country* on public television or on our websites. Listen in to test kitchen experts on public radio (SplendidTable.org) to hear insights that illuminate the truth about real home cooking. Want to hone your cooking skills or finally learn how to bake—with an America's Test Kitchen test cook? Enroll in one of our online cooking classes. However you choose to visit us, we welcome you into our kitchen, where you can stand by our side as we test our way to the best recipes in America.

FACEBOOK.COM/AMERICASTESTKITCHEN
TWITTER.COM/TESTKITCHEN
YOUTUBE.COM/AMERICASTESTKITCHEN
INSTAGRAM.COM/TESTKITCHEN
PINTEREST.COM/TESTKITCHEN

AMERICASTESTKITCHEN.COM
COOKSILLUSTRATED.COM
COOKSCOUNTRY.COM
ONLINECOOKINGSCHOOL.COM

INTRODUCTION

In any cluttered kitchen (the test kitchen included), there are some pots and pans that gather dust and others that rarely get put away. After many years of careful testing, we've identified the truly hardworking tools, the must-have utensils that we reach for time and again. Some are pretty obvious—a chef's knife, a cutting board, a pasta pot—but one that might come as a surprise is a cast-iron skillet. And this unassuming, sturdy pan doesn't just stand out on the well-stocked shelves of the test kitchen; cast iron also has a special place in our home kitchens, where we don't have room for cabinets full of specialized gear. A cast-iron skillet is an incredibly versatile, durable, and completely chemical-free way to cook. This consummate multitasking powerhouse is essential to have on hand when the right recipe comes along—and you might not realize just how many recipes are perfect in cast iron.

Most people already know that cast iron is just the thing for searing or blackening food quickly over high heat; when we're after a really dark, even crust on steaks or chops, there's nothing better. But a cast-iron skillet is not just for the stovetop; it's also equally at home in the oven for perfect roasts and baked goods. In addition, cast iron's great heat retention makes it a natural fit for hot, melty dips like fondue and solves the problem of soggy crusts on pies and quiches. Other surprising uses of this adaptable pan include baking perfect loaves of bread and making stick-free eggs and stir-fries, just to name a few. The cast-iron skillet is the one pan that does it all. This supertool is definitely a star in the test kitchen and our home kitchens, and with the recipes and techniques in this book, we're convinced it will become the star of yours, too.

THE TEST KITCHEN'S CAST IRON DISCOVERIES

The cast-iron skillet has been a test kitchen favorite since day one. Yet while we have tons of practical experience with this pan, there were still questions that puzzled us. We knew that cast iron cooks in certain ways, but we didn't quite understand why. We knew that developing and maintaining a layer of seasoning is key for a nonstick cast-iron pan, but we didn't really understand what seasoning actually is or how it works. We had also heard all kinds of conflicting information and myths about the best ways to clean and use cast-iron skillets. So we set out to learn everything we could about cast iron and to develop recipes that were designed specifically for the strengths of the skillet. Here are some of the most surprising discoveries we made in the process:

- **You CAN use soap on a cast-iron pan.** After months of recipe tests and thousands of dirty skillets, we developed simple, straightforward procedures for cleaning your cast iron. (See more on page 11.)

- **Food cooks faster in a cast-iron pan.** As we were testing our recipes, we noticed that compared to similar recipes cooked in other kinds of pans, the cast iron versions cooked quite a bit faster, largely because of cast iron's remarkable powers of heat retention. (See more on pages 4–5.)

- **You CAN cook tomatoes, vinegar, and other acidic ingredients in a cast-iron pan.** Acidic ingredients can cause problems in cast iron, so in order to avoid any unwanted flavors in our food or damage to our pans while still cooking with all our favorites, we came up with some ways to work around this issue. (See more on page 13.)

- **There's more than one right way to preheat a cast-iron pan.** Sometimes you want a perfect sear on a big piece of meat, and other times you just need to quickly sauté some onions. The environment in your cast-iron skillet can be customized for different types of cooking. During our testing we developed some rules for the best ways to preheat your skillet based on the cooking techniques used in a particular recipe. (See more on page 13.)

- **Seasoning and maintaining cast iron is not as difficult as you think it is.** A well-seasoned and cared-for cast-iron skillet can definitely rival a traditional nonstick pan. With our simple advice you can create and maintain a perfect cooking surface in your skillet. (See more on pages 10–11.)

TIPS FOR COOKING WITH CAST IRON

- **Use a pan that's the correct size for your recipe.** Some recipes in this book call for a 10-inch skillet and others use a 12-inch skillet. Cooking a recipe in a larger or smaller skillet can cause problems, so check the requirements of each recipe. We recommend buying both a 10-inch and a 12-inch pan so you can make every recipe in the book.

- **Scale the burner size to your pan.** The skillet will heat more evenly if it's properly matched to the size of the heating element on your stove. This applies to both gas and electric stoves.

- **Protect your hands.** Since cast iron retains heat extremely well, the handle of your skillet will stay very, very hot for quite a while after cooking. Always use a towel or potholder when taking a skillet out of the oven or moving it on the stovetop, and consider leaving the towel or potholder on the handle to remind yourself not to grab the bare metal.

- **Lift responsibly.** Cast iron is heavy, and while we try to minimize the time spent lifting or moving the skillet in our recipes, you will sometimes have to pick it up to transfer the pan from stove to oven or from cooking to serving. To make this easier, look for a skillet that has a helper handle opposite the pan handle. Be sure to protect your hands when using the helper handle as you do with the pan handle; use a towel, potholder, or silicone cover.

- **Use a vegetable- or plant-based oil to season your skillet.** While it's fine to cook with animal fats in your cast iron, fats that are more unsaturated are better for seasoning (for more information see page 10).

An All-American Pan with Chinese Roots

For centuries before DuPont invented Teflon in 1938, people cooked on naturally nonstick pans made of cast iron. The cast iron manufacturing process originated in China in the sixth century BCE and has barely changed since. The only major difference in modern manufacturing is that machines are used to partially or fully automate the work of pouring the insanely hot molten metal into the molds—it gets up to over 2,500 degrees at some points in the fabrication process!

Because of its great heat retention, cast iron has historically been a favorite material for cookware across a variety of cultures. Pots made of cast iron were particularly effective over open cooking fires before the invention of the kitchen stove. In U.S. history, cast iron's adaptability to open-flame cooking made it a natural fit for early American settlers and pioneers, leading to cast iron's modern reputation as a rustic accessory associated with campfires, cowboys, and covered wagons. Cast-iron pots and kettles that could be suspended over an open hearth or fire were very popular in early America, as were pots with legs that could sit over the coals and embers to cook.

Call It a Comeback

Due to its affordability and durability, cast iron was the material of choice for cookware in America until the early 20th century, when aluminum became cheaper and more widely available and subsequently took over as the cookware material of choice. By the end of the 20th century, nonstick skillets had become more common than cast iron in most homes. However, as worrying reports about the effects of chemical nonstick coatings on the environment and our health came to light, more and more cooks returned to the original "green" pan, the cast-iron skillet, as an alternative and rediscovered all the advantages it has to offer. This began a new era in the history of this unique pan.

This renaissance has also been a visible force in cast iron manufacturing. At one time, there were dozens of American companies making cast-iron cookware, but because of the embrace of new materials in the early 1900s, those numbers dwindled and now there is only one major company producing cast-iron cookware in the United States: Lodge. (Lodge makes our favorite traditional cast-iron skillet—see page 8.) Many of the pans currently available on the market are made in China. However, in recent years a new wave of American companies has begun producing small, artisanal batches of this classic cookware. Manufacturers in the United States and elsewhere have also experimented with innovative design tweaks to handles, shapes, and coatings in an attempt to modernize the classic bare-bones skillets, all of which has helped to bring this timeless pan firmly into the 21st century.

The Many Benefits of Cast Iron

There are a host of practical and culinary reasons why cast iron is experiencing a comeback. One of its greatest advantages is that a cast-iron pan is possibly the only piece of kitchen gear you can buy that noticeably improves after years of heavy use. As you cook in it, a cast-iron pan gradually develops a natural, slick patina, called seasoning, which releases food easily. A well-seasoned cast-iron skillet can become just as nonstick as an aluminum or stainless-steel pan and will definitely outlast them.

Cast iron doesn't heat very evenly because its thermal conductivity, or ability to transfer heat from one part of the metal to another, is very low. What cast iron does do well is hold on to heat: Once a cast-iron pan is hot, it will stay that way much more effectively than stainless steel. This makes cast iron the ideal material for high-heat applications like searing steak. The initial drop in temperature caused by adding the relatively low-temperature steak to the hot skillet will be much smaller in cast iron, allowing for higher heat and better browning. And better browning means a more delicious steak.

The durability of cast iron is legendary—many people are still cooking on cast-iron pans handed down through their family for generations. Cast iron is virtually indestructible and easily restored if mistreated (see pages 10–11). Cast iron's ability to develop a nonstick coating also makes it incredibly versatile. This is a boon for minimalist cooks who are looking to downsize their pot and pan collections to a few key pieces that can work in almost any application, but cast iron is also beloved by gourmet cooks who appreciate the particular benefits it offers for essential techniques like browning and searing.

Casting Doubts?

Cast-iron cookware has long been perceived as difficult and fussy to work with—it's heavy, it needs special care, there are some ingredients you can't cook in it, it's hard to clean—but it turns out that many of these points have been largely disproved or alleviated by modern developments in cast iron manufacturing. Pans now come factory preseasoned and require less effort to maintain and clean. Yes, cast iron is still heavy, but that is actually an advantage to both the durability and the cooking power of this kitchen workhorse. And yes, cast-iron pans do require a slightly greater investment of time and attention than cutting-edge nonstick cookware, but that investment pays off in spades. With a little love and effort, the cast-iron skillet you cook on today will be with you for decades, looking exactly the same and cooking better and better with every use.

TOP 10 RECIPES FOR CAST IRON NEWCOMERS

If you're new to cast iron cooking, it can feel a little intimidating. Here are some recipes we recommend to help you get used to your new cooking buddy:

1 **Warm Marinated Artichoke Hearts with Olives and Feta** (page 32)

2 **Thick-Cut Steaks with Herb Butter** (page 57)

3 **Crisp-Skin Salmon with Honey-Lime Sauce** (page 69)

4 **Classic Roast Chicken with Lemon-Thyme Pan Sauce** (page 82)

5 **Skillet Macaroni and Cheese** (page 110)

6 **Ultimate Indoor Burger**s (page 160)

7 **Fried Eggs** (page 187)

8 **Southern-Style Cornbread** (page 220)

9 **Bananas Foster** (page 250)

10 **Chocolate Chip Skillet Cookie** (page 270)

A CAST IRON PERSONALITY TEST

Which pan is right for you? Once you've decided to buy a cast-iron skillet, there are some other choices you'll face. One of the biggest questions is whether you want a traditional skillet (the classic black kind that you probably picture when you hear the words "cast-iron skillet") or an enameled skillet. Take the quiz below to figure out which cast-iron option best fits you and your kitchen, and then check out our equipment testing results on pages 8–9 to see which models we recommend.

PICK THE STATEMENT THAT BEST DESCRIBES YOU

When it comes to price
A I don't mind spending more for extra features.
B I'm a thrifty shopper and I love a bargain above all.

If I'm washing something
A I feel like long soaking times and using plenty of soap are the only ways to get it totally clean.
B I think that hot water and scrubbing are enough, so I'm OK with using little-to-no soap and no soaking.

If my pans could talk
A They'd probably be pretty happy—I'm fairly careful with my things.
B They might complain a little—I'm kind of tough on them!

My kitchen style could be summed up as
A I'm always interested in trying the newest thing and I tend to collect gadgets.
B I try to keep my collection pretty minimalist; if it's not broken, I don't fix it.

My patience level for a pan that needs some work is
A I'd rather have something that performs consistently right out of the box.
B I'm willing to put in some extra effort for something I really like, as long as it's going to pay off in the end.

I want my cast-iron skillet to be
A A specialty tool I use for recipes that really benefit from its singular characteristics.
B Basically a complete replacement for my nonstick skillet whenever possible.

RESULTS

If you mostly picked option A
Try one of the newer enameled cast-iron skillets. You'll pay a slightly higher price, but seasoning is never an issue and cleanup is much more straightforward. Plus, you can color coordinate! Our recommended 12-inch enameled skillets range from $50 to $180.

If you mostly picked option B
Stick with a traditional skillet. They're hardy, inexpensive, and long-lasting, with just a few simple rules to follow about care and maintenance to keep them in perfect working order. Our favorite 12-inch traditional skillet costs around $30 and lasts a lifetime—or longer.

EVALUATING CAST-IRON SKILLETS

While you may think of a cast-iron skillet as one of the most straightforward, no-frills options on the market, there are actually a surprising number of factors to take into account when buying one, and there are many more options today than there were 50 years ago. One of the most noticeable changes on the market has been the increasing presence of enameled cast-iron skillets. On an enameled skillet, the rough surface of the pan is cloaked inside and out with the same kind of porcelain coating found on Dutch ovens, and they're available in a rainbow of colors. Enamel promises a cast-iron pan with advantages: The glossy coating prevents the metal from rusting or reacting with acidic foods, both of which can be concerns with traditional cast iron (see pages 13–14). It also lets you thoroughly soak and scrub dirty pans with soap—generally taboo with traditional pans since too much soap and soaking will remove the patina, or top layer of seasoning on the cooking surface. While a handful of expensive enameled skillets have been around for years, new models are now appearing at lower prices. We tested these enameled versions against traditional cast iron to see if there was any reason to replace our old standby with one of these new arrivals.

The Cast Iron Cookoff

We purchased 10 cast-iron skillets, six enameled and four traditional, each about 12 inches in diameter. We then set about scrambling eggs, searing steaks, making a tomato-caper pan sauce (to check if its acidity reacted with the pan surface), skillet-roasting thick fish fillets that went from stove to oven, baking cornbread, and shallow-frying breaded chicken cutlets. At the end of testing, we scrambled more eggs to see whether the pans' surfaces had evolved. To simulate years of kitchen use, we plunged hot pans into ice water, banged a metal spoon on their rims, cut in them with a chef's knife, and scraped them with a metal spoon. We also considered special features that helped make the pans easy to use and clean.

Based on all these tests, neither enameled nor traditional cast iron was "best." Both offer great heat retention and superior browning, but beyond that it's a matter of determining what's best for your own needs (see our quiz on page 6 for some help figuring that out). There are standout options for both types of pans at a variety of price points. Our top picks for both traditional and enameled are listed in the chart on the next two pages in order of preference. Ovensafe temperature ratings are from the manufacturers.

WHAT ABOUT LIGHTWEIGHT CAST IRON?

Another new option on the market in recent years is lightweight cast iron. Unlike traditional cast-iron pans (which are made by pouring molten metal into a sand mold, which is broken apart when the pan cools, allowing the pan to emerge in one piece, handle included), lightweight cast-iron pans are made in a metal mold, which allows them to be made thinner. They are also machined or milled to thin them further, and their handles are attached separately with rivets. We tried three lightweight cast-iron skillets, comparing them with our favorite traditional cast-iron skillet in several tests.

All of the pans we tried were indeed lighter than a traditional cast-iron skillet—but that was pretty much their only advantage. All three lightweight pans heated up and cooled down faster than the thicker traditional cast iron. While they were easier to lift and handle, they were also far more reactive to heat changes, which caused them to cook much less evenly, with a distinct tendency to scorch along the outer edges. Overall, lightweight cast-iron skillets proved a disappointment, so they aren't included in our recommendations.

EVALUATING CAST-IRON SKILLETS

TRADITIONAL CAST IRON

HIGHLY RECOMMENDED

Lodge Classic Cast Iron Skillet, 12"
Model: L10SK3 **Price:** $33.31
Weight: 7 lb, 10⅛ oz
Cooking Surface: 10 in
Ovensafe to: At least 1,000°

Browning ★★★
Sticking ★★★
Ease of Use ★★★
Durability ★★★

Our winner arrived with the slickest preseasoned interior, and it only got better. It browned foods deeply, and its thorough seasoning ensured that our acidic pan sauce picked up no off-flavors. Though its handle is short, the pan has a helper handle that made lifting easy. It survived abuse testing without a scratch.

Calphalon 12-In. Pre-Seasoned Cast Iron Skillet
Model: 1873975 **Price:** $34.95
Weight: 6 lb, 12 oz
Cooking Surface: 10¼ in
Ovensafe to: "Well above broiler level"

Browning ★★★
Sticking ★★½
Ease of Use ★★★
Durability ★★★

Even browning made this pan stand out; we also liked the unusual helper handle and curved sides, which added to its cooking area. However, food stuck to its pebbly surface a bit more than to our smoother top-rated pan, and it took a little more effort to scrub it clean.

RECOMMENDED

Camp Chef 12" Seasoned Cast Iron Skillet
Model: SK12 **Price:** $21.99
Weight: 7 lb, ¾ oz
Cooking Surface: 9¾ in
Ovensafe to: 600°

Browning ★★★
Sticking ★★
Ease of Use ★★½
Durability ★★★

This inexpensive choice browned steak, chicken, and cornbread beautifully and made a pan sauce with no off-flavors. Nevertheless, its preseasoning seemed thin, looking patchy after washing; fish and eggs stuck at first, but the pan acquired good seasoning in time and endured abuse well.

RECOMMENDED WITH RESERVATIONS

T-fal Pre-Seasoned Cast Iron Skillet, 12"
Model: E8340763 **Price:** $34.97
Weight: 8 lb, 8¾ oz
Cooking Surface: 10 in
Ovensafe to: 600°

Browning ★★
Sticking ★★
Ease of Use ★★
Durability ★★½

This pan is supposedly preseasoned, but instructions had us season it again in the oven. Its nonstick quality improved slowly, and eggs continued to stick after several uses. When we flipped steaks, the pan seemed to lose heat, leading to uneven browning. It turned the pan sauce faintly metallic, and spatula scrapes left scratches. We did love the long, rounded handle.

ENAMELED CAST IRON

HIGHLY RECOMMENDED

Le Creuset Signature 11¾" Iron Handle Skillet
Model: LS2024-30 **Price:** $179.95
Weight: 6 lb, 8⅝ oz
Cooking Surface: 10 in
Ovensafe to: No maximum set by company

Browning ★★★
Sticking ★★½
Ease of Use ★★★
Durability ★★★

With flaring sides, an oversize helper handle, wide pour spouts, a satiny interior, and balanced weight, this expensive but beautifully made pan is a pleasure to cook in. Our only quibbles: A small piece of cornbread stuck, and scrambled eggs stuck a little (but scrubbed out easily). After abuse testing, the pan still looked nearly new.

RECOMMENDED

BEST BUY **Mario Batali by Dansk 12"**
Open Sauté Pan
Model: 826782 (cobalt color)
Price: $59.95
Weight: 8 lb, 10½ oz
Cooking Surface: 10¼ in
Ovensafe to: 475°

Browning ★★★
Sticking ★★★
Ease of Use ★★½
Durability ★★

This pan felt well balanced, and its ample size and great heat capacity rendered deep browning on every food we cooked. Its surface resisted sticking, releasing cornbread perfectly. It's a bit less durable than others: Half-inch areas of enamel chipped off both of the handles' tips, and the pan bottom looked blotchy.

Lodge Enamel Coated Cast Iron Skillet, 11"
Model: EC11S43 **Price:** $48.90
Weight: 6 lb, 13⅜ oz
Cooking Surface: 9¼ in
Ovensafe to: 400°

Browning ★ ★ ★
Sticking ★ ★ ½
Ease of Use ★ ★ ½
Durability ★ ★

The long handle on this small pan made it comfortable to lift, and its curved sides were easy to swipe with a spatula. It released cornbread perfectly but performed slightly less well with fish and eggs. Foods browned evenly, but two big steaks barely fit and steamed rather than seared. Good for small households.

RECOMMENDED WITH RESERVATIONS

Rachael Ray Cast Iron 12-Inch Open Skillet with Helper Handle
Model: 59161 **Price:** $79.95
Weight: 7 lb, 14⅝ oz
Cooking Surface: 11 in
Ovensafe to: 500°

Browning ★ ★ ½
Sticking ★ ★ ½
Ease of Use ★ ★
Durability ★ ★

This pan is roomy but sluggish to heat up and then prone to run too hot. Once we'd adjusted, the pan behaved well, with good browning; however, fish and cornbread stuck and took some scrubbing. Knife scratches remained.

Staub Cast Iron 12" Fry Pan
Model: 1223025 **Price:** $174.99
Weight: 6 lb, 6⅜ oz
Cooking Surface: 10 in
Ovensafe to: 500°

Browning ★ ★
Sticking ★ ★
Ease of Use ★ ★ ½
Durability ★ ★

We liked its low, flared sides, but this pan felt clunky and browned fish and steak unevenly. The cooking surface was prone to sticking. It was slower to heat and tended to run hot. The exterior scratched easily, and the bottom blackened in spots.

Tramontina Gourmet Enameled Cast Iron 12 In Skillet with Lid
Model: 80131/058DS
Price: $69.60
Weight: 7 lb, 8⅝ oz
Cooking Surface: 9¾ in
Ovensafe to: 450°

Browning ★ ★ ½
Sticking ★ ★
Ease of Use ★ ½
Durability ★ ★ ½

While it browned steaks fairly well, delicate foods stuck to this pan and broke the biggest chunk off cornbread. Thick, heavy, and deep, with a narrow cooking surface, it felt awkward, heated sluggishly, and was prone to run hot. The uncoated rim required seasoning to prevent rust.

OUR FAVORITE CAST IRON ACCESSORIES

UNIVERSAL LIDS

Several of the recipes in this book require the use of a lid. Lodge, which makes our winning traditional cast-iron skillet, also sells tempered-glass and cast-iron lids for their skillets. We recommend the **Lodge 12 Inch Tempered Glass Cover** because it's more lightweight and doesn't need any special treatment for seasoning or cleaning. If you don't want to invest in a special lid for your cast-iron pans, you can also use a regular universal lid. Most universal pan lids sport grooved rings ranging from 8 to 12 inches in diameter in order to fit a variety of standard-size pans. Our favorite, the **RSVP Endurance Stainless-Steel Universal Lid with Glass Insert**, has a small vent to help release steam and a heat-resistant handle.

CHAIN-MAIL SCRUBBER

Since soaking a cast-iron pan in soapy water can damage the seasoning, we've found other ways to remove cooked-on food, including the method on page 12 that uses kosher salt as an abrasive, but there are also gadgets that promise to make this task easier, including the innovative **CM Scrubber by KnappMade**. To test it out, we passed this 4-inch square of stainless-steel chain mail over a cast-iron pan encrusted with charred bits of sausage and another that we'd used for frying bacon. The linked steel rings effortlessly lifted away any stuck-on bits without damaging the pan's finish. The scrubber itself took some scrubbing to become completely grit- and oil-free for the next use, but it dried quickly and didn't rust.

Cast-iron skillets used to be sold as raw, uncoated, unseasoned iron, so the home cook would have to season them entirely from scratch to prevent rusting and sticking. But all that is in the past: New cast-iron skillets are now sold factory preseasoned. This means that the manufacturer sprays on a proprietary food-safe oil and bakes it onto the pan at a very high temperature. However, if the seasoning on a new pan becomes damaged or if you acquire an old-fashioned uncoated pan—inherited from a family member or found at a yard sale—you will still need to know how to season (or reseason) it yourself, in which case you might be wondering: What exactly is seasoning, why do you need it, and how does it work?

In this context, seasoning is what we call a coating of polymerized triglyceride molecules that is many molecules thick. When fat is heated at a certain temperature for a particular length of time, it polymerizes. For cooking oils, polymerization means the linking together of hundreds of molecules through the formation of new chemical bonds between the fatty acids in the oil. This bonding creates a plastic-like layer of large polymers (many hundreds of molecules linked together) that is physically trapped within the pitted surface of a cast-iron pan and partly bonded to the metal itself. The metal atoms catalyze, or speed up, the reaction.

In other words, by applying oil to the surface of your skillet and heating that oil, you can cause the fat molecules in the oil to break down and reorganize into a layer of new molecules that adhere to the pan, creating a fairly durable coating that acts much like an all-natural Teflon.

Heating the pan is crucial to seasoning. The degree of polymerization is directly related to the temperature to which the oil is heated. An oil at its smoke point is rapidly oxidizing, which is great for polymerization. However, heating the pan too hot can actually cause the coating to break down, or depolymerize. A 500-degree oven is the easiest way to bring the pan's temperature just past the smoke point without allowing it to get too hot, so we use the oven for our recommended seasoning technique. However, the stovetop also works

well; simply heat the pan to the oil's smoke point for a few minutes. Heat helps activate the creation of polymers and encourages the seasoning process, building up the layer of protective molecules that will form a barrier between the reactive iron in the pan and water or food that will cause it to rust. Because the main component of cast iron is iron, which combines more easily with oxygen than other metals do, cast iron that is not seasoned tends to rust quickly and easily when exposed to moisture. In theory this whole process may seem like a lot to worry about, but it's actually pretty simple in practice—see our straightforward instructions on the next page to get started with your skillet. And remember: Every time you cook in your cast-iron pan, exposing it to heat and oil, you're improving the pan's seasoning.

OIL CHOICE

The more unsaturated the oil, the more readily it will oxidize and polymerize. Oils such as canola, sunflower, soybean, and corn are highly unsaturated. We have found that flaxseed oil, which is especially rich in omega-3 fatty acids, forms a particularly durable seasoning layer.

HOW CAN I TELL IF MY SKILLET IS WELL SEASONED?

A well-seasoned skillet should have a smooth, dark black, semiglossy finish. It should not be sticky or greasy to the touch. It will not have any rusty, dull, or dry patches. One of the easiest ways we've found for testing the seasoning in your skillet is to cook a fried egg. If your skillet is well seasoned, you should not experience any major sticking.

MINOR SEASONING REPAIRS

You can perform a simple touch-up on a pan with small areas of damaged seasoning by heating up the skillet over medium-high heat and repeatedly wiping it with a wad of paper towels dipped in vegetable oil (hold the towels with tongs to protect yourself) until the surface looks dark black and semiglossy but isn't sticky or greasy to the touch.

HOW TO SEASON AND MAINTAIN YOUR CAST-IRON SKILLET

All well-maintained cast-iron pans will become more nonstick with time. While you might think this will take years, we found a significant difference in our pans after just a few weeks of regular use in the test kitchen. However, as we noted in our equipment test (see pages 7–9), even new preseasoned skillets are not always 100% nonstick when you first cook with them, and a well-seasoned skillet will still become less nonstick without proper maintenance, so it's important to treat your cast-iron skillet with care. Properly maintaining the seasoning on your skillet begins with properly cleaning it. Here are a few guidelines for keeping your pan in optimal shape (these guidelines are for traditional cast-iron skillets; enameled skillets can be treated more like other pots and pans).

1 While the skillet is still warm, wipe it clean with paper towels to remove excess food bits and oil.

2 Rinse the skillet under hot running water, scrubbing with a brush or nonabrasive scrub pad to remove traces of food. Use a small amount of soap if you like, but make sure to rinse it all off.

3 Dry the skillet thoroughly (do not let it drip-dry) and put it back on the burner over medium-low heat until all traces of moisture disappear (this keeps rusting at bay). Never put a wet cast-iron skillet away or stack anything on top of a skillet that hasn't been properly dried.

4 Add ½ teaspoon of vegetable oil to the warm, dry skillet and wipe the interior with a wad of paper towels until it is lightly covered with oil.

5 Continue to rub oil into the skillet, replacing the paper towels as needed, until the skillet looks dark and shiny and does not have any remaining oil residue.

6 Turn off the heat and allow the skillet to cool completely before putting it away.

A well-seasoned skillet should have a smooth, dark black, semiglossy finish.

SEASONING FROM SCRATCH

Our recommended procedure for seasoning a completely unseasoned pan or reseasoning a stripped skillet uses flaxseed oil, which has six times more omega-3 fatty acids than vegetable oil; over prolonged exposure to high heat, these combine to form a strong, solid matrix on the pan's surface. If you're starting with a clean, unseasoned pan, jump right in with step 2. If you have a pan with heavily damaged seasoning or serious rust, you'll want to strip it first. The best way we've found to completely strip the seasoning on a pan is to run it through your oven's self-cleaning cycle. Make sure you check the owner's manual for your oven before doing this, as not all manufacturers recommend it.

1 If your cast-iron skillet has any residual seasoning, strip it completely by running it through your oven's self-cleaning cycle. Let the skillet cool to room temperature, then wipe it clean with paper towels.

2 Adjust an oven rack to the middle position and heat the oven to 500 degrees. Place 1 tablespoon of flaxseed oil (for a 12-inch skillet) or 2 teaspoons of oil (for a 10-inch skillet) in the stripped, dry skillet and rub the oil onto the entire surface with paper towels. With fresh paper towels, thoroughly wipe the skillet to remove any excess oil (the skillet should look dry, not glistening with oil). Place the skillet upside down in the oven and bake for 1 hour.

3 Using potholders, remove the skillet from the oven and let it cool for 30 minutes. Being careful of the hot skillet handle, repeat oiling and baking the skillet five more times until the skillet has a smooth, dark black, semiglossy finish.

PROBLEM #1

A Stinky Skillet

Some sources recommend adding a thin layer of oil to the pan and heating it to its smoking point on the stovetop to remove stinky, stubborn fish oils, but this method leaves an oily mess to clean up. Luckily, it turns out that heat alone is enough to eliminate the two sources of fishy funk: compounds called trialkylamines, which evaporate at around 200 to 250 degrees, and oxidized fatty acids, which vaporize at temperatures above 350 degrees. Next time your skillet needs a little aromatherapy, simply heat the empty, smelly pan in a 400-degree oven for 10 minutes. This method is fast, neat, and effective and doesn't stink up the kitchen.

PROBLEM #2

An Extra-Dirty Skillet

If your skillet has stubborn stuck-on food or is a little rusty, the best fix we've found is to scrub it with kosher salt. Start by rubbing the pan with fine steel wool (we normally don't use steel wool on cast iron, but it's necessary when you're dealing with serious grime). Wipe out the loose dirt with a cloth and pour in vegetable oil to a depth of ¼ inch, then heat the pan over medium-low heat for 5 minutes. Remove the pan from the heat and add ¼ cup of kosher salt. Using a potholder to grip the handle, scrub the pan with a thick cushion of paper towels (hold the paper towels with tongs to protect yourself). The warm oil will loosen any remaining crud, and the salt will have an abrading effect without posing any danger to the pan's seasoning. Rinse the pan under hot running water, dry well, and repeat, if necessary.

Scrub with salt and oil

PROBLEM #3

A Patchy or Scratched Skillet

Cooking acidic foods or following improper cleaning procedures can damage the seasoning on your pan, creating spots of dull, patchy, dry-looking metal on the inside of the pan instead of the smooth, rich black of well-seasoned cast iron. When this happens, you can restore the pan by following the instructions for Minor Seasoning Repairs (page 10). Wiping the warm pan with oil will help reseason the small areas of the surface that have been damaged, evening out the protective coating on the skillet. (If your pan looks really bad, follow the instructions for Seasoning from Scratch on page 11.)

Slick down the rough spots

PROBLEM #4

A Stained Enameled Skillet

While all of the enameled cast-iron skillets featured in our review on pages 8–9 have dark-colored interiors like traditional cast-iron skillets, other enameled pans have light-colored interiors like those you may have seen on enameled Dutch ovens. The interiors of those pans can sometimes become stained or discolored by foods. If this happens, you can use bleach to clean them. Le Creuset recommends a stain-removal solution of 1 teaspoon of bleach per pint of water. We found that stained pots were slightly improved by this but still far from their original hue. We then tried a much stronger solution (which was OK'd by the manufacturer) of 1 part bleach to 3 parts water. After standing overnight, a lightly stained pot was just as good as new, but a heavily stained one required an additional night of soaking before it, too, was looking natty.

THE MYTH

You can't cook wine, tomatoes, or other acidic ingredients in a cast-iron pan.

THE TESTING When acidic ingredients are cooked in cast iron for an extended amount of time, trace amounts of molecules from the metal can loosen and leach into the food. Although these minute amounts are not harmful to consume, they may impart unwanted metallic flavors, and the pan's seasoning can be damaged as well. To test how fast this happens and how noticeable it is, we made a highly acidic tomato sauce and simmered it in a well-seasoned skillet, testing it every 15 minutes to check for off-flavors and damage to the pan.

THE TAKEAWAY In the end, our tasters could detect metallic flavors in the tomato sauce only after it had simmered for a full 30 minutes. So, while you can definitely cook with acidic ingredients in your cast-iron skillet, you have to be careful. First, make sure your pan is well seasoned; seasoning keeps the acid from interacting with the iron—to a point. An acidic sauce can afford a brief stay in a well-seasoned pan with no dire consequences. You should also be careful to remove acidic dishes from the skillet after they finish cooking; don't let them sit too long in the warm skillet and transfer any leftovers to an airtight container. (These rules do not apply to enameled cast-iron skillets; the enameled coating makes it safe to cook acidic ingredients for any length of time.)

All of the recipes in this book have been carefully developed to work in cast iron, even when they use highly acidic ingredients like vinegar, wine, tomatoes, cherries, and stone fruits. We use tricks like shorter simmering times, diluting the problematic ingredients to make the pH less of an issue, and waiting until late in the recipe to add the acidic ingredients. If you do accidentally oversimmer an acidic ingredient, you may have to throw out the food, but you can simply reseason your skillet using the procedures outlined on pages 10–11 and get back to cooking in it again.

THE MYTH

One of cast iron's greatest advantages is that it heats really evenly.

THE TESTING We were interested in this question because it would affect the way we went about preheating our skillets for cooking. To see just how the pans reacted when placed over heat, we designed a test that would give us a visual indication of the way heat traveled through the cast iron. We spread 1 tablespoon of all-purpose flour in both our favorite cast-iron skillet and a traditional stainless-steel skillet and heated them over medium heat until the flour started to toast. As the flour browned in the hot pans, it essentially created a map of how each skillet heated up.

THE TAKEAWAY While the flour in the stainless-steel skillet toasted evenly to a uniform golden brown, the flour in our cast-iron skillet started to burn in some spots before other areas of the skillet had any browning at all. It turns out that because cast iron is such a poor conductor, it in fact heats very unevenly on the stove—and more or less so depending on the level of heat you use. To work around this, we preheat the skillet in a 500-degree oven when we need a really good, even, fast sear. The better heat distribution in the oven helps the pan heat more evenly, creating a superior surface for searing. For recipes where a strong sear isn't necessary, we preheat the pan for either 3 or 5 minutes over medium-high heat on the stovetop, which we found to be the best way to get relatively even heat without too much work.

Stainless-Steel Skillet

Cast-Iron Skillet

THE MYTH

Cast-iron skillets work only on gas stoves; you can't cook with them on an electric range.

THE TESTING Part of our testing procedure for the recipes in this book was to make them not only in both traditional and enameled cast-iron skillets but also on both gas and electric stoves. We know that almost half of our readers are likely to use electric stoves in their home kitchens, so we wanted to make sure our recipes would work for them, especially since some people think that cast iron and electric stoves don't mix well.

THE TAKEAWAY We mostly found that cast iron works great on electric, although it may take a little longer to achieve the same results since cast iron is slightly slower to heat on an electric heating element. If you're using a cast-iron skillet on an electric range, you may find that you need to cook things slightly longer—use the upper ends of the timing ranges given in our recipes. If you have a glass-top range, you should also take extra care when moving the heavy cast-iron pan around on the stove to avoid any scratching or damage.

THE MYTH

You should never wash cast iron with soap.

THE TESTING During our extensive recipe-testing process we generated hundreds of dirty skillets and thus had plenty of opportunities to test different cleaning methods. While developing our recommended procedure (see page 11), we experimented with a variety of cleansers, including dish soap and scouring powders.

THE TAKEAWAY We found that a few drops of dish soap are not enough to interfere with the polymerized bonds on the surface of a well-seasoned cast-iron skillet. Don't scrub the pan with abrasives like steel wool or use harsh cleansers like Comet, and don't soak the pan, since those things can definitely affect the seasoning, but it's OK to use a few drops of dish soap if you need to clean up a particularly greasy pan, or even if that just makes you feel more comfortable with your cast iron. Just make sure you rinse the pan clean and wipe it dry when you're finished.

THE MYTH

If a cast-iron pan gets rusted, it's ruined.

THE TESTING Because cast iron is so durable, old cast-iron pans are a common find at thrift stores, antique shops, and flea markets. But older cast iron may not always be in tip-top shape. To find out whether even the most damaged cast iron could still be salvaged, we took the most abused skillets we could find; completely stripped them of all their dirt, rust, and ruined seasoning by sending them through the self-cleaning cycle on our oven; and then tried reseasoning them from scratch.

THE TAKEAWAY It takes a lot to kill a cast-iron skillet. If yours has a crack in it from improper use or storage, or if it has literally rusted through, it's time to throw it out, but unless the structure of the pan has been truly compromised, there isn't much that can "ruin" cast iron. Even if the seasoning gets seriously marred or the pan starts to rust, you can clean it off and start fresh. See our guidelines on page 11 for detailed instructions on how to deal with a pan that's seen better days.

THE MYTH

When you cook in a cast-iron skillet, your food will absorb a lot of extra iron so you can effectively supplement your diet by using this type of pan.

THE TESTING We simmered tomato sauce in a stainless-steel pan and in seasoned and unseasoned cast-iron pans. We then sent samples of each sauce to an independent lab to test for the presence of iron. The unseasoned cast iron released the most molecules of metal. The sauce from this pot contained nearly 10 times as much iron (108 mg/kg) as the sauce from the seasoned cast-iron pot, which contained only a few more milligrams than the sauce from the stainless-steel pot.

THE TAKEAWAY Since this occurs in pronounced amounts only with unseasoned skillets, which you wouldn't use for cooking, we don't consider this an issue. A seasoned cast-iron skillet will not leach any appreciable amount of iron into food cooked in it.

Sure, this book will show you dozens of ways to use your cast-iron skillet in recipes both traditional and surprising, but this irreplaceable tool also has other unusual uses in the kitchen that you've probably never thought of before. Here are just a few tips for jobs your cast-iron skillet can help with in the kitchen besides straightforward cooking (plus some unexpected ways to keep it in top-notch shape).

Creative Cast Iron Cleaning

We have our favorite recommended techniques for cleaning and scrubbing your cast-iron skillet, but over time we've also come up with some alternative methods that double as creative ways to recycle common items from your kitchen. Here are two tricks for scrubbing your pans when the built-up, burnt-on food gets too bad for a simple rinse and wipe. After using either of these, be sure to follow the procedures for cleaning, drying, and oiling your pan outlined on page 11.

PLASTIC MESH BAG Let the dirty pan cool, then use a plastic mesh produce bag (the kind that holds lemons or onions) to wipe the pan clean. The mesh bag doesn't damage the seasoning the way steel wool would, and you don't have to ruin a scrubber with grease.

ALUMINUM FOIL A wad of heavy-duty aluminum foil also makes a great cast-iron skillet cleaner. After using paper towels to wipe any excess grease from a cooled pan, simply use the foil to scrub off stuck-on food or dirt.

In-a-Pinch Pie Plate

If you find yourself short a pie plate, a seasoned cast-iron skillet can be the perfect alternative for just about any pie (see page 257 or 258 for recipes we have specially developed for this purpose). Just make sure your skillet is 9 or 10 inches in diameter to keep the recipe volume and baking times consistent.

Cast Iron Double-Team

Here's a trick for panini (like the ones on page 156) without a griddle, panini press, or Dutch oven.

1 Set a large, seasoned, oiled cast-iron skillet over medium-high heat; place your assembled sandwiches in the middle.

2 Place a smaller cast-iron skillet on top of the sandwich to press. Cook until the bottom of the sandwich is golden brown, then flip and repeat the process on the other side.

Thawing in a Hurry

Your cast-iron skillet can help you even before you start cooking. Place thin, frozen cuts of meat in the skillet at room temperature and let them sit for an hour. The rapid transfer of ambient heat from the metal to the food will quickly, safely thaw the meat.

Skillet Stove Helper

Tired of burning butter that you're trying to melt or scorching mashed potatoes while keeping them warm on the stovetop? Let your cast-iron skillet help you out. It makes a great flame tamer to keep things over gentle heat for a long time; simply place the skillet over a low flame, then place your pot or saucepan right in the skillet. The skillet will moderate the heat.

SIZZLING HOT STARTERS

Warm Marinated Artichoke Hearts
with Olives and Feta

BAKED PEPPERONI PIZZA DIP

SERVES 8 TO 10

WHY THIS RECIPE WORKS To bring pizza party flavor to a fun, easy appetizer, we turned classic pepperoni pie into a rich, cheesy dip that we could bake and serve right in the skillet. The cast iron's excellent heat retention ensured that the cheese didn't separate or become congealed but stayed warm and gooey until the skillet had been scraped clean, with no need for Sterno or a hot plate. For the rich base of our dip, we combined cream cheese, mozzarella, and pizza sauce. Stirring in crisped pepperoni finalized the familiar flavor profile. Naturally, the perfect partner for our creamy, saucy dip was pizza dough. We rolled out ½-ounce dough balls, tossed them with garlic oil, and baked them right in the skillet. The cast iron created a crisp, golden bottom on these pull-apart garlic rolls. The dip mixture was then spooned into the center of the skillet, inside the ring of parbaked mini rolls, and the whole thing was baked in the oven. We topped the dip with fresh basil and reserved pepperoni crisps. Partygoers can simply pull off a garlicky roll and use it to scoop out some cheesy dip. We like the convenience of using ready-made pizza dough from the local pizzeria or supermarket; however, you can use our Classic Pizza Dough (page 43). For the pizza sauce, consider using our No-Cook Pizza Sauce (page 176). To soften the cream cheese quickly, microwave it for 20 to 30 seconds.

- 3 ounces thinly sliced pepperoni, quartered
- 1 tablespoon extra-virgin olive oil
- 3 garlic cloves, minced
- 1 pound pizza dough
- 8 ounces cream cheese, cut into 8 pieces and softened
- ¾ cup pizza sauce
- 4 ounces mozzarella cheese, shredded (1 cup)
- 2 tablespoons chopped fresh basil

1 Adjust oven rack to middle position and heat oven to 400 degrees. Cook pepperoni in 10-inch cast-iron skillet over medium heat until crisp, 5 to 7 minutes. Using slotted spoon, transfer pepperoni to paper towel–lined plate; set aside. Off heat, add oil and garlic to fat left in skillet and let sit until fragrant, about 1 minute; transfer to medium bowl.

2 Place dough on lightly floured counter, pat into rough 8-inch square, and cut into 32 pieces (½ ounce each). Working with 1 piece of dough at a time, roll into tight ball, then coat with garlic oil. Evenly space 18 balls around edge of skillet, keeping center of skillet clear. Place remaining 14 balls on top, staggering them between seams of balls underneath. Cover loosely with greased plastic wrap and let sit until slightly puffed, about 20 minutes.

3 Remove plastic. Transfer skillet to oven and bake until balls are just beginning to brown, about 20 minutes, rotating skillet halfway through baking. Meanwhile, whisk cream cheese and pizza sauce together in large bowl until thoroughly combined and smooth. Stir in mozzarella and three-quarters of crisped pepperoni.

4 Spoon cheese mixture into center of skillet, return to oven, and bake until dip is heated through and rolls are golden brown, about 10 minutes. Sprinkle with basil and remaining crisped pepperoni. Serve.

ASSEMBLING BAKED PEPPERONI PIZZA DIP

Evenly space 18 balls around edge of skillet. Place remaining 14 balls on top, staggering between seams of lower row. There will be some gaps in top row.

BAKED CRAB DIP WITH CROSTINI

SERVES 8 TO 10

WHY THIS RECIPE WORKS In its ideal form, crab dip is a decadent, finger-friendly party pleaser served warm as a cocktail appetizer full of creamy, meaty seafood and savory spices. Here, the cast-iron skillet provides the perfect oven-to-table cooking vessel, ensuring that your guests will enjoy the dip while it's hot. For a serving option that was sturdy enough to scoop into the rich dip without any need for a spoon, we made a quick batch of crostini from sliced baguettes. Prebaking the bread before adding it to the skillet ensured that the toasts stayed crisp when loaded up with dip. To make a savory base for the crab dip, we first cooked onion in the skillet, adding just a bit of Old Bay seasoning and coriander. We then removed the sautéed onions from the skillet and combined them with cream cheese, mayonnaise, and parsley. After gently folding the crabmeat into the mixture, we put the whole thing back in the skillet and baked it until warmed and bubbly throughout, with crostini fanned around the perimeter. Unlike other versions of this popular appetizer, our crab dip has a high ratio of crab to cheese, allowing the sweet crab flavor to come through. Do not substitute imitation crabmeat here. To soften the cream cheese quickly, microwave it for 20 to 30 seconds.

2 (12-inch) baguettes, sliced ¼ inch thick on bias
¼ cup extra-virgin olive oil
  Salt and pepper
1 onion, chopped fine
1 teaspoon Old Bay seasoning
1 teaspoon ground coriander
8 ounces cream cheese, cut into 8 pieces and softened
½ cup mayonnaise
4 teaspoons minced fresh parsley
12 ounces lump crabmeat, picked over for shells and pressed dry between paper towels

1 Adjust oven racks to upper-middle and lower-middle positions and heat oven to 400 degrees. Arrange bread slices in even layer in 2 rimmed baking sheets and bake until dry and crisp, about 10 minutes, rotating sheets and flipping slices halfway through baking. Brush crostini with 2 tablespoons oil and season with salt and pepper; set aside.

2 Heat 10-inch cast-iron skillet over medium heat for 3 minutes. Add remaining 2 tablespoons oil and heat until shimmering. Add onion and cook until softened, about 5 minutes. Stir in Old Bay and coriander and cook until fragrant, about 30 seconds; transfer to large bowl. Stir cream cheese, mayonnaise, 1 tablespoon parsley, ¼ teaspoon salt, and ¼ teaspoon pepper into onion mixture until thoroughly combined. Gently fold in crabmeat.

3 Spread dip evenly in now-empty skillet, then shingle crostini around edge, submerging narrow ends in crab mixture. Transfer skillet to oven and bake until dip is heated through and crostini are golden brown, about 10 minutes. Sprinkle with remaining 1 teaspoon parsley. Serve.

ASSEMBLING BAKED CRAB DIP

Shingle crostini around edge of skillet, submerging narrow ends in crab mixture.

MEXICAN LAYER DIP

SERVES 8 TO 10

WHY THIS RECIPE WORKS While cool and creamy seven-layer dip holds lots of appeal, we wanted to heat things up and make a sizzling-hot take on this classic that was layered with beans and spicy ground meat, plus a variety of fresh toppings. We also wanted to keep this ultimate appetizer simple, not fussy. For ease and simplicity, we used the cast-iron skillet for every step of the cooking process, from sautéing on the stovetop, to baking in the oven, to serving. We really wanted the meat layer to pack a punch, so instead of simply using browned ground beef, we created a bold mixture by using ground pork seasoned with tomato paste, chipotle chile powder, garlic, oregano, and cumin. On its own, the seasoned pork was slightly dry, so we moistened it with a little chicken broth and incorporated some shredded Monterey Jack cheese to produce a saucy, cheesy, meaty mixture. We then briefly removed the meat from the skillet so we could create the base for our dip by simmering pinto beans with chicken broth and then mashing them to a smooth, scoopable consistency. When the meat mixture was layered back in the pan, our dip was ready to go into the oven to bake until hot. Once it was out of the oven, we finished the dish with assorted fresh garnishes for a colorful final presentation. Our dip might not have seven layers, but it definitely has more than enough flavor for your next fiesta. Serve with tortilla chips and lime wedges.

3 tablespoons vegetable oil

1 pound ground pork

1½ tablespoons tomato paste

1½ tablespoons chipotle chile powder

3 garlic cloves, minced

1½ teaspoons minced fresh oregano
or ½ teaspoon dried

1 teaspoon ground cumin

¼ teaspoon salt

1½ cups chicken broth

6 ounces Monterey Jack cheese,
shredded (1½ cups)

1 large red onion, chopped fine

2 (15-ounce) cans pinto beans, rinsed

1 tomato, cored and chopped

1 avocado, halved, pitted, and chopped

¼ cup fresh cilantro leaves

1 Adjust oven rack to middle position and heat oven to 350 degrees. Heat 10-inch cast-iron skillet over medium heat for 3 minutes. Add 1 tablespoon oil and heat until shimmering. Add ground pork and cook, breaking up meat with wooden spoon, until no longer pink, about 5 minutes. Stir in tomato paste, chile powder, garlic, oregano, cumin, and salt and cook until fragrant, about 1 minute.

2 Stir in ½ cup broth, scraping up any browned bits, and cook until sauce is thickened slightly, about 1 minute. Transfer mixture to medium bowl and stir in Monterey Jack until well combined.

3 Heat remaining 2 tablespoons oil in now-empty skillet over medium heat until shimmering. Add 1 cup onion and cook until softened, about 5 minutes. Stir in beans and remaining 1 cup broth, bring to simmer, and cook until beans are heated through, about 5 minutes. Using potato masher, mash beans until smooth, then continue to cook, stirring constantly, until beans are thick and creamy, about 3 minutes.

4 Off heat, spread beans into even layer, then spread pork mixture over top. Transfer skillet to oven and bake until heated through, about 10 minutes. Sprinkle with tomato, avocado, remaining onion, and cilantro. Serve.

BEER AND CHEDDAR FONDUE

SERVES 8 TO 10

WHY THIS RECIPE WORKS Making fondue tends to be a tricky, fussy project requiring specialty pots and chafing dishes and incessant stirring to help the cheese melt evenly and stay molten. We wanted to take advantage of the heat-retaining powers of cast iron to make a beer and cheddar fondue that would stay creamy without constant attention. A combination of mild cheddar and highly meltable American cheese provided a nice creamy base, but it turned grainy when combined with the acidic beer. To stabilize it, we added cornstarch, which acted as an emulsifier, plus garlic and dry mustard to complement the flavor of the cheddar. This dip is served right in the skillet; the residual heat of the cast iron helps the fondue stay warm and melty. The fondue tasted best when made with block cheese that we shredded ourselves; we recommend that you buy a block of American cheese from the deli counter. Preshredded cheese will work, but the fondue will be much thicker. A mild American lager, such as Budweiser, works best here. For dipping we like to use bread cubes, apple slices, steamed broccoli and cauliflower florets, and cured meats. The fondue will stay warm in the skillet for about 15 minutes. To reheat, return the skillet to low heat and cook, stirring constantly, until the fondue is smooth and begins to bubble, 5 to 10 minutes. Adjust the consistency with warm water, 1 tablespoon at a time, as needed.

8 ounces mild cheddar cheese, shredded (2 cups)

8 ounces American cheese, shredded (2 cups)

3 tablespoons cornstarch

1½ teaspoons dry mustard

¼ teaspoon pepper

¼ teaspoon cayenne pepper

1½ cups beer

1 garlic clove, minced

Toss cheddar, American cheese, cornstarch, mustard, pepper, and cayenne together in bowl until well combined. Bring beer and garlic to boil in 10-inch cast-iron skillet over medium-high heat. Reduce heat to medium-low and slowly whisk in cheese mixture, 1 handful at a time. Continue to cook, whisking constantly, until fondue is smooth and begins to bubble, 4 to 6 minutes. Serve.

VARIATION

Tex-Mex Fondue

Substitute 2 cups shredded pepper Jack cheese for cheddar cheese and 1 teaspoon chipotle chile powder for dry mustard.

SHREDDING SEMISOFT CHEESE

To prevent grater from becoming clogged when shredding semisoft cheeses, use vegetable oil spray to lightly coat holes, then shred away.

BAKED BRIE WITH HONEYED APRICOTS

SERVES 8 TO 10

WHY THIS RECIPE WORKS Baked Brie topped with jam or fruit—we like dried apricots and honey— is a popular party snack, and for good reason. When the cheese is warmed, it magically transforms into a rich, dippable concoction. Baking the cheese in a cast-iron skillet seemed like a no-brainer; since the skillet holds onto heat so well, it would keep the cheese in the ideal luscious, fluid state longer than any other pan. For sweet and creamy flavor in every bite, we reengineered the traditional whole wheel of baked Brie by trimming off the rind (which doesn't melt that well) and slicing the cheese into cubes. The result? Our honey-apricot mixture was evenly distributed throughout the dish, not just spooned on top. We finished the dish with an extra drizzle of honey and some minced chives to reinforce the sweet-savory flavor profile. Be sure to use a firm, fairly unripe Brie for this recipe. Serve with crackers or Melba toast.

¼ cup dried apricots, chopped

¼ cup honey

1 teaspoon minced fresh rosemary

¼ teaspoon salt

¼ teaspoon pepper

2 (8-ounce) wheels firm Brie cheese, rind removed, cheese cut into 1-inch pieces

1 tablespoon minced fresh chives

1 Adjust oven rack to middle position and heat oven to 400 degrees. Microwave apricots, 2 tablespoons honey, rosemary, salt, and pepper in medium bowl until apricots are softened and mixture is fragrant, about 1 minute, stirring halfway through microwaving. Add Brie and toss to combine.

2 Transfer mixture to 10-inch cast-iron skillet and bake until cheese is melted, 10 to 15 minutes. Drizzle with remaining 2 tablespoons honey and sprinkle with chives. Serve.

CUTTING RIND OFF BRIE

1 Using serrated knife, carefully slice top and bottom rind off wheel of Brie.

2 Trim rind from sides.

HUSHPUPPIES WITH CHIPOTLE AÏOLI

SERVES 8

WHY THIS RECIPE WORKS Hushpuppies are a classic Southern take on cornmeal dumplings that feature crispy outsides, fluffy insides, and big corn flavor. To get the best crunch, we looked to our 12-inch cast-iron skillet. A classic frying vessel, it holds onto heat extremely well; even after we had dropped the first batch of hushpuppy batter into the heated oil its temperature didn't fluctuate dramatically, which ensured a crunchy finish for even the last dumplings in the batch. For truly delicate interiors, we strayed from tradition and lightened the cornmeal batter with a little all-purpose flour. We stuck with tradition by using buttermilk as the liquid component in our batter, however. This ingredient not only added a nice tang, it also allowed us to incorporate baking soda into our recipe. Baking soda reacts with the acidic buttermilk, producing carbon dioxide bubbles that further lightened the batter. While we were at it, we added a little baking powder, which was activated when the batter was dropped into the hot oil, causing the dumplings to expand slightly and opening up their interior crumb. With our hushpuppies sufficiently tender, we looked to jazz up their relatively plain flavor. Cayenne pepper was an obvious addition, and scallions and Dijon mustard really helped to make these crowd favorites. While these hushpuppies are delicious on their own, we also whipped together a chipotle aïoli with a few pantry staples for the perfect dipping sauce to go along with them. Do not use stone-ground cornmeal in this recipe; it will make the texture of the hushpuppies too gritty. You will need a 12-inch cast-iron skillet with at least 2-inch sides for this recipe.

½ cup mayonnaise

5 teaspoons minced canned chipotle chile in adobo sauce

1 teaspoon lime juice

¾ cup cornmeal

½ cup all-purpose flour

1½ teaspoons baking powder

½ teaspoon baking soda

¼ teaspoon salt

¼ teaspoon cayenne pepper

¾ cup buttermilk

2 large eggs

2 scallions, sliced thin

2 tablespoons Dijon mustard

1 quart peanut or vegetable oil

1 Adjust oven rack to middle position and heat oven to 200 degrees. Whisk mayonnaise, chipotle, and lime juice together in bowl; set aside for serving.

2 Whisk cornmeal, flour, baking powder, baking soda, salt, and cayenne together in large bowl. In separate bowl, whisk buttermilk, eggs, scallions, and mustard together until well combined. Stir buttermilk mixture into cornmeal mixture with rubber spatula until just combined. Let batter sit at room temperature for 10 minutes.

3 Set wire rack in rimmed baking sheet and line with triple layer of paper towels. Add oil to 12-inch cast-iron skillet until it measures about ¾ inch deep and heat over medium-high heat to 375 degrees.

4 Carefully drop one-third of batter, 1 tablespoon at a time, into oil. Fry until deep golden brown, 2 to 4 minutes, flipping hushpuppies halfway through frying. Adjust burner, if necessary, to maintain oil temperature between 350 and 375 degrees. Transfer hushpuppies to prepared rack and keep warm in oven. (Hushpuppies can be kept warm in oven for up to 30 minutes.)

5 Return oil to 375 degrees and repeat with remaining batter in 2 batches. Serve with chipotle aïoli.

CHARRED GRAPE TOMATO BRUSCHETTA

SERVES 8 TO 10

WHY THIS RECIPE WORKS Traditional tomato bruschetta is a classic appetizer, but this Italian garlic bread can be a bit boring, especially when tomatoes aren't at their peak. We decided to enhance the bruschetta topping by charring grape tomatoes in a superhot cast-iron skillet. Cooking them for about 10 minutes created a beautiful, even blistering that drew out the natural sweetness of the tiny tomatoes while adding a deeper flavor profile and great color contrast. Simply tossing the tomatoes with oil and salt before cooking encouraged uniform blistering. Adding shallot, fresh oregano, and balsamic vinegar at the end balanced the sweetness of the mixture while complementing the charred tomatoes. Our updated, flavor-packed topping paired perfectly with the traditional toasted bread rubbed with raw garlic and olive oil. We finished the toasts with parsley, shaved Parmesan, and extra olive oil for a colorful, savory starter. A combination of red and yellow grape tomatoes makes for an attractive presentation. Cherry tomatoes can be substituted for grape tomatoes. If the tomatoes are out of season, add sugar to taste to enhance their sweetness as necessary.

1 (10 by 5-inch) loaf Italian bread,
   sliced ¾ inch thick
1 large garlic clove, halved
5 tablespoons extra-virgin olive oil
   Salt and pepper
2 pounds grape tomatoes
1 shallot, minced
1 tablespoon minced fresh oregano
   or 1 teaspoon dried
2 teaspoons balsamic vinegar
   Sugar
1 ounce Parmesan cheese, shaved
1 tablespoon minced fresh parsley

1 Adjust oven rack to middle position and heat oven to 400 degrees. Arrange bread slices in even layer in rimmed baking sheet and bake until dry and crisp, about 10 minutes, flipping slices halfway through baking. Rub cut side of garlic clove over 1 side of crostini, brush with 2 tablespoons oil, and season with salt and pepper; set aside.

2 Heat 12-inch cast-iron skillet over medium heat for 5 minutes. Toss tomatoes with 1 tablespoon oil and 1 teaspoon salt. Add tomatoes to skillet and cook, stirring occasionally, until lightly charred and blistered, about 10 minutes.

3 Stir in shallot, oregano, and ½ teaspoon pepper and cook until fragrant, about 30 seconds. Off heat, coarsely mash tomatoes using potato masher. Stir in vinegar and season with salt, pepper, and sugar to taste. Spoon tomato mixture onto crostini, sprinkle with Parmesan and parsley, and drizzle with remaining 2 tablespoons oil. Serve.

SHAVING PARMESAN

Using light touch, run vegetable peeler over block of Parmesan to achieve paper-thin slices.

WARM MARINATED ARTICHOKE HEARTS
WITH OLIVES AND FETA

SERVES 6 TO 8

WHY THIS RECIPE WORKS Although jars of artichoke hearts marinated in heavily seasoned oil line grocery store shelves, we wouldn't recommend serving that mushy, one-dimensional convenience food at your next dinner party. But you also don't have to tackle the leaves and spines of whole, fresh artichokes to make easy, elegant party fare with an inspired flavor profile. Our take on this appetizer began with jarred whole artichoke hearts packed in water. We halved the artichokes and seared them in a hot cast-iron pan to bring out their nutty flavor, then simmered them in olive oil over low heat to infuse the oil with flavor. The mild artichokes were the perfect base for aromatic herbs and spices—thyme, lemon, garlic, and fennel seeds—which increased the complexity of our dish. A dose of red pepper flakes made our artichokes a little zestier. We also added kalamata olives and simmered them with the artichokes and seasonings to mellow their brininess. We waited until the very end to stir in cubed feta and a little parsley, which ensured that the cubes wouldn't lose their shape and the parsley wouldn't discolor. We prefer the flavor and tenderness of jarred artichoke hearts here, but you can substitute frozen artichokes; if using, be sure to thaw them and pat them dry before cooking. Do not use marinated or oil-packed artichoke hearts. Serve with crusty bread for dipping in the infused oil.

1 cup extra-virgin olive oil

2 cups jarred whole artichoke hearts packed in water, halved and patted dry

Salt and pepper

3 sprigs fresh thyme

2 (2-inch) strips lemon zest plus 1 tablespoon juice

2 garlic cloves, sliced thin

1 teaspoon fennel seeds

½ teaspoon red pepper flakes

½ cup pitted kalamata olives, halved

4 ounces feta cheese, cut into ½-inch pieces (1 cup)

1 tablespoon minced fresh parsley

1 Heat 10-inch cast-iron skillet over medium heat for 3 minutes. Add 1 tablespoon oil and heat until shimmering. Add artichoke hearts and ½ teaspoon salt and cook until spotty brown, 7 to 9 minutes. Stir in thyme sprigs, lemon zest, garlic, fennel seeds, and pepper flakes and cook until fragrant, about 30 seconds.

2 Stir in olives and remaining oil. Reduce heat to low and cook until flavors meld and mixture is heated through, about 20 minutes.

3 Discard thyme sprigs and lemon zest, if desired. Gently stir in feta and lemon juice and season with salt and pepper to taste. Sprinkle with parsley. Serve.

VARIATION
Warm Marinated Artichoke Hearts
with Sun-Dried Tomatoes
Omit feta. Substitute 2 sprigs fresh rosemary for thyme, ½ cup coarsely chopped oil-packed sun-dried tomatoes for olives, and 2 tablespoons chopped fresh basil for parsley.

SPICY GARLIC SHRIMP

SERVES 6 TO 8

WHY THIS RECIPE WORKS Shrimp in garlicky olive oil is a Spanish tapas classic, but making this appetizer at home often results in rubbery, overcooked shrimp and flavorless oil. To solve these problems, we moved this dish to our cast-iron skillet. Searing in cast iron is an ideal way to prepare shrimp; it produces the ultimate combination of a well-caramelized exterior and a moist, tender interior. Executed properly, this cooking method also preserves the shrimp's plumpness and trademark briny sweetness. We simply seasoned the shrimp with salt and pepper before searing it in two batches. We sometimes add sugar to shrimp to encourage browning, but that proved unnecessary in this case as the high heat retention of the cast-iron skillet was enough to create the ideal dark golden sear without any help from additional ingredients. Searing just one side of the shrimp created a colorful presentation and a robust flavor without any danger of overcooking. We then thinly sliced a big handful of garlic cloves and gently simmered them in oil with a bay leaf and red pepper flakes for just a few minutes to create an aromatic, spicy dipping oil. Sherry vinegar and minced fresh parsley added at the end of cooking brightened the final flavor profile of the dish while echoing its Spanish roots. Note that the cooking time listed here is for large shrimp (26 to 30 per pound). If using smaller or larger shrimp, be sure to adjust the cooking time as needed. Serve with crusty bread for dipping in the infused oil.

1 pound large shrimp (26 to 30 per pound), peeled, deveined, and tails removed
Salt and pepper
½ cup extra-virgin olive oil
8 garlic cloves, sliced thin
1 bay leaf
½ teaspoon red pepper flakes
2 teaspoons sherry vinegar
1 tablespoon minced fresh parsley

1 Pat shrimp dry with paper towels and season with salt and pepper. Heat 10-inch cast-iron skillet over medium heat for 5 minutes. Add 1 tablespoon oil and heat until just smoking. Add half of shrimp in even layer and cook, without moving, until browned on 1 side, about 2 minutes; transfer to bowl. Repeat with 1 tablespoon oil and remaining shrimp; transfer to bowl.

2 Reduce heat to low and add remaining 6 tablespoons oil, garlic, bay leaf, and pepper flakes to now-empty skillet. Cook, stirring occasionally, until garlic is tender and beginning to brown, 4 to 7 minutes.

3 Increase heat to high and add shrimp and any accumulated juices. Cook, stirring constantly, until shrimp are opaque throughout, about 1 minute.

4 Discard bay leaf. Off heat, stir in vinegar and parsley and season with salt and pepper to taste. Serve.

PEELING AND DEVEINING SHRIMP

1 Break shell under swimming legs, which will come off as shell is removed. Leave tail intact if desired, or tug tail to remove shell.

2 Use paring knife to make shallow cut along back of shrimp to expose vein. Use tip of knife to lift out vein. Discard vein by wiping blade against paper towel.

LOADED BEEF NACHOS

SERVES 6 TO 8

WHY THIS RECIPE WORKS Who doesn't like nachos? A heaping pile of warm tortilla chips loaded with flavorful, spicy beef and gooey cheese holds undeniable appeal. But all too often, just a few minutes after emerging from the oven the chips end up soggy, the beef is cold, and the cheese is congealed. For nachos that could hold their hot-out-of-the-oven appeal until the very last chip is snagged, we moved this happy-hour favorite to the cast-iron skillet. While it may not be traditional, it turned out to be the perfect vessel for nachos; not only did it mean we could use fewer dishes (you can both cook the beef and serve the nachos in the same skillet), but cast iron also holds onto heat longer than aluminum or stainless steel, so the nachos stay warmer longer after you take them out of the oven. To ensure that every bite was loaded with toppings, we layered the nachos in the skillet, so even the chips on the bottom had an even coating of warm cheese and spicy beef. Serve with fresh tomato salsa, guacamole, sour cream, and lime wedges.

---

2 tablespoons vegetable oil

1 onion, chopped fine

8 ounces 90 percent lean ground beef

1 tablespoon chili powder

1 garlic clove, minced

1 teaspoon minced fresh oregano
   or ¼ teaspoon dried

½ teaspoon ground cumin

½ teaspoon ground coriander

¼ teaspoon cayenne pepper

⅛ teaspoon salt

½ cup chicken broth

8 ounces Monterey Jack cheese, shredded (2 cups)

8 ounces sharp cheddar cheese, shredded (2 cups)

8 ounces tortilla chips

¼ cup jarred jalapeños, chopped

2 scallions, sliced thin

1 Adjust oven rack to middle position and heat oven to 400 degrees. Heat 12-inch cast-iron skillet over medium heat for 3 minutes. Add oil and heat until shimmering. Add onion and cook until softened, about 5 minutes. Add ground beef and cook, breaking up meat with wooden spoon, until no longer pink, about 5 minutes. Stir in chili powder, garlic, oregano, cumin, coriander, cayenne, and salt and cook until fragrant, about 1 minute.

2 Stir in broth, scraping up any browned bits, and cook until nearly evaporated, about 2 minutes. Transfer mixture to medium bowl and stir in 1 cup Monterey Jack and 1 cup cheddar.

3 Wipe skillet clean with paper towels. Spread half of tortilla chips evenly in now-empty skillet. Sprinkle ½ cup Monterey Jack and ½ cup cheddar over chips, then top with half of beef mixture, followed by half of jalapeños. Repeat layering with remaining chips, ½ cup Monterey Jack, ½ cup cheddar, beef mixture, and jalapeños. Transfer skillet to oven and bake until cheese is melted and just beginning to brown, 10 to 15 minutes. Sprinkle with scallions and serve.

GREEN CHILE CHEESEBURGER SLIDERS

SERVES 10 TO 12

WHY THIS RECIPE WORKS We're not quite sure how sliders became all the rage, but for burger lovers this is one party snack that is far from waning in popularity. Our goal was a diminutive burger that delivered great char, juicy meat, and some chile spice. To create a flavorful crust on a small burger while retaining a moist interior, you need a real blast of heat that can char the outside quickly, and a well-seasoned cast-iron skillet is the best tool for the job. For an extra flavor kick that made these sliders perfect as an appetizer, we added a double dose of green chiles, both in the meat and on top of the burgers. To infuse flavor into the patties we sautéed onion, garlic, and canned green chiles, then pureed that mixture and added it to the ground beef. Refrigerating the burgers for half an hour ensured that the thin, delicate patties were easy to handle. For the topping, we reserved ½ cup of the sautéed green chile mixture before pureeing and combined it with mayonnaise, lime juice, and salt for a spread that added moisture and extra flavor to the sliders. Using shredded pepper Jack helped ensure that the cheese melted evenly on the burgers. Form the patties ½ inch wider than the slider buns; after the patties shrink during cooking, they will be the perfect size. We found Martin's 12 Sliced Potato Rolls to be a great slider bun. Using two spatulas when flipping these thin, moist patties is helpful.

5 tablespoons vegetable oil

1 onion, chopped fine

1½ cups canned chopped green chiles, rinsed and patted dry

1 garlic clove, minced

¼ cup mayonnaise

1 tablespoon lime juice

Salt and pepper

1 pound 85 percent lean ground beef

4 ounces pepper Jack cheese, shredded (1 cup)

12 soft white dinner rolls, sliced and toasted

1 Heat 12-inch cast-iron skillet over medium heat for 3 minutes. Add 2 tablespoons oil and heat until shimmering. Add onion and cook until softened, about 5 minutes. Stir in chiles and garlic and cook until fragrant, about 1 minute. Transfer mixture to food processor and process to smooth paste, about 1 minute, scraping down sides of bowl as needed. Combine ½ cup processed chile paste, mayonnaise, lime juice, and ¼ teaspoon salt in bowl; set aside for serving.

2 Add remaining chile paste, beef, ½ teaspoon salt, and ¼ teaspoon pepper to large bowl and knead with hands until uniformly combined. Divide meat mixture into 12 lightly packed balls, then flatten into ¼-inch-thick patties. Transfer patties to platter and refrigerate until chilled, about 30 minutes or up to 24 hours.

3 Wipe now-empty skillet clean with paper towels and heat over medium heat for 5 minutes. Add 1 tablespoon oil and heat until just smoking. Place 4 burgers in skillet and cook, without moving, until well browned on first side, about 2 minutes. Flip burgers and top with 1 heaping tablespoon pepper Jack. Cover and continue to cook until well browned on second side and cheese is melted, about 2 minutes.

4 Repeat with remaining 2 tablespoons oil, burgers, and pepper Jack in 2 batches. Serve burgers with buns and chile sauce.

LAMB MEATBALLS WITH YOGURT SAUCE

SERVES 8 TO 10

WHY THIS RECIPE WORKS Bite-size meatballs are a cocktail party staple. We wanted to try a new flavor twist on this traditional appetizer, so we looked for international inspiration from the heavily spiced lamb patties known as *kofte* that are a popular street food in the Middle East. In most authentic recipes, ground lamb is charred over an outdoor grill, so for our indoor version we achieved that charred lamb flavor by swapping out a fiery grill for a smoking-hot cast-iron skillet. With a Middle Eastern flavor profile in mind, we created a meatball mixture with ground lamb as our base and added fresh mint, cumin, garlic, cinnamon, and clove for the seasonings. For our binder we stuck with a standard egg yolk, but instead of a traditional panade of bread and milk to help bind the meat and ensure moistness, we used Greek yogurt and crushed saltines. The yogurt added a welcome tang to our meatballs that fit nicely within the flavor profile, and using dry saltines instead of fresh bread ensured that our meatballs held their shape but weren't too moist. We browned the meatballs in just one batch; it took only a few minutes in the hot cast-iron skillet to create a perfectly seared exterior. A tangy and refreshing Greek yogurt sauce provided the perfect pairing for these tasty morsels. To crush the saltines quickly and easily, place them in a zipper-lock bag and use a rolling pin to smash them.

---

1 cup plain Greek yogurt

3 tablespoons minced fresh mint

2 tablespoons extra-virgin olive oil

1 garlic clove, minced

½ teaspoon grated lemon zest plus ½ teaspoon juice
   Salt and pepper

6 square or 7 round saltines, crushed (3 tablespoons)

2 tablespoons water

1 pound ground lamb

1 large egg yolk

1 teaspoon ground cumin

¾ teaspoon ground cinnamon

⅛ teaspoon ground cloves

1 Combine ⅔ cup yogurt, 1 tablespoon mint, 1 tablespoon oil, half of garlic, lemon zest and juice, and ¼ teaspoon salt in bowl. Season with salt and pepper to taste. Cover and refrigerate until ready to serve.

2 Mash remaining ⅓ cup yogurt, crushed saltines, and water together with fork in large bowl to form paste. Add ground lamb, egg yolk, cumin, cinnamon, cloves, ¾ teaspoon salt, ⅛ teaspoon pepper, remaining 2 tablespoons mint, and remaining garlic and knead with hands until uniformly combined. Pinch off and roll mixture into 1-inch meatballs (about 35 meatballs).

3 Heat 12-inch cast-iron skillet over medium heat for 5 minutes. Add remaining 1 tablespoon oil and heat until just smoking. Brown meatballs on all sides, 5 to 8 minutes; using slotted spoon, transfer to serving platter. Serve with yogurt sauce.

CARAMELIZED ONION, PEAR, AND BACON TART

SERVES 8 TO 10

WHY THIS RECIPE WORKS A cast-iron skillet retains heat like a pizza stone with the functionality of a skillet, making it the perfect tool for a tart. We topped our version with bacon, which also helped grease the pan, and onions that we caramelized in the bacon fat. To ensure that this tart had broad appeal, we mixed in pear and goat cheese to balance the savory-sweet flavor profile. We like the convenience of using ready-made pizza dough here; however, you can use our Classic Pizza Dough.

8 slices bacon, chopped fine

2 pounds onions, halved and sliced ¼ inch thick

1 teaspoon minced fresh thyme or ¼ teaspoon dried

1½ teaspoons packed brown sugar

Salt and pepper

2 tablespoons balsamic vinegar

1 pound pizza dough

1 Bosc pear, quartered, cored, and sliced ¼ inch thick

4 ounces goat cheese, crumbled (1 cup)

2 tablespoons minced fresh chives

1 Adjust oven rack to upper-middle position and heat oven to 500 degrees. Cook bacon in 12-inch cast-iron skillet over medium heat until crisp, 7 to 9 minutes. Using slotted spoon, transfer bacon to bowl. Measure out and reserve ¼ cup fat; discard remaining fat.

2 Add 2 tablespoons reserved fat, onions, thyme, sugar, and ¾ teaspoon salt to now-empty skillet. Cover and cook, stirring occasionally, until onions are softened, 8 to 10 minutes. Uncover and continue to cook, stirring occasionally, until onions are deep golden brown, about 10 minutes. Stir in vinegar and cook until almost completely evaporated, about 2 minutes; transfer to bowl.

3 Wipe skillet clean with paper towels, then grease with 1 tablespoon reserved fat. Place dough on lightly floured counter, divide in half, and cover with greased plastic wrap. Press and roll 1 piece of dough (keeping remaining dough covered) into 11-inch round. Transfer dough to prepared skillet and gently push it to corners of pan. Spread half of onion mixture over dough, leaving ½-inch border around edge. Scatter half of pear, half of crisp bacon, and ½ cup goat cheese evenly over top.

4 Set skillet over medium-high heat and cook until outside edge of dough is set, tart is lightly puffed, and bottom crust is spotty brown when gently lifted with spatula, 2 to 4 minutes. Transfer skillet to oven and bake until edge of tart is golden brown, 7 to 10 minutes.

5 Using potholders, remove skillet from oven and slide tart onto wire rack; let cool slightly. Being careful of hot skillet handle, repeat with remaining 1 tablespoon reserved fat, dough, and toppings. Sprinkle tarts with chives and cut into wedges. Serve.

CLASSIC PIZZA DOUGH

MAKES 1 POUND

This recipe can easily be doubled.

2 cups (11 ounces) plus 2 tablespoons bread flour

1⅛ teaspoons instant or rapid-rise yeast

¾ teaspoon salt

1 tablespoon olive oil

¾ cup warm water (110 degrees)

1 Pulse flour, yeast, and salt together in food processor to combine, about 5 pulses. With processor running, add oil, then water, and process until rough ball forms, 30 to 40 seconds. Let dough rest for 2 minutes, then process for 30 seconds longer. (If after 30 seconds dough is very sticky and clings to blade, add extra flour as needed.)

2 Transfer dough to lightly floured counter and knead by hand to form smooth, round ball, about 1 minute. Place dough in large, lightly greased bowl, cover tightly with greased plastic wrap, and let rise until doubled in size, 1 to 1½ hours. (Alternatively, dough can be refrigerated for at least 8 hours or up to 16 hours.)

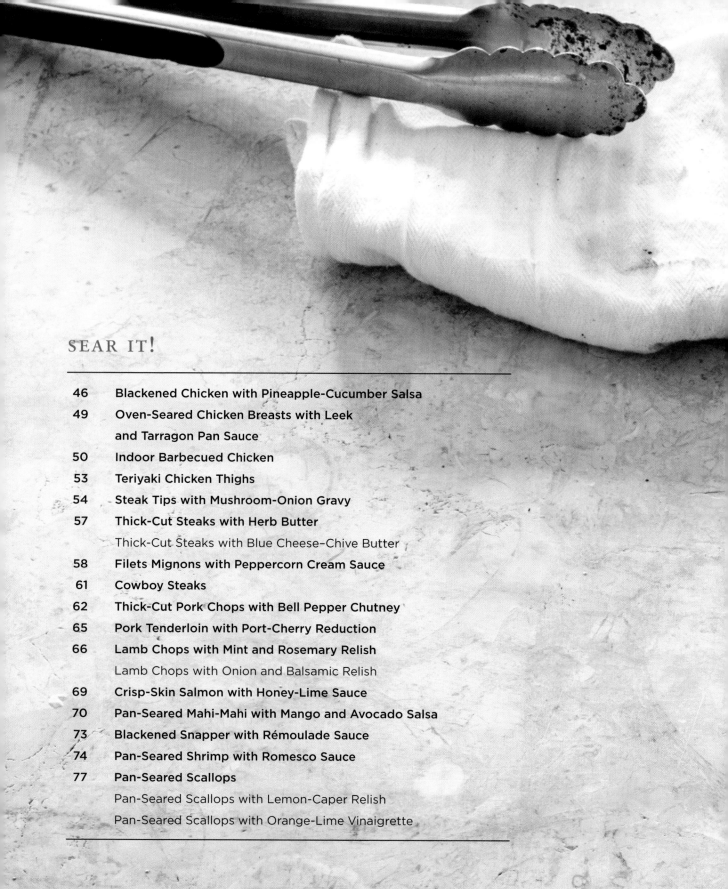

SEAR IT!

Cowboy Steaks

BLACKENED CHICKEN WITH PINEAPPLE-CUCUMBER SALSA

SERVES 4

WHY THIS RECIPE WORKS The appeal of blackened chicken lies in a complex, flavorful, crisp crust that envelops a juicy chicken breast. However, most of the time this dish ends up with a burnt-tasting exterior and chalk-dry meat. The key to cooking blackened boneless, skinless chicken breasts with a flavorful, moist interior is the heat level. Cooking over low or even moderate heat pushes the meat's moisture to the surface, and once the juices hit the exterior of the meat, the breasts will not brown at all. Cooking over high heat, however, burns the spices in the rub before the meat has a chance to cook through. To keep the spices from burning, we first pounded the thicker ends of the breasts to make them even so that they would cook through faster, ensuring that the spice rub spent less time exposed to intense heat. We got a great initial sear over medium-high heat and then finished the chicken at a lower, gentler temperature. The other key to a flavorful blackened-but-not-burned chicken is the rub. We chose a robust combination of ingredients: Brown sugar, coriander, ground ginger, garlic powder, allspice, and cayenne all lent their potent flavors to create a deeply complex mixture. A fruity salsa balanced the sharp, bold flavors in the rub. We turned to tangy pineapple and cooling cucumber to perfectly complement our spicy chicken.

2 cups ½-inch pineapple pieces

½ cucumber, peeled, halved lengthwise, seeded, and cut into ½-inch pieces

1 small shallot, minced

1 serrano chile, stemmed, seeded, and minced

2 tablespoons chopped fresh mint

1 tablespoon lime juice

Salt and pepper

1 tablespoon packed brown sugar

2 teaspoons ground coriander

1½ teaspoons ground ginger

1½ teaspoons garlic powder

¾ teaspoon ground allspice

½ teaspoon cayenne pepper

4 (6- to 8-ounce) boneless, skinless chicken breasts, trimmed

2 tablespoons vegetable oil

1 Adjust oven rack to middle position, place 12-inch cast-iron skillet on rack, and heat oven to 500 degrees. Meanwhile, combine pineapple, cucumber, shallot, serrano, mint, lime juice, and ½ teaspoon salt in bowl; set aside for serving.

2 Combine sugar, coriander, ginger, garlic powder, allspice, cayenne, 1 teaspoon salt, and ¾ teaspoon pepper in bowl, breaking up any lumps. Pound thicker ends of chicken breasts as needed to achieve even thickness. Pat chicken dry with paper towels and rub evenly with spice mixture.

3 When oven reaches 500 degrees, remove skillet from oven using potholders and place over medium-high heat; turn off oven. Being careful of hot skillet handle, add oil and heat until just smoking. Cook chicken, without moving, until lightly browned on first side, about 2 minutes. Flip chicken and continue to cook until lightly browned on second side, about 2 minutes.

4 Flip chicken, reduce heat to medium, and cook until very dark brown and chicken registers 160 degrees, 4 to 7 minutes, flipping chicken halfway through cooking. Serve with salsa.

OVEN-SEARED CHICKEN BREASTS WITH LEEK AND TARRAGON PAN SAUCE

SERVES 4

WHY THIS RECIPE WORKS Bone-in, skin-on chicken breasts are more flavorful than boneless, skinless breasts, but getting the skin to crisp without overcooking the delicate meat can be a challenge. We developed a streamlined method that starts by preheating a cast-iron skillet in a very hot oven, then dropping the oven temperature and adding the chicken to both sear the skin and roast the breasts at the same time. The trick was to start the breasts skin side down. This allowed the heat of the skillet and the heat from the oven to crisp the skin while the weight of the breast pressed down on it. The result was ultracrisp skin on a perfectly moist chicken breast. While the chicken rested, we made a quick pan sauce that captured all the tasty browned bits the meat left behind. We started by sweating a leek, then added some flour to help thicken the sauce. Next we poured in savory chicken broth and flavorful vermouth, which we then reduced for a thicker consistency. Fresh tarragon, whole-grain mustard, and a little butter gave our sauce a distinctive flavor identity and richness.

4 (12-ounce) bone-in split chicken breasts, trimmed
1 tablespoon vegetable oil
Salt and pepper
1 leek, white and light green parts only, halved lengthwise, chopped fine, and washed thoroughly
1 teaspoon all-purpose flour
1 cup chicken broth
½ cup dry vermouth or dry white wine
1 tablespoon unsalted butter
1 tablespoon minced fresh tarragon
1 teaspoon whole-grain mustard

1 Adjust oven rack to middle position, place 12-inch cast-iron skillet on rack, and heat oven to 500 degrees. Meanwhile, pat chicken dry with paper towels, rub with oil, and season with salt and pepper.

2 When oven reaches 500 degrees, place chicken skin side down in hot skillet. Reduce oven temperature to 450 degrees and roast until chicken is well browned and registers 160 degrees, 25 to 30 minutes, flipping chicken halfway through roasting.

3 Using potholders, remove skillet from oven. Transfer chicken to serving platter, tent loosely with aluminum foil, and let rest while making sauce.

4 Being careful of hot skillet handle, pour off all but 1 tablespoon fat from skillet. Add leek, cover, and cook over medium heat, stirring occasionally, until softened, 5 to 10 minutes. Stir in flour and cook, uncovered, for 1 minute. Slowly whisk in broth and vermouth, scraping up any browned bits and smoothing out any lumps. Bring to simmer and cook until sauce is thickened and reduced to about 1 cup, 5 to 10 minutes.

5 Stir in any accumulated chicken juices. Off heat, whisk in butter, tarragon, and mustard. Season with salt and pepper to taste. Spoon sauce over chicken and serve.

INDOOR BARBECUED CHICKEN

SERVES 4

WHY THIS RECIPE WORKS You don't need a grill for classic barbecue tang and tender, juicy chicken; you can get the same deep flavor and great browning indoors with your cast-iron skillet. To build levels of flavor, we first rubbed the chicken with a spicy mixture of chili powder, brown sugar, garlic powder, cumin, salt, and pepper. We then employed the method from our Oven-Seared Chicken Breasts with Leek and Tarragon Pan Sauce (page 49), which uses a superhot preheated pan and a hot oven to crisp up the skin and develop flavorful browning on the chicken while still retaining moisture. While the meat rested, we made a quick but deeply flavored ketchup-molasses barbecue sauce in the empty skillet. To finish, we simply tossed the chicken thoroughly with the sauce before serving. Waiting to make the sauce until after cooking the chicken kept it from burning and gave the skin on the chicken a chance to develop color first. The bright, tangy flavors of the sauce were complemented by the deeper, smoky flavors of the spice rub.

1 tablespoon vegetable oil

2½ teaspoons chili powder

1½ teaspoons packed brown sugar

1 teaspoon garlic powder

½ teaspoon ground cumin

   Salt and pepper

3 pounds bone-in chicken pieces (split breasts cut in half, drumsticks, and/or thighs), trimmed

½ onion, chopped fine

⅔ cup ketchup

⅓ cup water

3 tablespoons molasses

1 tablespoon Worcestershire sauce

1 tablespoon Dijon mustard

2 teaspoons cider vinegar

1 Adjust oven rack to middle position, place 12-inch cast-iron skillet on rack, and heat oven to 500 degrees. Meanwhile, combine oil, chili powder, sugar, garlic powder, cumin, 1 teaspoon salt, and 1 teaspoon pepper in bowl. Pat chicken dry with paper towels and rub evenly with spice mixture.

2 When oven reaches 500 degrees, place chicken skin side down in hot skillet. Reduce oven temperature to 450 degrees and roast until chicken is well browned, breasts register 160 degrees, and drumsticks/thighs register 175 degrees, 25 to 30 minutes, flipping chicken halfway through roasting.

3 Using potholders, remove skillet from oven. Transfer chicken to serving platter and let rest while making sauce.

4 Being careful of hot skillet handle, pour off all but 1 tablespoon fat from skillet. Add onion and cook over medium heat until softened, about 5 minutes. Whisk in ketchup, water, molasses, Worcestershire, and mustard and cook, stirring occasionally, until thickened and reduced to about 1 cup, 2 to 5 minutes.

5 Stir in any accumulated chicken juices. Off heat, whisk in vinegar and season with salt and pepper to taste. Return chicken to skillet and turn to coat with sauce. Return chicken to serving platter and serve, passing remaining sauce separately.

HALVING BONE-IN CHICKEN BREASTS

After smoothing skin to cover breast, cut breast in half until knife hits bone. To get through bone, rock knife back and forth, applying pressure from heel of your other hand, until separated.

TERIYAKI CHICKEN THIGHS

SERVES 4

WHY THIS RECIPE WORKS For a truly great, fuss-free method that delivered the ultimate chicken teriyaki—crisp skin and juicy meat slathered with a perfectly balanced sweet-salty glaze—we started with bone-in, skin-on chicken thighs. The rich, meaty flavor of this cut stood up nicely to the strong flavors of traditional teriyaki sauce. To ensure that the maximum amount of skin came in contact with the skillet, we pressed the meat down with a weighted Dutch oven. This method forced the thighs flat against the preheated cast-iron skillet to ensure even, direct contact with the hot pan and resulted in ultracrisp skin. For the glaze, our mixture balanced salty soy sauce with the sweetness of sugar and mirin, a sweet Japanese rice wine, and spicy ginger and savory garlic provided depth. For the perfect consistency, we cooked the teriyaki sauce down in the skillet and added a bit of cornstarch, which gave it extra clinging power. Mirin is a key component of teriyaki; it can be found in the international section of most major supermarkets and in most Asian markets. If you cannot find it, use 2 tablespoons of white wine and an extra teaspoon of sugar.

8 (5- to 7-ounce) bone-in chicken thighs, trimmed
  Salt and pepper
1 tablespoon vegetable oil
½ cup soy sauce
½ cup sugar
2 tablespoons mirin
1 garlic clove, minced
½ teaspoon grated fresh ginger
½ teaspoon cornstarch
2 scallions, thinly sliced on bias

1 Adjust oven rack to middle position, place 12-inch cast-iron skillet on rack, and heat oven to 500 degrees. Meanwhile, pat chicken dry with paper towels and season with pepper.

2 When oven reaches 500 degrees, remove skillet from oven using potholders and place over medium heat; turn off oven. Being careful of hot skillet handle, add oil and heat until just smoking. Place chicken skin side down in skillet. Place weighted Dutch oven on top of chicken and cook until skin is deep brown and very crisp, 16 to 20 minutes, checking browning after 10 minutes and adjusting heat as needed.

3 Remove weighted pot and flip chicken. Continue to cook, without weight, until chicken is lightly browned on second side and registers 175 degrees, about 2 minutes; transfer to serving platter.

4 Whisk soy sauce, sugar, mirin, garlic, ginger, and cornstarch together in bowl. Pour off fat from skillet, then add soy sauce mixture and bring to simmer over medium heat. Cook, stirring occasionally, until sauce is thick and glossy, about 2 minutes. Stir in any accumulated chicken juices. Return chicken to skillet and turn to coat with sauce. Return chicken to serving platter, sprinkle with scallions, and serve, passing remaining sauce separately.

PRESSING CHICKEN THIGHS

Place chicken skin side down in skillet. Place Dutch oven, weighted with cans, on top of chicken to press chicken fully and evenly against hot pan surface.

STEAK TIPS WITH MUSHROOM-ONION GRAVY

SERVES 4

WHY THIS RECIPE WORKS Steak tips smothered with mushroom and onion gravy is a classic combination. But this dish is too often plagued by chewy, overcooked beef, bland gravy, and prefab ingredients like canned cream of mushroom soup. We wanted tender, meaty steak and full-flavored gravy, enriched by fresh mushrooms and onions, and we wanted to do it all in one pan, so naturally we turned to our cast-iron skillet. We started by searing the meat in batches, creating flavorful browning and fond without overcrowding the pan. After removing the meat from the skillet, we added our mushrooms and onions, covered them, and let the mushrooms release their liquid. We then cooked off the liquid, scraping up all the flavorful browned bits the beef left behind and concentrating the mushroom flavor. We finished our gravy by adding savory garlic, tomato paste, thyme, and Worcestershire sauce. Allowing the meat to finish cooking in the gravy blended the flavors and built depth. A touch of fresh parsley and bright red wine vinegar added at the very end rounded out the dish. Sirloin steak tips, also known as flap meat, can be sold as whole steaks, cubes, and strips. To ensure uniform pieces, we prefer to purchase whole steaks and cut them ourselves.

2 pounds sirloin steak tips, trimmed and cut into 1½-inch pieces

Salt and pepper

¼ cup vegetable oil

1 pound white mushrooms, trimmed and sliced ¼ inch thick

1 large onion, halved and sliced thin

2 garlic cloves, minced

2 teaspoons tomato paste

1 teaspoon minced fresh thyme or ¼ teaspoon dried

3 tablespoons all-purpose flour

1¾ cups beef broth

1 tablespoon Worcestershire sauce

1 tablespoon chopped fresh parsley

2 teaspoons red wine vinegar

1 Adjust oven rack to middle position, place 12-inch cast-iron skillet on rack, and heat oven to 500 degrees. Meanwhile, pat steak tips dry with paper towels and season with salt and pepper.

2 When oven reaches 500 degrees, remove skillet from oven using potholders and place over medium heat; turn off oven. Being careful of hot skillet handle, add 2 tablespoons oil and heat until just smoking. Brown half of steak tips on all sides, 6 to 8 minutes; transfer to bowl. Repeat with 1 tablespoon oil and remaining steak tips; transfer to bowl.

3 Add remaining 1 tablespoon oil to fat left in skillet and heat over medium heat until shimmering. Add mushrooms, onion, and ¼ teaspoon salt, cover, and cook, stirring occasionally, until mushrooms have released all their liquid, about 5 minutes. Uncover and continue to cook until liquid has evaporated and vegetables begin to brown, 4 to 6 minutes.

4 Stir in garlic, tomato paste, and thyme and cook until fragrant, about 30 seconds. Stir in flour and cook for 1 minute. Stir in broth and Worcestershire, scraping up any browned bits and smoothing out any lumps.

5 Bring gravy to simmer, then stir in browned beef and any accumulated juices. Reduce heat to medium-low and simmer, stirring occasionally, until beef registers 130 to 135 degrees (for medium), 3 to 5 minutes. Off heat, stir in parsley and vinegar and season with salt and pepper to taste. Serve.

THICK-CUT STEAKS WITH HERB BUTTER

SERVES 4

WHY THIS RECIPE WORKS Pan-searing a thick-cut steak presents a real challenge: How do you keep the perimeter from overcooking while the center of the steak reaches the desired temperature for the perfect balance of crisp crust and tender, juicy interior? We've found that searing the steak over high heat and then gently finishing it in the oven works well. But we were looking for a way to make a steak with the ultimate crust entirely on the stovetop—so we turned to a cast-iron skillet, since its heat-retention properties are ideal for a perfect sear. We chose the moderately expensive boneless strip steak for its big, beefy flavor. The first step to a great sear was an evenly heated cooking surface, which we accomplished by preheating the cast-iron skillet in the oven. This also gave us time to prepare a zesty compound butter with shallot, garlic, parsley, and chives—and to let the steaks warm up to room temperature, which helped them cook more quickly and evenly. Salting the outside of the steaks while they rested pulled moisture from the steaks while also seasoning the meat. This helped us get a better sear. We started out flipping our steaks only once, halfway through cooking. However, we found that flipping the steaks more often led to a shorter cooking time and a smaller gray band of dry, overcooked meat just under the surface of the steaks. After testing different flipping techniques and heating levels, we found that flipping the steaks every 2 minutes and transitioning from medium-high to medium-low heat partway through cooking resulted in a perfectly browned, crisp crust and a juicy, evenly cooked interior every time.

2 (1-pound) boneless strip steaks, 1½ inches thick, trimmed

Salt and pepper

4 tablespoons unsalted butter, softened

2 tablespoons minced shallot

1 tablespoon minced fresh parsley

1 tablespoon minced fresh chives

1 garlic clove, minced

2 tablespoons vegetable oil

1 Adjust oven rack to middle position, place 12-inch cast-iron skillet on rack, and heat oven to 500 degrees. Meanwhile, season steaks with salt and let sit at room temperature. Mix butter, shallot, parsley, chives, garlic, and ¼ teaspoon pepper together in bowl; set aside until needed.

2 When oven reaches 500 degrees, pat steaks dry with paper towels and season with pepper. Using potholders, remove skillet from oven and place over medium-high heat; turn off oven. Being careful of hot skillet handle, add oil and heat until just smoking. Cook steaks, without moving, until lightly browned on first side, about 2 minutes. Flip steaks and continue to cook until lightly browned on second side, about 2 minutes.

3 Flip steaks, reduce heat to medium-low, and cook, flipping every 2 minutes, until steaks are well browned and meat registers 120 to 125 degrees (for medium-rare), 7 to 9 minutes. Transfer steaks to carving board, dollop 2 tablespoons herb butter on each steak, tent loosely with aluminum foil, and let rest for 5 to 10 minutes. Slice steaks into ½-inch-thick slices and serve.

VARIATION

Thick-Cut Steaks with Blue Cheese–Chive Butter

Omit shallot and parsley. Increase chives to 2 tablespoons and add ⅓ cup crumbled mild blue cheese to butter with chives.

FILETS MIGNONS WITH PEPPERCORN CREAM SAUCE

SERVES 4

WHY THIS RECIPE WORKS For our filets mignons, we took what we learned from our Thick-Cut Steaks with Herb Butter (page 57) and applied it to this leaner but still thick piece of meat. Using the oven to preheat the pan ensured an evenly heated, superhot cooking surface. This step also gave us time to season the filets with salt and let them sit at room temperature, a move that drew out moisture from the steaks. Since moisture is the enemy of browning, this was an important step in creating an evenly browned surface on the filets. Searing the filets over medium-high heat in the hot skillet before finishing them gently over lower heat created a crisp crust and a perfectly medium-rare, juicy interior. Because filets are relatively lean, they pair well with a rich pan sauce. We turned to white wine, chicken broth, and heavy cream for the backbone of our sauce, which we then reduced to concentrate the flavors. Using the same skillet for the meat and the sauce allowed us to incorporate all the tasty browned bits left in the pan for additional flavor. Once reduced, the creamy sauce boasted savory depth and richness but needed something more. Bold, fresh tarragon and spicy, coarsely ground black pepper—both classic complementary flavors for beef—finished the sauce and gave it a flavorful punch.

4 (6- to 7-ounce) center-cut filets mignons, 1½ inches thick, trimmed

Salt and coarsely ground pepper

2 tablespoons vegetable oil

1 shallot, minced

¾ cup dry white wine

½ cup chicken broth

½ cup heavy cream

1 tablespoon minced fresh tarragon

1 Adjust oven rack to middle position, place 12-inch cast-iron skillet on rack, and heat oven to 500 degrees. Meanwhile, season steaks with salt and let sit at room temperature.

2 When oven reaches 500 degrees, pat steaks dry with paper towels and season with pepper. Using potholders, remove skillet from oven and place over medium-high heat; turn off oven. Being careful of hot skillet handle, add oil and heat until just smoking. Cook steaks, without moving, until lightly browned on first side, about 2 minutes. Flip steaks and continue to cook until lightly browned on second side, about 2 minutes.

3 Flip steaks, reduce heat to medium-low, and cook, flipping every 2 minutes, until steaks are well browned and meat registers 120 to 125 degrees (for medium-rare), 6 to 8 minutes. Transfer steaks to serving platter, tent loosely with aluminum foil, and let rest while making sauce.

4 Add shallot to fat left in skillet and cook over medium-high heat until softened, about 30 seconds. Stir in wine, broth, and cream, scraping up any browned bits. Bring to simmer and cook until slightly thickened, 6 to 8 minutes. Stir in any accumulated meat juices and cook for 1 minute. Off heat, whisk in tarragon and 1 teaspoon pepper and season with salt to taste. Serve steaks, passing sauce separately.

COWBOY STEAKS

SERVES 4

WHY THIS RECIPE WORKS Cowboy steaks are traditionally thick-cut bone-in rib eyes that are grilled over a hot fire, and they are known for their big, beefy, smoky flavor. We turned to a cast-iron skillet to replicate this Southwestern classic indoors. Fitting four bone-in rib eyes in a single skillet and still getting an even sear on both sides of each steak proved too cumbersome. Instead, we chose the thinner and less expensive (yet still tender and flavorful) top sirloin steak. To replicate the smoky flavor of meat slow-cooked on the grill, we used two smoked spices in our rub: smoked paprika and chipotle chile powder. This combination ensured levels of smokiness and spice in every bite for a quick, easy barbecue fix. Garlic powder, salt, and pepper rounded out our simple yet deeply flavorful rub. We began by searing each side of the steaks over medium-high heat on the stovetop in a preheated cast-iron skillet for an ideal brown crust, then gently finished the steaks to a perfect medium-rare over medium-low heat.

2 teaspoons smoked paprika

1½ teaspoons salt

1 teaspoon chipotle chile powder

1 teaspoon garlic powder

½ teaspoon pepper

2 (1-pound) boneless top sirloin steaks, 1 inch thick, trimmed and halved crosswise

2 tablespoons vegetable oil

1 Adjust oven rack to middle position, place 12-inch cast-iron skillet on rack, and heat oven to 500 degrees. Meanwhile, combine paprika, salt, chile powder, garlic powder, and pepper in bowl. Pat steaks dry with paper towels and rub evenly with spice mixture.

2 When oven reaches 500 degrees, remove skillet from oven using potholders and place over medium-high heat; turn off oven. Being careful of hot skillet handle, add oil and heat until just smoking. Cook steaks, without moving, until lightly browned on first side, about 2 minutes. Flip steaks and continue to cook until lightly browned on second side, about 2 minutes.

3 Flip steaks, reduce heat to medium-low, and cook until very dark brown and meat registers 120 to 125 degrees (for medium-rare), 4 to 6 minutes, flipping steaks halfway through cooking. Transfer steaks to serving platter, tent loosely with aluminum foil, and let rest for 5 to 10 minutes. Serve.

TAKING THE TEMPERATURE OF STEAKS AND CHOPS

To determine internal temperature for steaks, chops, and other small cuts, insert instant-read thermometer deep into side of meat, away from bone (if applicable).

THICK-CUT PORK CHOPS WITH BELL PEPPER CHUTNEY

SERVES 4

WHY THIS RECIPE WORKS We wanted a foolproof method for producing juicy, tender pork chops with great browning. Preheating a cast-iron skillet in the oven before moving it to the stovetop over medium-high heat gave us a perfect sear, which we followed by gently finishing the chops over lower heat. To keep the pork chops flat, we made two slits through the fat and connective tissue surrounding them; since it contracts faster than the rest of the meat, it can cause buckling and lead to an uneven sear. The chops are best cooked to 145 degrees, so we started checking the temperature on the earlier side of the time range to avoid overcooking them. We brined the pork chops to ensure that they stayed moist and juicy. To accent our chops, we made a quick savory red bell pepper chutney while they rested. We sautéed shallot and red bell pepper before adding chicken broth, pork chop drippings, sugar, garlic, and an assortment of spices. Vinegar and fresh parsley added at the very end contributed brightness. If your pork is enhanced (injected with a salt solution), do not brine in step 1, but season with salt in step 2.

Salt and pepper

7 tablespoons sugar

4 (12-ounce) bone-in pork rib chops, 1½ inches thick, trimmed

1 tablespoon vegetable oil

2 red bell peppers, stemmed, seeded, and chopped fine

2 shallots, minced

1 garlic clove, minced

1 teaspoon grated fresh ginger

½ teaspoon yellow mustard seeds

¼ teaspoon red pepper flakes

⅓ cup chicken broth

1 tablespoon white wine vinegar

1 tablespoon minced fresh parsley

1 Dissolve 3 tablespoons salt and 3 tablespoons sugar in 1½ quarts cold water in large container. Cut 2 slits about 2 inches apart through fat and connective tissue on edges of each pork chop. Submerge chops in brine, cover, and refrigerate for at least 30 minutes or up to 1 hour.

2 Adjust oven rack to middle position, place 12-inch cast-iron skillet on rack, and heat oven to 500 degrees. Meanwhile, remove chops from brine, pat dry with paper towels, and season with pepper.

3 When oven reaches 500 degrees, remove skillet from oven using potholders and place over medium-high heat; turn off oven. Being careful of hot skillet handle, add oil and heat until just smoking. Cook chops, without moving, until lightly browned on first side, about 3 minutes. Flip chops and continue to cook until lightly browned on second side, about 3 minutes.

4 Flip chops, reduce heat to medium-low, and cook until well browned and pork registers 145 degrees, 14 to 18 minutes, flipping chops halfway through cooking. Transfer chops to serving platter, tent loosely with aluminum foil, and let rest while making chutney.

5 Pour off all but 1 tablespoon fat from skillet. Add bell peppers, shallots, and ½ teaspoon salt, cover, and cook over medium heat, stirring occasionally, until softened, about 5 minutes. Stir in garlic, ginger, mustard seeds, and pepper flakes and cook until fragrant, about 30 seconds.

6 Stir in broth and remaining ¼ cup sugar, scraping up any browned bits. Bring to simmer and cook, stirring occasionally, until chutney is thickened, 5 to 7 minutes. Stir in any accumulated pork juices. Off heat, stir in vinegar and parsley. Season with salt and pepper to taste. Spoon chutney over chops and serve.

PORK TENDERLOIN WITH PORT-CHERRY REDUCTION

SERVES 4

WHY THIS RECIPE WORKS Pork tenderloin has a lot going for it: It's supertender with a buttery, fine-grained texture; it's easy to prepare; it cooks quickly; and its mild flavor is the perfect backdrop for a variety of sauces. But because pork tenderloin is so lean, it frequently ends up dry and overcooked. We wanted a recipe that would produce flavorful and juicy pork tenderloin every time. Preheating the skillet in the oven before adding the tenderloins ensured that they cooked quickly but still developed a great crust. For a flavorful pan sauce, we made a sweet-tart reduction of ruby port, tart balsamic vinegar, tangy dried cherries, and savory thyme that perfectly complemented the pork. The sauce came together in the same skillet in which we cooked the meat while the tenderloins rested after cooking. To ensure that the tenderloins don't curl during cooking, remove the silverskin from the meat.

2 (12- to 16-ounce) pork tenderloins, trimmed
   Salt and pepper
2 tablespoons vegetable oil
1 shallot, minced
¾ cup port
¼ cup balsamic vinegar
¼ cup dried cherries, chopped
1 sprig fresh thyme
2 tablespoons unsalted butter

1 Adjust oven rack to middle position, place 12-inch cast-iron skillet on rack, and heat oven to 500 degrees. Meanwhile, season pork with salt and let sit at room temperature.

2 When oven reaches 500 degrees, pat pork dry with paper towels and season with pepper. Using pot holders, remove skillet from oven and place over medium-high heat; turn off oven. Being careful of hot skillet handle, add oil and heat until just smoking. Brown pork on all sides, about 10 minutes.

3 Reduce heat to medium-low and continue to cook pork, turning as needed, until well browned and pork registers 145 degrees, 8 to 12 minutes. Transfer pork to carving board, tent loosely with aluminum foil, and let rest while making reduction.

4 Add shallot to fat left in skillet and cook over medium heat until softened, about 30 seconds. Stir in port, vinegar, cherries, and thyme sprig, scraping up any browned bits. Bring to simmer and cook until slightly thickened and reduced to about ½ cup, 4 to 6 minutes. Off heat, discard thyme sprig and whisk in butter. Season with salt and pepper to taste. Slice pork into ½-inch-thick slices and serve with reduction.

REMOVING PORK SILVERSKIN

Silverskin is connective tissue between meat and surface fat. To remove, slip knife under silverskin, angle knife slightly upward, and cut with gentle back-and-forth motion.

LAMB CHOPS WITH MINT AND ROSEMARY RELISH

SERVES 4

WHY THIS RECIPE WORKS Lamb and cast iron have great chemistry. The intense heat of a preheated cast-iron pan can produce a great crust on lamb and also melt away the meat's abundance of fat, distributing flavor throughout. We wanted to develop a technique that would complement the mild, sweet flavor of lamb chops with no risk of overcooking this delicate cut. Simply searing the chops quickly on both sides over medium-high heat and then gently finishing them over lower heat created a crisp crust and juicy interior. For seasoning, we stuck to the basics with just salt and pepper, and to add flavor and complement the lamb, we created a quick olive oil–based mint and rosemary relish, similar to a chimichurri sauce. The bold mint and rosemary combination, along with garlic, spicy red pepper flakes, and tangy red wine vinegar, was the perfect pairing with the flavor of the lamb. Unlike shoulder chops, rib or loin chops are best cooked to medium-rare in order to retain their delicate flavor and tender texture; chops cooked past medium were dry and less flavorful and juicy.

RELISH

- ½ cup minced fresh mint
- 5 tablespoons extra-virgin olive oil
- 2 teaspoons minced fresh rosemary
- 2 teaspoons red wine vinegar
- 1 garlic clove, minced
- ⅛ teaspoon red pepper flakes
  Salt and pepper

LAMB

- 8 (5- to 6-ounce) lamb rib or loin chops, 1¼ to 1½ inches thick, trimmed
  Salt and pepper
- 2 tablespoons vegetable oil

1 FOR THE RELISH Adjust oven rack to middle position, place 12-inch cast-iron skillet on rack, and heat oven to 500 degrees. Meanwhile, combine all ingredients in serving bowl. Season with salt and pepper to taste; set aside for serving.

2 FOR THE LAMB Pat chops dry with paper towels and season with salt and pepper. When oven reaches 500 degrees, remove skillet from oven using potholders and place over medium-high heat; turn off oven. Being careful of hot skillet handle, add oil and heat until just smoking. Cook chops, without moving, until lightly browned on first side, about 2 minutes. Flip chops and continue to cook until lightly browned on second side, about 2 minutes.

3 Flip chops, reduce heat to medium-low, and cook until well browned and meat registers 120 to 125 degrees (for medium-rare), 3 to 5 minutes, flipping chops halfway through cooking. Transfer chops to serving platter, tent loosely with aluminum foil, and let rest for 5 to 10 minutes. Serve with relish.

VARIATION

Lamb Chops with Onion and Balsamic Relish
Omit mint relish. While chops rest, pour off all but 1 tablespoon fat from skillet. Add 1 finely chopped small red onion and ¼ teaspoon salt and cook over medium heat until softened and lightly browned, about 5 minutes. Stir in 2 minced garlic cloves and cook until fragrant, about 30 seconds. Off heat, stir in 2 tablespoons balsamic vinegar. Transfer onion mixture to small serving bowl and let cool slightly. Stir in 3 tablespoons extra-virgin olive oil and 2 tablespoons minced fresh parsley. Season with salt and pepper to taste, then serve with chops.

CRISP-SKIN SALMON WITH HONEY-LIME SAUCE

SERVES 4

WHY THIS RECIPE WORKS Rich, meaty salmon and sweet-tangy flavors are a fantastic pairing, but most recipes fall short, producing soggy skin that gets pushed to the side of the plate, unevenly cooked fish, and an overly sweet sauce. To make a foolproof recipe using this combination, we turned to a cast-iron skillet and its excellent searing abilities. Preheating the skillet in the oven ensured that it was hot enough to cook the outside of the fish quickly without overcooking the inside. We first seared the flesh side over medium heat until we got a gorgeous brown crust, then we flipped the salmon skin side down and crisped the skin over medium-low heat. Making three or four shallow slashes in the skin helped to render some of the excess fat and ensured that the skin was supercrisp for a perfect contrast to the rich fish. For our sauce, we balanced honey with tangy lime zest and juice to keep its sweetness in check, plus a bit of cayenne for added complexity and heat. To ensure uniform pieces of salmon that cooked at the same rate, we found it best to buy a whole center-cut fillet and cut it into four pieces ourselves. If your knife is not sharp enough to cut through the skin easily, try a serrated knife.

2 tablespoons honey

1 tablespoon minced fresh chives

2 teaspoons grated lime zest plus 4 teaspoons juice

⅛ teaspoon cayenne pepper

1 (2-pound) skin-on salmon fillet, 1½ inches thick, sliced crosswise into 4 equal pieces

1 tablespoon vegetable oil

Salt and pepper

1 Adjust oven rack to middle position, place 12-inch cast-iron skillet on rack, and heat oven to 500 degrees. Meanwhile, combine honey, chives, lime zest and juice, and cayenne in bowl; set aside for serving.

2 Using sharp knife, make 3 to 4 shallow slashes about 1 inch apart on skin side of each fillet, being careful not to cut into flesh. Pat salmon dry with paper towels, rub with oil, and season with salt and pepper.

3 When oven reaches 500 degrees, remove skillet from oven using potholders and place over medium heat; turn off oven. Being careful of hot skillet handle, place salmon flesh side down in skillet and cook until well browned, 3 to 4 minutes.

4 Gently flip salmon, reduce heat to medium-low, and continue to cook until skin is crisp and center is still translucent when checked with tip of paring knife and registers 125 degrees (for medium-rare), 9 to 12 minutes. Transfer salmon to serving platter and spoon sauce over top. Serve.

SCORING FISH SKIN

Using sharp knife, make 3 to 4 shallow slashes, about 1 inch apart, on skin side of each fillet, being careful not to cut into flesh.

PAN-SEARED MAHI-MAHI
WITH MANGO AND AVOCADO SALSA

SERVES 4

WHY THIS RECIPE WORKS Mahi-mahi boasts a hearty, meaty texture that makes it a perfect candidate for high-heat cooking in a cast-iron skillet where it can get a great sear on both sides. To complement this mild-tasting fish, we seasoned the fillets with a combination of salt, pepper, and lemony coriander. After searing the flesh side over medium heat for even browning, we flipped the fillets and reduced the heat to gently cook the fish through. We then created a mango salsa to sweeten things up: Diced mango tossed with avocado, red onion, cilantro, and lime juice gave us a bright and zingy accompaniment to our perfectly charred fish. Halibut is a good substitute for mahi-mahi in this recipe.

1 mango, peeled, pitted, and cut into ½-inch pieces
1 avocado, halved, pitted, and cut into ½-inch pieces
¼ cup finely chopped red onion
3 tablespoons lime juice, plus extra for seasoning (2 limes)
2 tablespoons chopped fresh cilantro
Salt and pepper
½ teaspoon ground coriander
4 (8-ounce) skin-on mahi-mahi fillets, 1 to 1½ inches thick
2 tablespoons vegetable oil

1 Adjust oven rack to middle position, place 12-inch cast-iron skillet on rack, and heat oven to 500 degrees. Meanwhile, combine mango, avocado, onion, lime juice, and cilantro in bowl. Season with salt, pepper, and extra lime juice to taste; set aside for serving.

2 Combine 1 teaspoon salt, coriander, and ¼ teaspoon pepper in small bowl. Pat mahi-mahi dry with paper towels and sprinkle with salt mixture.

3 When oven reaches 500 degrees, remove skillet from oven using potholders and place over medium heat; turn off oven. Being careful of hot skillet handle, add oil and heat until just smoking. Place mahi-mahi flesh side down in skillet and cook until lightly browned, 3 to 4 minutes.

4 Gently flip mahi-mahi, reduce heat to medium-low, and continue to cook until lightly browned on second side, fillets flake apart when gently prodded with paring knife, and fish registers 140 degrees, 7 to 12 minutes. Serve with salsa.

CUTTING MANGO

1 After cutting thin slice from 1 end of mango, rest mango on trimmed bottom and cut off skin in thin strips, top to bottom.

2 Cut down along each side of flat pit to remove flesh.

3 Trim any remaining flesh off sides of pit. Once fruit is peeled and sliced, it can be cut as desired.

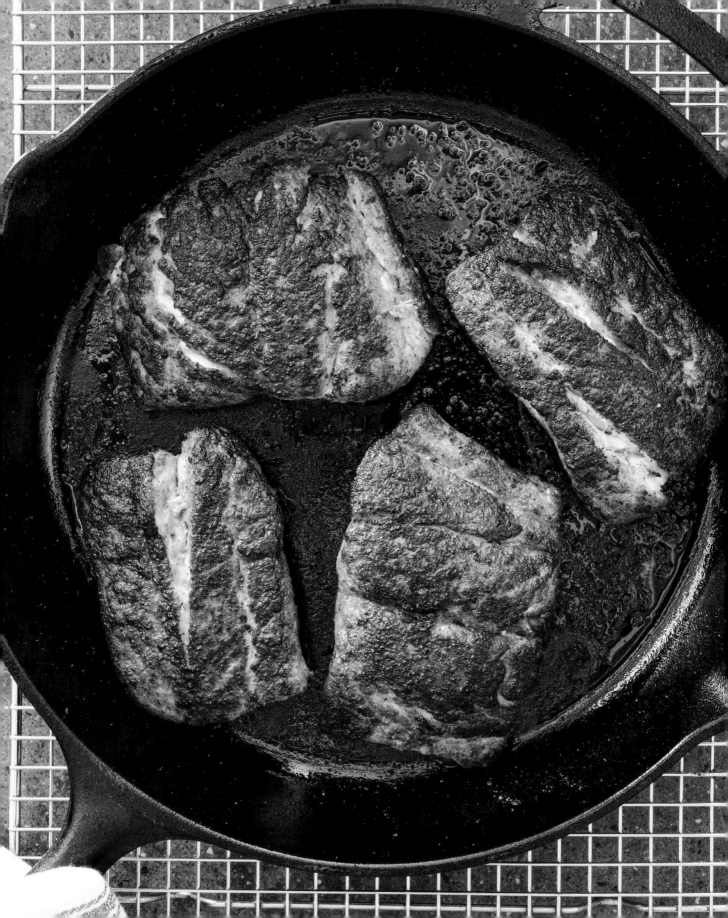

BLACKENED SNAPPER WITH RÉMOULADE SAUCE

SERVES 4

WHY THIS RECIPE WORKS A cast-iron skillet is the ideal vessel for getting perfectly blackened fish. The pan can be heated until it is white-hot and it retains the heat beautifully, which is key to creating the dark brown, crusty, sweet-smoky, toasted-spice exterior that is the hallmark of this Creole dish. But we also encountered some challenges. To begin with, the snapper fillets tended to curl up in the pan and cook unevenly. To prevent curling, we simply scored the skin. Next, we turned to the coating on the fish fillets. For a blackened but not burnt exterior, we made a small amount of a superflavorful spice mixture with sweet paprika, garlic powder, coriander, fennel, and cayenne and coated our fish on both sides. However, this produced fish with harsh, raw flavors. To address this, we made sure that we added enough oil to the pan with the lean snapper fillets to bloom our spices properly. To complement the smoky, spicy snapper, we made a tangy, cooling rémoulade sauce with creamy mayonnaise, briny capers, spicy Dijon mustard, sweet pickle relish, and bright lemon juice. If your knife is not sharp enough to cut through the skin easily, try a serrated knife. It is important to keep the skin on during cooking; remove it afterward if you choose not to serve it.

½ cup mayonnaise

1 tablespoon lemon juice

1½ teaspoons sweet pickle relish

1 teaspoon capers, rinsed and minced

½ teaspoon Dijon mustard

4 (6- to 8-ounce) skin-on red snapper fillets,
    ¾ inch thick

2 teaspoons paprika

1 teaspoon garlic powder

½ teaspoon ground coriander

Salt and pepper

¼ teaspoon ground fennel

⅛ teaspoon cayenne pepper

2 tablespoons vegetable oil

1 Adjust oven rack to middle position, place 12-inch cast-iron skillet on rack, and heat oven to 500 degrees. Meanwhile, whisk mayonnaise, lemon juice, relish, capers, and mustard together in bowl; set aside for serving.

2 Using sharp knife, make 3 to 4 shallow slashes about 1 inch apart on skin side of each fillet, being careful not to cut into flesh. Combine paprika, garlic powder, coriander, ½ teaspoon salt, ¼ teaspoon pepper, ground fennel, and cayenne in bowl. Pat snapper dry with paper towels and rub evenly with spice mixture.

3 When oven reaches 500 degrees, remove skillet from oven using potholders and place over medium-high heat; turn off oven. Being careful of hot skillet handle, add oil and heat until just smoking. Place snapper flesh side down in skillet and cook until very dark brown, about 2 minutes.

4 Gently flip snapper and continue to cook until very dark brown on second side, fillets flake apart when gently prodded with tip of paring knife, and fish registers 140 degrees, about 2 minutes. Serve with rémoulade.

PAN-SEARED SHRIMP WITH ROMESCO SAUCE

SERVES 4

WHY THIS RECIPE WORKS Pan-searing shrimp often results in shrimp that are either dry and flavorless or pale and gummy. We wanted shrimp that were well caramelized but still moist, sweet, and tender. Brining peeled shrimp inhibited browning, so instead we seasoned them with a flavorful mixture of paprika, salt, pepper, cayenne, and sugar, which brought out their natural sweetness and aided in browning. We cooked the shrimp in batches in a large, piping-hot cast-iron skillet. The cast iron's great heat retention helped us get perfectly even browning all over the shrimp. To accompany the shrimp, we created a batch of quick, classic Spanish romesco, which is made with roasted red peppers and traditionally served with fish. We started with a base of extra-virgin olive oil, hearty sandwich bread, and almonds, which we toasted for added richness and texture. To keep things simple, we skipped roasting our own red peppers and stuck with boldly flavored jarred roasted red peppers. Note that the cooking time listed here is for jumbo shrimp (16 to 20 per pound). If using smaller or larger shrimp, be sure to adjust the cooking time as needed.

½ slice hearty white sandwich bread,
   cut into ½-inch pieces
¼ cup slivered almonds
2 tablespoons extra-virgin olive oil
2 garlic cloves, sliced thin
1 cup jarred roasted red peppers, rinsed and
   patted dry
1½ tablespoons sherry vinegar
1 teaspoon honey
   Salt and pepper
½ teaspoon smoked paprika
½ teaspoon sugar
   Pinch cayenne pepper
1½ pounds jumbo shrimp (16 to 20 per pound),
   peeled and deveined
2 tablespoons vegetable oil

1 Cook bread, almonds, 1 tablespoon olive oil, and garlic in 12-inch cast-iron skillet over medium heat, stirring constantly, until bread and almonds are golden brown and fragrant, about 5 minutes. Transfer bread mixture to food processor and pulse until coarsely chopped, about 5 pulses. Add red peppers, vinegar,

honey, ½ teaspoon salt, and remaining 1 tablespoon olive oil and pulse until finely ground, about 10 pulses, scraping down sides of bowl as needed. Transfer sauce to bowl and set aside for serving.

2 Wipe skillet clean with paper towels. Adjust oven rack to middle position, place now-empty skillet on rack, and heat oven to 500 degrees. Meanwhile, combine paprika, sugar, ¼ teaspoon salt, ¼ teaspoon pepper, and cayenne in bowl. Pat shrimp dry with paper towels and sprinkle with paprika mixture.

3 When oven reaches 500 degrees, remove skillet from oven using potholders and place over medium-high heat; turn off oven. Being careful of hot skillet handle, add 1 tablespoon vegetable oil and heat until just smoking. Add half of shrimp to skillet in single layer and cook, without moving, until well browned on first side, about 2 minutes. Flip shrimp and continue to cook until lightly browned on second side and shrimp are opaque throughout, 30 to 60 seconds.

4 Transfer shrimp to serving platter and tent loosely with aluminum foil. Wipe skillet clean with paper towels and repeat with remaining 1 tablespoon vegetable oil and remaining shrimp. Serve with sauce.

PAN-SEARED SCALLOPS

SERVES 4

WHY THIS RECIPE WORKS Producing restaurant-style scallops with perfectly browned exteriors and moist, tender centers at home requires overcoming a major obstacle: a weak stovetop. The heat-retaining power of a cast-iron pan was the perfect solution. Blotting the scallops dry, preheating the pan in the oven, and then bringing oil to just smoking over medium-high heat were steps in the right direction, but it wasn't until we tried a common restaurant technique—butter basting—that our scallops really improved. We seared the scallops in oil on one side and added butter to the skillet before flipping them. We then used a large spoon to ladle the foaming butter over the scallops. Adding the butter midway through ensured that it had enough time to work its browning magic on the scallops, but not enough time to burn. For extra flavor, try one of our zesty variations. Be sure to purchase "dry" scallops, which don't have chemical additives. Dry scallops look ivory or pinkish; wet scallops are bright white.

1½ pounds large sea scallops, tendons removed
   Salt and pepper
¼ cup vegetable oil
2 tablespoons unsalted butter
   Lemon wedges

1 Adjust oven rack to middle position, place 12-inch cast-iron skillet on rack, and heat oven to 500 degrees. Meanwhile, place scallops in rimmed baking sheet lined with clean dish towel and top with second towel; let sit at room temperature.

2 When oven reaches 500 degrees, season scallops with salt and pepper. Using potholders, remove skillet from oven and place over medium-high heat; turn off oven. Being careful of hot skillet handle, add 2 tablespoons oil and heat until just smoking. Add half of scallops in single layer, flat side down, and cook, without moving, until well browned on first side, about 2 minutes.

3 Add 1 tablespoon butter to skillet. Using tongs, flip scallops. Continue to cook, using large spoon to baste scallops with melted butter (tilt skillet so butter pools on one side) until sides of scallops are firm and centers are opaque, 30 to 90 seconds (remove smaller scallops as they finish cooking).

4 Transfer scallops to serving platter and tent loosely with aluminum foil. Wipe skillet clean with paper towels and repeat with remaining 2 tablespoons oil, remaining scallops, and remaining 1 tablespoon butter. Serve with lemon wedges.

VARIATIONS

Pan-Seared Scallops with Lemon-Caper Relish
Combine ¼ cup minced fresh parsley, 1 minced shallot, 3 tablespoons capers, rinsed and minced, 3 tablespoons extra-virgin olive oil, and 4 teaspoons lemon juice in bowl. Season with pepper to taste. Serve with scallops.

Pan-Seared Scallops with Orange-Lime Vinaigrette
Whisk 2 tablespoons orange juice, 2 tablespoons lime juice, 1 small minced shallot, 1 tablespoon minced fresh cilantro, and ⅛ teaspoon red pepper flakes together in medium bowl, then slowly whisk in ¼ cup extra-virgin olive oil. Season with salt and pepper to taste. Serve with scallops.

PREPPING SCALLOPS

Use your fingers to peel away small, crescent-shaped muscle that is sometimes attached to scallops, as this tendon becomes incredibly tough when cooked.

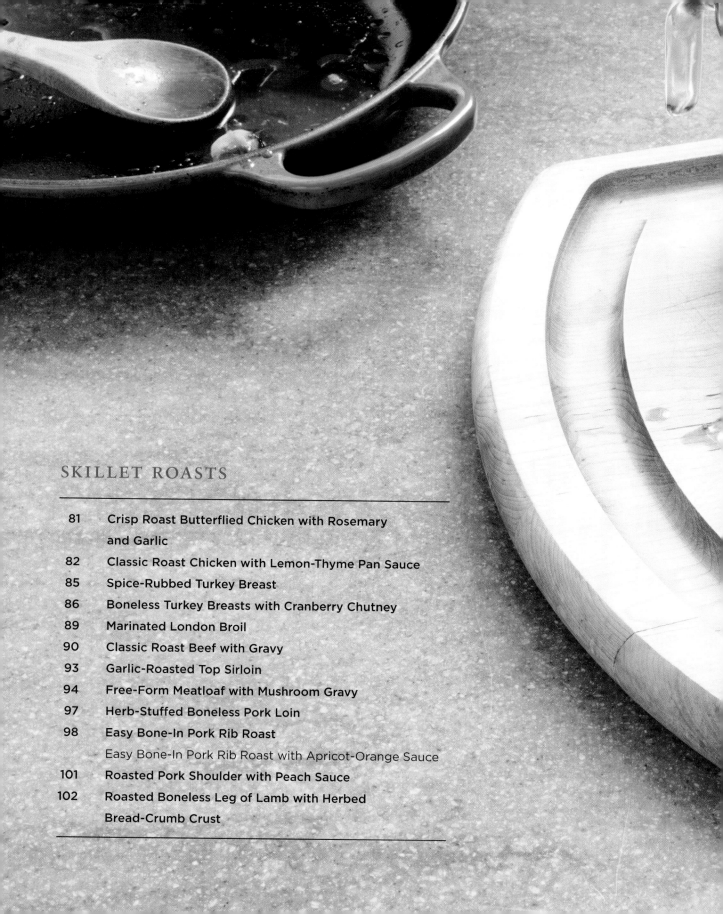

SKILLET ROASTS

Garlic-Roasted Top Sirloin

CRISP ROAST BUTTERFLIED CHICKEN
WITH ROSEMARY AND GARLIC

SERVES 4

WHY THIS RECIPE WORKS A butterflied chicken cooks considerably quicker than a traditional whole bird. Flattening the chicken also encourages crisp skin, since most of the skin is in contact with the hot pan. Achieving crisp skin is even easier with a cast-iron skillet, because the pan is able to maintain very high cooking temperatures. However, during our testing we found that after initially crisping up, the skin turned soggy as the chicken continued to cook skin side down in its own juices. We set out to produce perfectly cooked chicken with crisp skin that could be on the table in less than an hour. We started by heating a skillet in a very hot oven. We then put the chicken into the preheated skillet skin side down and cooked it until the skin was golden brown. Flipping the chicken over for the remainder of the cooking time allowed us to take advantage of the hot, dry air of the oven to ensure that the skin remained crisp and intact. A simple mixture of extra-virgin olive oil, rosemary, and garlic brushed on the chicken during roasting elevated the flavor and crisped the skin further. We had four-star, perfectly browned roast chicken with spectacular skin on the table in under an hour, thanks to the great heat retention of the cast-iron skillet; and as a bonus, the butterflied bird was a cinch to carve. Be aware that the chicken may slightly overhang the skillet at first, but once browned it will shrink to fit; do not use a chicken larger than 4 pounds. Serve with lemon wedges.

---

2 tablespoons extra-virgin olive oil

1 teaspoon minced fresh rosemary

1 garlic clove, minced

1 (3½- to 4-pound) whole chicken, giblets discarded
   Salt and pepper

1 Adjust oven rack to lowest position, place 12-inch cast-iron skillet on rack, and heat oven to 500 degrees. Meanwhile, combine 1 tablespoon oil, rosemary, and garlic in bowl; set aside.

2 With chicken breast side down, use kitchen shears to cut through bones on either side of backbone; discard backbone. Flip chicken over, tuck wingtips behind back, and press firmly on breastbone to flatten. Pat chicken dry with paper towels, then rub with remaining 1 tablespoon oil and season with salt and pepper.

3 When oven reaches 500 degrees, place chicken breast side down in hot skillet. Reduce oven temperature to 450 degrees and roast chicken until well browned, about 30 minutes.

4 Using potholders, remove skillet from oven. Being careful of hot skillet handle, gently flip chicken breast side up. Brush chicken with oil mixture, return skillet to oven, and continue to roast chicken until breast registers 160 degrees and thighs register 175 degrees, about 10 minutes. Transfer chicken to carving board, tent loosely with aluminum foil, and let rest for 15 minutes. Carve chicken and serve.

BUTTERFLYING A WHOLE CHICKEN

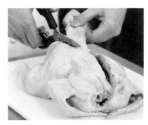

1 Using kitchen shears, cut through bones on either side of backbone and trim away any excess fat or skin at neck. Discard backbone.

2 Flip chicken over, tuck wingtips behind back, and use heel of your hand to flatten breastbone.

CLASSIC ROAST CHICKEN
WITH LEMON-THYME PAN SAUCE

SERVES 4

WHY THIS RECIPE WORKS Roast chicken is often described as a simple dish, but the actual process—brining or salting, trussing, and turning—is anything but easy. We wanted a truly simple way to get roast chicken on the table in just an hour without sacrificing flavor. We quickly realized that trussing was unnecessary; we could simply tie the legs together and tuck the wings underneath the bird. We also found we could skip flipping the chicken during cooking by taking advantage of the great heat retention of cast iron. We cooked the chicken breast side up in a preheated skillet to give the thighs a head start and allow the skin to crisp up. Starting in a 450-degree oven and then turning the oven off while the chicken finished cooking slowed the evaporation of juices, ensuring moist, tender meat, even without brining or salting. A traditional pan sauce pairing lemon and thyme was the perfect complement, and it took just minutes to make while the chicken rested. Pan drippings contributed meatiness, and finishing the sauce with butter gave it the perfect velvety texture. We prefer to use a 3½- to 4-pound chicken for this recipe. If roasting a larger bird, increase the time when the oven is on in step 2 to 30 to 40 minutes.

1 (3½- to 4-pound) whole chicken, giblets discarded
1 tablespoon extra-virgin olive oil
  Salt and pepper
1 lemon, quartered
1 shallot, minced
1 cup chicken broth
2 teaspoons Dijon mustard
2 tablespoons unsalted butter
1½ teaspoons minced fresh thyme

1 Adjust oven rack to middle position, place 12-inch cast-iron skillet on rack, and heat oven to 450 degrees. Meanwhile, pat chicken dry with paper towels, rub with oil, and season with salt and pepper. Tie legs together with kitchen twine and tuck wingtips behind back.

2 When oven reaches 450 degrees, place chicken breast side up in hot skillet. Roast chicken until breast registers 120 degrees and thighs register 135 degrees, 20 to 30 minutes.

3 Arrange lemon quarters cut side down around chicken. Turn off oven and leave chicken in oven until breast registers 160 degrees and thighs register 175 degrees, 15 to 20 minutes.

4 Using potholders, remove skillet from oven. Transfer chicken to carving board, tent loosely with aluminum foil, and let rest for 15 minutes. Let roasted lemon cool slightly, then squeeze into fine-mesh strainer set over bowl, extracting as much juice and pulp as possible; press firmly on solids to yield 2 teaspoons juice.

5 While chicken rests, pour off all but 1 tablespoon fat from skillet, being careful of hot skillet handle. Add shallot and cook over medium heat until softened, about 30 seconds. Whisk in broth and mustard, scraping up any browned bits. Bring to simmer and cook until mixture is reduced to ¾ cup, about 3 minutes. Stir in any accumulated chicken juices. Off heat, whisk in butter, lemon juice, and thyme. Season with pepper to taste; cover to keep warm. Carve chicken and serve with sauce.

TUCKING THE WINGS

To secure wings while roasting whole chicken and prevent them from burning, fold them firmly behind neck. They should hold themselves in place.

SPICE-RUBBED TURKEY BREAST

SERVES 6 TO 8

WHY THIS RECIPE WORKS Outside of Thanksgiving and other crowd-worthy gatherings, roasting an entire turkey seems excessive. Downsizing to a turkey breast is a more practical option; the challenge is to get moist, juicy meat and crisp skin on this smaller cut. To accomplish this, we used a technique that incorporated both high-temperature searing for crisp skin and roasting at a lower temperature to ensure moist meat. We started with a preheated cast-iron skillet and then transferred the pan to a 325-degree oven to let the breast cook through. The addition of a potent spice paste gave this mild cut mellow heat and deep flavor. Rubbing the mixture (five-spice powder, cumin, garlic powder, cayenne, and cardamom, along with oil) under the skin and over the exterior of the turkey ensured a burst of flavor in every bite. Lifting the skin to apply the spice rub had the added advantage of creating pockets of air that made it easier for the fat to render and the skin to crisp. Many supermarkets now sell "hotel-cut" turkey breasts, which still have the wings and rib cage attached. If this is the only type of breast you can find, you will need to remove the wings and cut away the rib cage with kitchen shears before proceeding with the recipe. If you are using a self-basting turkey breast (such as a frozen Butterball) or a kosher turkey breast, do not brine in step 1, but season with salt in step 2.

Salt and pepper

1 (6-pound) bone-in whole turkey breast, trimmed

2 tablespoons vegetable oil

2 teaspoons five-spice powder

1½ teaspoons ground cumin

1 teaspoon garlic powder

¼ teaspoon cayenne pepper

¼ teaspoon ground cardamom

1 Dissolve ½ cup salt in 4 quarts cold water in large container. Submerge turkey in brine, cover, and refrigerate for 3 to 6 hours.

2 Adjust oven rack to middle position and heat oven to 325 degrees. Combine 1 tablespoon oil, five-spice powder, cumin, garlic powder, cayenne, cardamom, and 1 teaspoon pepper in bowl.

3 Remove turkey from brine and pat dry with paper towels. Using your fingers or handle of wooden spoon, gently loosen skin covering each side of breast. Rub paste evenly over and under skin.

4 Heat 12-inch cast-iron skillet over medium heat for 5 minutes. Add remaining 1 tablespoon oil and heat until just smoking. Place turkey skin side down in skillet and cook, turning breast on its sides as needed, until lightly browned, 5 to 7 minutes.

5 Flip turkey skin side up, transfer skillet to oven, and roast until turkey registers 160 degrees, about 1½ hours. Transfer turkey to carving board, tent loosely with aluminum foil, and let rest for 20 minutes. Carve turkey and serve.

PREPARING A TURKEY BREAST FOR A RUB

In order to rub spice paste evenly under skin, first loosen skin covering each side of breast using your fingers or handle of wooden spoon.

BONELESS TURKEY BREASTS
WITH CRANBERRY CHUTNEY

SERVES 6 TO 8

WHY THIS RECIPE WORKS Boneless turkey breast offers all the hearty flavor of turkey without the challenges of cooking and carving a giant bird or bone-in breast, making it a quicker and more approachable everyday meal. For crisp, golden skin, we preheated our cast-iron skillet on the stovetop and browned the turkey on all sides before roasting. This meant that the meat needed much less time to finish cooking in the oven. We came across a problem during roasting, however; the boneless breasts were very unevenly shaped, so they cooked unevenly. Tucking the tapered ends underneath and tying the breasts with twine made them more uniform and easier to cook. Finally, we developed a chutney to add flavor to the mild meat. We used shallot, fresh ginger, mustard seeds, sugar, cranberries, and orange zest, with a splash of vinegar to round out the flavors. If you're using self-basting turkey breast halves (such as frozen Butterball) or kosher turkey breast halves, do not brine in step 1, but season with salt in step 2. Often, boneless turkey breast halves are sold in elastic netting; be sure to remove the netting before brining or cooking.

Salt and pepper

2 (2-pound) boneless, skin-on turkey breast halves, trimmed

1 tablespoon vegetable oil

1 shallot, minced

4 teaspoons grated fresh ginger

1 teaspoon yellow mustard seeds

12 ounces (3 cups) fresh or frozen cranberries

1 cup packed brown sugar

¾ cup water

1 tablespoon grated orange zest

2 tablespoons cider vinegar

1 Dissolve 6 tablespoons salt in 3 quarts cold water in large container. Submerge turkey in brine, cover, and refrigerate for at least 30 minutes or up to 1 hour.

2 Adjust oven rack to middle position and heat oven to 325 degrees. Remove turkey from brine and pat dry with paper towels. Tuck tapered end of each breast underneath and loosely tie lengthwise with kitchen twine. Tie breasts crosswise at 1½-inch intervals to make tidy, even roasts. Season turkey with pepper.

3 Heat 12-inch cast-iron skillet over medium heat for 5 minutes. Add oil and heat until just smoking. Brown turkey on all sides, about 10 minutes. Flip turkey skin side down, transfer skillet to oven, and roast until turkey registers 160 degrees, about 1 hour, flipping breasts halfway through roasting.

4 Using potholders, remove skillet from oven. Transfer turkey to carving board, tent loosely with aluminum foil, and let rest while making chutney.

5 Being careful of hot skillet handle, pour off all but 1 tablespoon fat. Add shallot, ginger, mustard seeds, and ½ teaspoon salt and cook over medium heat until shallot is softened, about 30 seconds. Stir in cranberries, sugar, water, and orange zest. Bring to simmer and cook, stirring occasionally, until cranberries have mostly broken down and mixture is thickened, about 15 minutes. Off heat, stir in vinegar and any accumulated turkey juices. Remove twine from turkey and slice into ¼-inch-thick slices. Serve with chutney.

TYING A BONELESS TURKEY BREAST

After folding tapered end of turkey breast underneath, loosely tie breast lengthwise with kitchen twine to secure. Tie breast crosswise at 1½-inch intervals to make tidy, even roast.

MARINATED LONDON BROIL

SERVES 4

WHY THIS RECIPE WORKS The term "London broil" doesn't actually refer to any particular cut of meat or cooking method. Instead, it's a generic term for large, inexpensive cuts. London broil recipes often call for grilling to get a good char that can add flavor to an otherwise uninspiring cut. We wanted to find a way to replicate these results on the stove. We decided to use shoulder steak, not only because it is economical but because it has a little bit of fat, which adds flavor. When it came to cooking the shoulder steak, we realized that the technique used in our Thick-Cut Steaks with Herb Butter (page 57) wouldn't work here—shoulder steak is simply too large and cumbersome to flip every few minutes. Besides, by the time the steak reached the desired temperature on the stovetop (120 to 125 degrees for medium-rare), the rub was burnt and the kitchen was filled with smoke. Instead, we took a cue from the usual London broil treatment and tried to replicate the sear from a grill using a preheated cast-iron pan. Our cast-iron skillet was preheated in a 500-degree oven and then placed on the stovetop over medium-high heat to guarantee that the steak would get well seared on both sides. We then returned the seared steak to the oven to minimize smoking and ensure even cooking. Prior to searing, the steak soaked in a savory marinade of soy sauce, vinegar, ketchup, garlic, and fresh herbs. Coating the marinated steak with black pepper and paprika helped to create nice char, not to mention a flavorful crust. Remember to slice the cooked steak thin against the grain; otherwise the meat will be tough and rubbery.

½ cup soy sauce

2½ tablespoons vegetable oil

2 tablespoons balsamic vinegar

2 tablespoons ketchup

2 tablespoons chopped fresh sage

5 garlic cloves, minced

1 teaspoon chopped fresh rosemary

1 (1½- to 2-pound) shoulder steak, 1½ inches thick, trimmed

1½ teaspoons coarsely ground pepper

1 teaspoon paprika

1 Process soy sauce, 1½ tablespoons oil, vinegar, ketchup, sage, garlic, and rosemary in blender until herbs and garlic are finely chopped, about 30 seconds. Combine marinade and steak in 1-gallon zipper-lock bag. Toss steak to coat, press out as much air as possible, and seal bag. Refrigerate for at least 2 hours or up to 8 hours, flipping bag halfway through marinating.

2 Adjust oven rack to lowest position, place 12-inch cast-iron skillet on rack, and heat oven to 500 degrees. Meanwhile, remove steak from marinade and pat dry with paper towels. Combine pepper and paprika in bowl, then sprinkle mixture onto steak. Let steak sit at room temperature.

3 When oven reaches 500 degrees, remove skillet from oven using potholders and place over medium-high heat. Being careful of hot skillet handle, add remaining 1 tablespoon oil to skillet and heat until just smoking. Cook steak until well browned on both sides, about 2 minutes per side. Transfer skillet to oven and roast until meat registers 120 to 125 degrees (for medium-rare), 5 to 7 minutes, flipping steak halfway through roasting.

4 Transfer steak to carving board, tent loosely with aluminum foil, and let rest for 15 minutes. Slice steak thin against grain. Serve.

CLASSIC ROAST BEEF WITH GRAVY

SERVES 8

WHY THIS RECIPE WORKS Reaching for a cast-iron skillet to cook a large roast may not be your first instinct, but this pan's unrivaled searing ability makes it great for browning meat and building flavorful gravy, the keys to great roast beef. Salting the meat for our roast beef and letting it sit overnight helped season the beef. To get a good crust and tender meat without overcooking, we first seared the roast on the stovetop in a hot skillet and then finished it in a low oven. The low roasting temperature (just 225 degrees) produced incredibly juicy meat and a uniformly rosy interior but left precious little liquid in the skillet. Without enough pan drippings to make gravy, we instead used the rendered fat and flavorful browned bits left behind from searing the meat on the stovetop as our gravy base and started making the sauce early in the cooking process, before finishing the roast in the oven. Setting the roast on top of a bed of sliced vegetables during its time in the oven eliminated the need for a V-rack and enhanced the flavor of the gravy. To get even more concentrated beef flavor without extra work, we turned to store-bought condensed beef consommé to deglaze the skillet after roasting. If desired, you can substitute top sirloin for the top round; look for an evenly shaped roast with a ¼-inch fat cap.

1 (4- to 5-pound) boneless top round roast, trimmed and tied at 1-inch intervals

Salt and pepper

1 tablespoon vegetable oil, plus extra as needed

2 carrots, peeled and cut into 2-inch pieces

1 onion, sliced into ½-inch-thick rounds

1 celery rib, cut into 2-inch pieces

4 tablespoons unsalted butter

⅓ cup all-purpose flour

1 teaspoon tomato paste

2 (10.5-ounce) cans beef consommé

1½ cups water

1 Sprinkle roast with 2 teaspoons salt, wrap tightly with plastic wrap, and refrigerate for at least 1 hour or up to 24 hours.

2 Adjust oven rack to middle position and heat oven to 225 degrees. Pat roast dry with paper towels and sprinkle with 2 teaspoons pepper. Heat 12-inch cast-iron skillet over medium heat for 5 minutes. Add oil and heat until just smoking. Brown roast on all sides, 8 to 12 minutes; transfer to plate.

3 Pour off all but 2 tablespoons fat from skillet. (If necessary, add extra oil as needed to equal 2 tablespoons.) Add carrots, onion, celery, and butter and cook until vegetables are softened and lightly browned, 5 to 7 minutes. Stir in flour and tomato paste and cook until mixture begins to darken, about 2 minutes. Off heat, push vegetables to center of skillet. Place browned roast on top of vegetables, transfer skillet to oven, and roast until meat registers 120 to 125 degrees (for medium-rare), 1½ to 2 hours.

4 Using potholders, remove skillet from oven. Transfer roast to carving board, tent loosely with aluminum foil, and let rest while making gravy.

5 Being careful of hot skillet handle, place skillet with vegetables over medium heat and cook, stirring occasionally, until vegetables are deep golden brown, about 5 minutes. Slowly whisk in consommé and water, scraping up any browned bits and smoothing out any lumps. Bring to simmer and cook until gravy is thickened, 10 to 15 minutes. Stir in any accumulated meat juices.

6 Strain gravy through fine-mesh strainer into serving bowl, pressing on vegetables to extract as much liquid as possible; discard solids. Season with salt and pepper to taste. Remove kitchen twine from roast and slice thin against grain. Serve with gravy.

GARLIC-ROASTED TOP SIRLOIN

SERVES 6 TO 8

WHY THIS RECIPE WORKS While developing this recipe, we envisioned a roast beef with a browned, flavorful crust complementing a juicy, tender interior. But this wouldn't be any old roast—we wanted tons of savory garlic flavor, not just sprinkled or dabbed on top but infused throughout. And we didn't want to break the bank either, so we turned to an affordable and well-marbled cut, top sirloin. A two-way approach yielded true garlic roast beef: We studded the roast with toasted garlic and, after browning it on the stovetop, coated it with a garlic paste before moving it to the oven to finish cooking. Rubbing the roast with herbed salt and letting it sit overnight also helped develop nuanced flavor and tenderness. The perfect finishing touch to our roast was a quick version of long-simmering jus, made by enriching a blend of store-bought beef and chicken broths with the browned bits left in the skillet, reducing the mixture for a few minutes to thicken, and adding the accumulated meat juices from the resting roast to round out the deep, meaty flavor of our jus. Look for an evenly shaped roast with a ¼-inch fat cap. When making the jus, taste the reduced broth before adding any of the accumulated meat juices from the roast. The meat juices are well seasoned and may make the jus too salty.

16 garlic cloves, unpeeled

1 (4-pound) boneless top sirloin roast, trimmed

1 tablespoon minced fresh thyme or 1 teaspoon dried
   Salt and pepper

2 tablespoons vegetable oil

1½ cups beef broth

1½ cups chicken broth

1 Toast garlic in 12-inch cast-iron skillet over medium heat, stirring frequently, until spotty brown, about 8 minutes; set aside. When cool enough to handle, peel 8 cloves and slice ¼ inch thick (you should have at least 24 slices). Peel and mince remaining 8 cloves; refrigerate until ready to use.

2 Using paring knife, make twenty-four 1-inch-deep slits all over roast, then insert garlic slices into slits. Combine thyme and 2 teaspoons salt in bowl, then rub mixture evenly over roast. Wrap roast tightly with plastic wrap and refrigerate for at least 1 hour or up to 24 hours.

3 Adjust oven rack to middle position and heat oven to 300 degrees. Combine minced garlic, 1 tablespoon oil, and ½ teaspoon salt in bowl. Pat roast dry with paper towels and season with pepper. Heat 12-inch cast-iron skillet over medium heat for 5 minutes. Add remaining 1 tablespoon oil and heat until just smoking. Brown roast on all sides, 8 to 12 minutes.

4 Flip roast fat side up and spread garlic mixture over top. Transfer skillet to oven and roast until meat registers 120 to 125 degrees (for medium-rare), 50 to 70 minutes.

5 Using potholders, remove skillet from oven. Transfer roast to carving board, tent loosely with aluminum foil, and let rest for 20 minutes.

6 Meanwhile, being careful of hot skillet handle, pour off fat from skillet. Add broths and bring to simmer over medium-high heat, using wooden spoon to scrape up any browned bits. Cook, stirring occasionally, until broth mixture is reduced to 2 cups, about 5 minutes. Stir in any accumulated meat juices and cook for 1 minute. Strain jus through fine-mesh strainer into serving bowl; discard solids. Season with salt and pepper to taste. Slice roast thin against grain. Serve with jus.

FREE-FORM MEATLOAF WITH MUSHROOM GRAVY

SERVES 6 TO 8

WHY THIS RECIPE WORKS Traditional meatloaf recipes call for using a loaf pan, which can be problematic: The meat stews in its own juices, and only the top of the meatloaf develops any browning. Adopting a free-form method in the skillet allowed the sides and top of our meatloaf to brown nicely. A triple dose of mushrooms contributed great texture and depth of flavor: We soaked earthy dried porcini mushrooms and then added their potent soaking liquid to the loaf along with processed white mushrooms; the rehydrated porcini and more white mushrooms added depth and texture to our gravy. The versatile cast-iron skillet was the perfect tool for sautéing the mushrooms, baking the meatloaf, and then building the accompanying rich, mushroom-studded gravy.

1 cup water
¼ ounce dried porcini mushrooms, rinsed
16 square or 18 round saltines
10 ounces white mushrooms, trimmed
1 tablespoon vegetable oil, plus extra as needed
1 onion, chopped fine
  Salt and pepper
4 garlic cloves, minced
1 pound ground pork
2 large eggs
1 tablespoon plus ¾ teaspoon Worcestershire sauce
1 pound 85 percent lean ground beef
¾ teaspoon minced fresh thyme
¼ cup all-purpose flour
2½ cups chicken broth

1 Adjust oven rack to middle position and heat oven to 375 degrees. Microwave water and porcini mushrooms in covered bowl until steaming, about 1 minute. Let sit until softened, about 5 minutes. Drain mushrooms in fine-mesh strainer lined with coffee filter, reserve ¾ cup liquid, and mince mushrooms.

2 Process saltines in food processor until finely ground, about 30 seconds; transfer to large bowl. Pulse half of white mushrooms in now-empty processor until finely ground, 8 to 10 pulses.

3 Heat 12-inch cast-iron skillet over medium heat for 3 minutes. Add oil and heat until shimmering. Add ground white mushrooms, onion, and ¼ teaspoon salt and cook until softened, 6 to 8 minutes. Stir in garlic and cook until fragrant, about 30 seconds. Transfer mushroom mixture to bowl with saltines and let cool completely, about 15 minutes.

4 Add ground pork, eggs, 1 tablespoon Worcestershire, 1 teaspoon salt, ¾ teaspoon pepper, and ¼ cup reserved porcini liquid to cooled mushroom-saltine mixture and gently knead with hands until mostly combined. Add ground beef and knead until well combined. Transfer meat mixture to now-empty skillet and shape into 10 by 6-inch loaf. Transfer skillet to oven and bake until meatloaf registers 160 degrees, about 30 minutes.

5 Using potholders, remove skillet from oven. Using spatula, transfer meatloaf to carving board, tent loosely with aluminum foil, and let rest while making gravy.

6 Thinly slice remaining white mushrooms. Being careful of hot skillet handle, discard any solids left in skillet and pour off all but 2 tablespoons fat. (If necessary, add extra oil to equal 2 tablespoons.) Add minced porcini mushrooms, sliced white mushrooms, and ¼ teaspoon salt and cook over medium heat until softened and lightly browned, 6 to 8 minutes. Stir in thyme and ¼ teaspoon salt and cook until fragrant, about 30 seconds. Stir in flour and cook for 2 minutes.

7 Whisk in broth, remaining ½ cup reserved porcini liquid, and remaining ¾ teaspoon Worcestershire, scraping up any browned bits and smoothing out any lumps. Bring to simmer and cook until gravy is thickened, 10 to 15 minutes. Season with salt and pepper to taste. Slice meatloaf and serve with mushroom gravy.

HERB-STUFFED BONELESS PORK LOIN

SERVES 6 TO 8

WHY THIS RECIPE WORKS A good pork loin roast makes an impressive dinner, but the leanness and mild flavor of this cut can cause problems. To avoid any pitfalls, we started by rubbing the pork with salt and sugar to season the meat and promote browning. To give every bite plenty of flavor, we butterflied the roast, coated its interior with an herb-Parmesan paste, then rolled it up and tied it. Searing the meat on the stovetop before finishing it in a low oven yielded a tender interior with a crisp crust. Look for an evenly shaped roast that is 8 to 9 inches long; it will fit best in the skillet. If your roast has a thick layer of fat on top, trim the fat until it measures about ¼ inch thick.

1 tablespoon packed brown sugar

Salt and pepper

6 tablespoons extra-virgin olive oil

3 garlic cloves, sliced thin

2 ounces Parmesan cheese, grated (1 cup)

¾ cup minced fresh parsley

½ cup chopped fresh basil

¼ cup capers, rinsed and minced

3 anchovy fillets, rinsed and minced

1 (3- to 4-pound) boneless center-cut pork loin roast, trimmed

Lemon wedges

1 Combine sugar and 1½ teaspoons salt in bowl. Heat ¼ cup oil and garlic in 12-inch cast-iron skillet over medium heat until garlic is tender and beginning to brown, 3 to 5 minutes. Transfer garlic oil to medium bowl, let cool slightly, then stir in Parmesan, parsley, basil, capers, anchovies, and ½ teaspoon pepper.

2 Position roast fat side up on cutting board. Insert knife one-third of way up from bottom of roast along 1 long side and cut horizontally, stopping ½ inch from edge. Open roast and press flat; 1 side will be twice as thick. Continue cutting thicker side of roast in half, stopping ½ inch from edge; open roast and press flat.

3 Sprinkle cut surface of roast with half of sugar-salt mixture, then spread herb mixture evenly over meat, leaving ½-inch border on all sides. Starting from short side farthest from exterior fat cap, roll roast tightly, then tie with kitchen twine at 1-inch intervals. Sprinkle with remaining sugar-salt mixture. Wrap roast tightly with plastic wrap and refrigerate for at least 1 hour or up to 24 hours.

4 Adjust oven rack to middle position and heat oven to 275 degrees. Pat roast dry with paper towels and season with pepper. Heat now-empty skillet over medium heat for 5 minutes. Add remaining 2 tablespoons oil and heat until just smoking. Brown roast on all sides, about 10 minutes. Flip roast fat side down, transfer skillet to oven, and roast until meat registers 135 degrees, 30 to 45 minutes, flipping roast halfway through roasting.

5 Transfer roast to carving board, tent loosely with aluminum foil, and let rest for 20 minutes. Remove twine from roast and slice into ½-inch-thick slices. Serve with lemon wedges.

BUTTERFLYING A PORK LOIN

1 With roast fat side up, insert knife one-third of way up from bottom along 1 long side and cut horizontally, stopping ½ inch from edge. Open roast and press flat.

2 Continue cutting thicker side of roast in half, stopping ½ inch from edge; open roast and press flat.

EASY BONE-IN PORK RIB ROAST

SERVES 6

WHY THIS RECIPE WORKS A center-cut pork rib roast is the pork version of prime rib. Treated the right way, it can be truly impressive: moist, tender, and full of rich meatiness. To ensure that the natural flavor of our roast was the star of this recipe, we seasoned the meat simply with thyme, salt, pepper, and garlic powder. We started by searing the meat in our cast-iron skillet to promote browning and start rendering the flavorful fat cap. After this step, the pork loin was transferred to the oven to finish cooking through. The fat cap continued to melt and moisten the meat as it roasted. The rack of bones along the side of the roast helped slow the cooking process and protect the delicate white meat. To guarantee perfectly cooked pork, we removed the roast from the oven once its temperature reached 140 degrees and allowed it to come to the desired final doneness while it rested, covered, on a carving board. Look for an evenly shaped roast that is 8 to 9 inches long; it will fit best in the skillet. If your roast has a thick layer of fat on top, trim the fat until it measures about ¼ inch thick. For easier carving, ask the butcher to remove the tip of the chine bone and to cut the remainder of the chine bone between the ribs.

1 (4-pound) center-cut bone-in pork rib roast,
    chine bone removed, trimmed
1 tablespoon minced fresh thyme
1 tablespoon kosher salt
1½ teaspoons pepper
1½ teaspoons garlic powder
1 tablespoon vegetable oil

1 Adjust oven rack to lower-middle position and heat oven to 250 degrees. Using sharp knife, cut slits in surface fat layer of roast, spaced 1 inch apart, in crosshatch pattern, being careful to cut down to but not into meat. Pat roast dry with paper towels. Combine thyme, salt, pepper, and garlic powder in bowl, then rub mixture evenly over roast. Wrap roast tightly with plastic wrap and refrigerate for at least 1 hour or up to 24 hours.

2 Heat 12-inch cast-iron skillet over medium heat for 5 minutes. Add oil and heat until just smoking. Place roast fat side down in skillet and cook until well browned, 4 to 6 minutes. Flip roast fat side up, transfer skillet to oven, and roast until pork registers 140 degrees, 1½ to 2 hours.

3 Transfer roast to carving board, tent loosely with aluminum foil, and let rest for 30 minutes. Carve roast into thick slices by cutting between ribs. Serve.

VARIATION

Easy Bone-In Pork Rib Roast with Apricot-Orange Sauce
Combine 1 cup apricot preserves, ½ cup orange juice, ¼ cup quartered dried apricots, and 3 tablespoons lemon juice in bowl. After transferring roast to carving board, pour off fat from skillet and add glaze, scraping up any browned bits. Bring glaze to simmer over medium heat and cook until thickened slightly, about 3 minutes, then transfer to serving bowl.

SCORING A PORK ROAST

Using sharp knife, cut slits in surface fat layer, spaced 1 inch apart, in crosshatch pattern, being careful not to cut into meat.

ROASTED PORK SHOULDER WITH PEACH SAUCE

SERVES 8 TO 12

WHY THIS RECIPE WORKS Pork shoulder is loaded with flavorful fat, making it a natural choice for roasting. But cooking it in a roasting pan can take upward of 6 hours. To shorten the cooking time without compromising taste or texture, we turned to our cast-iron skillet. Cast iron's excellent heat retention makes it ideal for long-cooking applications. We got great results from our pork shoulder in as little as 4 hours in the oven. Rubbing the meat with brown sugar and salt and letting it sit overnight dried out the exterior and boosted browning, and elevating the pork shoulder with onion slices and adding water to the skillet during roasting kept the drippings from burning and also created a flavorful jus in the pan. While the meat rested, we combined the jus with peaches, white wine, sugar, vinegar, thyme, and mustard to create a sweet-and-sour sauce to cut the richness of the roasted pork. Pork butt roast is often labeled Boston shoulder, Boston butt, or pork butt in the supermarket. Add more water to the roasting pan as necessary during the last hours of cooking to prevent the fond from burning. For more information on scoring a pork roast, see page 98. This recipe requires refrigerating the salted meat for at least 12 hours before cooking.

1 (6- to 8-pound) bone-in pork butt roast, trimmed
   Kosher salt and pepper
⅓ cup packed light brown sugar
1 onion, sliced into ½-inch-thick rounds
1 pound frozen peaches, cut into ½-inch pieces
2 cups dry white wine
½ cup granulated sugar
5 tablespoons rice vinegar
2 sprigs fresh thyme
1 tablespoon whole-grain mustard

1 Using sharp knife, cut slits in surface of fat layer of roast, spaced 1 inch apart, in crosshatch pattern, being careful to cut down to but not into meat. Combine ⅓ cup salt and brown sugar in bowl, then rub mixture evenly over roast. Wrap roast tightly with plastic wrap and refrigerate for at least 12 hours or up to 24 hours.

2 Adjust oven rack to lowest position and heat oven to 325 degrees. Brush any excess salt mixture from surface of roast and season with pepper. Arrange onion rounds in single layer on bottom of 12-inch cast-iron skillet and place roast fat side up on top. Add 2 cups water to skillet.

3 Transfer skillet to oven and roast, basting twice during cooking, until pork is extremely tender and meat near (but not touching) bone registers 190 degrees, 4 to 5 hours.

4 Using potholders, remove skillet from oven. Transfer roast to carving board, tent loosely with aluminum foil, and let rest while making peach sauce.

5 Being careful of hot skillet handle, discard onion rounds and transfer remaining juices to fat separator. Let liquid settle for 5 minutes, then measure out and reserve ¼ cup jus; discard fat and remaining jus. (If necessary, add water as needed to equal ¼ cup.)

6 Bring reserved jus, peaches, wine, granulated sugar, ¼ cup vinegar, and thyme sprigs to simmer in now-empty skillet over medium-low heat. Cook, stirring occasionally, until reduced to 2 cups, about 30 minutes. Stir in any accumulated meat juices. Off heat, discard thyme sprigs. Using potato masher, mash portion of peaches to thicken sauce as desired. Stir in mustard and remaining 1 tablespoon vinegar and season with salt and pepper to taste.

7 Using sharp paring knife, cut around inverted T-shaped bone until it can be pulled free from roast (use clean dish towel to grasp bone). Using serrated knife, slice roast thin. Serve with sauce.

ROASTED BONELESS LEG OF LAMB
WITH HERBED BREAD-CRUMB CRUST

SERVES 6 TO 8

WHY THIS RECIPE WORKS A leg of lamb that comes already boned, rolled, and neatly tied from the meat case sounds like an easy shortcut to a great dinner. However, it turns out that cooking this cut is not so simple—the meat often turns out brown and rubbery, and the outer layer of fat is prone to scorching, which can result in an unappealing gamy flavor. We wanted a foolproof method for a crisp crust and perfectly cooked interior every time. We started at the supermarket; whole boneless legs are impractical for the average dinner table, but a half leg is just the right amount for six to eight people. We relied on our cast-iron skillet to jump-start the cooking process on the stovetop. Moving the roast to a gentle 375-degree oven guaranteed a juicy, tender interior. A savory crumb crust with fresh herbs, garlic, and Parmesan was the ideal complement to the tender lamb. We brushed Dijon mustard on the roast to help the crust adhere and to lend additional flavor. Applying the crust partway through cooking (after removing the twine) ensured that the roast would hold its shape and the crust would stay in place. A quick blast under the broiler at the end of cooking helped the crumbs turn crisp and brown. We prefer the sirloin end rather than the shank end of the lamb leg in this recipe for its more uniform shape, though either will work well.

¼ cup minced fresh parsley

3 tablespoons minced fresh rosemary

3 tablespoons extra-virgin olive oil

2 tablespoons minced fresh thyme

3 garlic cloves, peeled

¾ cup panko bread crumbs

1 ounce Parmesan cheese, grated (½ cup)

1 (3½- to 4-pound) boneless half leg of lamb, untied, trimmed

Salt and pepper

1 tablespoon Dijon mustard

1 Adjust oven rack to middle position and heat oven to 375 degrees. Process parsley, rosemary, 1 teaspoon oil, thyme, and garlic in food processor until finely ground, scraping down sides of bowl as needed, about 1 minute. Measure out and reserve 1½ tablespoons herb mixture. Combine remaining herb mixture, panko, Parmesan, and 1 tablespoon oil in bowl; set aside.

2 Position roast with rough interior side (which was against bone) facing up on cutting board. Cover roast with plastic wrap and pound to even ¾-inch thickness with meat pounder. Rub surface of roast with

2 teaspoons oil and season with salt and pepper. Spread reserved herb mixture evenly over surface of meat, leaving 1-inch border on all sides. Starting from short side, roll roast tightly, then tie with kitchen twine at 1-inch intervals. Season with salt and pepper.

3 Heat 12-inch cast-iron skillet over medium heat for 5 minutes. Add remaining 1 tablespoon oil and heat until just smoking. Brown roast on all sides, 8 to 12 minutes. Transfer skillet to oven and roast until meat registers 110 to 115 degrees, 25 to 35 minutes.

4 Using potholders, remove skillet from oven; heat broiler. Transfer roast to carving board and remove twine. Brush top and sides of roast with mustard, then firmly press bread-crumb mixture onto coated sides with your hands to form solid, even coating that adheres to meat.

5 Being careful of hot skillet handle, return roast to skillet and broil until crust is golden brown and meat registers 120 to 125 degrees (for medium-rare), about 5 minutes. Transfer roast to carving board and let rest for 20 minutes. Slice roast into ½-inch-thick slices. Serve.

ONE-DISH DINNERS

Paella

SAUSAGE LASAGNA

SERVES 6

WHY THIS RECIPE WORKS A big, bubbling lasagna is the pinnacle of comfort food. We wanted a version that could be made quickly, with minimal effort (and minimal dishes) and without sacrificing any flavor. We started building a flavorful sauce by sautéing onion, garlic, and red pepper flakes. We then browned some sausage and added tomatoes, simmering only briefly to meld the flavors yet keep it fresh tasting. After cooking the sauce, we emptied the skillet and layered the lasagna as we would in a casserole dish with the tomato-sausage sauce, a ricotta-egg mixture, no-boil lasagna noodles, and plenty of Parmesan and mozzarella. Once our lasagna was assembled, we topped it with extra cheese and transferred the skillet to the oven. After a short 30-minute stint, we had the bubbly, cheesy top and perfectly cooked pasta we were looking for, all made in a single pan. Do not use nonfat ricotta or fat-free mozzarella here.

3 (14.5-ounce) cans whole peeled tomatoes
2 tablespoons extra-virgin olive oil
1 onion, chopped fine
   Salt and pepper
3 garlic cloves, minced
¼ teaspoon red pepper flakes
1 pound hot or sweet Italian sausage, casings removed
12 ounces (1½ cups) whole-milk ricotta cheese
1 large egg yolk
1 teaspoon minced fresh thyme or ¼ teaspoon dried
8 ounces mozzarella cheese, shredded (2 cups)
¼ cup grated Parmesan cheese
12 no-boil lasagna noodles, broken in half
3 tablespoons chopped fresh basil

1 Adjust oven rack to middle position and heat oven to 400 degrees. Pulse tomatoes and their juice in food processor until coarsely ground, about 10 pulses.

2 Heat 12-inch cast-iron skillet over medium heat for 3 minutes. Add oil and heat until shimmering. Add onion and ½ teaspoon salt and cook until softened and lightly browned, 5 to 7 minutes. Stir in garlic and pepper flakes and cook until fragrant, about 30 seconds. Add sausage and cook, breaking up meat with wooden spoon, until no longer pink, about 5 minutes. Stir in processed tomatoes, bring to simmer, and cook until sauce is slightly thickened, about 10 minutes; transfer to bowl.

3 In separate bowl, combine ricotta, egg yolk, thyme, ½ teaspoon salt, and ½ teaspoon pepper. Combine mozzarella and Parmesan in third bowl.

4 Spread ¾ cup sauce over bottom of now-empty skillet. Shingle 7 noodle halves around edge of skillet and place 1 noodle half in center. Dollop one-third of ricotta mixture over noodles, then top with one-quarter of mozzarella mixture and one-third of remaining sauce (in that order). Repeat layering process twice, beginning with noodles and ending with sauce. Top with remaining mozzarella mixture.

5 Transfer skillet to oven and bake until cheese is golden brown and lasagna is bubbling around edges, 30 to 40 minutes. Let lasagna cool for 10 minutes, then sprinkle with basil and serve.

LAYERING NOODLES FOR SKILLET LASAGNA

After spreading sauce layer, shingle 7 noodle halves around edge of skillet and place 1 noodle half in center.

BAKED ZITI WITH CHARRED TOMATOES

SERVES 4

WHY THIS RECIPE WORKS Baked ziti, a hearty combination of pasta, tomato sauce, and gooey cheese, can be time-consuming and fussy between making the sauce, boiling the pasta, and then assembling and baking the dish. We were looking to streamline this dish, achieving the same delicious results in less time and without watching over, and dirtying, a multitude of pots. Our first priority was the sauce. We used a hot cast-iron skillet to get a nice blistery char on grape tomatoes, bringing a deep, caramelized flavor to the sauce. We further bolstered the sauce by sautéing garlic, red pepper flakes, and tomato paste with the charred tomatoes. We then mashed everything to a coarse consistency and diluted it with water so that we could cook the ziti right in the sauce. Cooking the ziti in the skillet with the sauce saved us from using an extra pot, and the starch released from the pasta during cooking helped thicken the sauce nicely. We finished the sauce by stirring in basil and Parmesan. We then sprinkled the whole dish with mozzarella and broiled it in the oven. Being able to go from the stovetop to the broiler was another perk of the cast-iron pan, and the dish needed only 5 minutes in the oven for a perfectly melty, browned cheese layer on top. You can substitute penne for the ziti. Do not use fat-free mozzarella here.

1½ pounds grape tomatoes

1 tablespoon extra-virgin olive oil

Salt and pepper

6 garlic cloves, minced

1 teaspoon tomato paste

¼ teaspoon red pepper flakes

12 ounces (3¾ cups) ziti

3 cups water, plus extra as needed

1 ounce Parmesan cheese, grated (½ cup)

¼ cup chopped fresh basil

4 ounces mozzarella cheese, shredded (1 cup)

1 Adjust oven rack 6 inches from broiler element and heat broiler. Heat 12-inch cast-iron skillet over medium heat for 5 minutes. Toss tomatoes with oil and 1 teaspoon salt. Add tomatoes to skillet and cook, stirring occasionally, until lightly charred and blistered, about 10 minutes. Stir in garlic, tomato paste, and pepper flakes and cook until fragrant, about 30 seconds. Off heat, coarsely mash tomatoes using potato masher.

2 Stir in pasta and water and bring to boil over medium-high heat. Reduce heat to vigorous simmer, cover, and cook, stirring often, until pasta is tender, 15 to 18 minutes.

3 Stir in Parmesan and adjust sauce consistency with extra hot water as needed. Stir in basil and season with salt and pepper to taste. Sprinkle with mozzarella. Transfer skillet to oven and broil until cheese is melted and spotty brown, about 5 minutes. Serve.

VARIATION

Baked Ziti with Puttanesca Sauce

Add 2 anchovies, rinsed and minced, to skillet with garlic and increase pepper flakes to ½ teaspoon. Substitute ½ cup dry red wine for ½ cup of water in step 2. Substitute ¼ cup minced fresh parsley for basil and stir ½ cup chopped pitted kalamata olives and 2 tablespoons capers, rinsed and minced, into cooked pasta with Parmesan.

SKILLET MACARONI AND CHEESE

SERVES 4

WHY THIS RECIPE WORKS While boxed or frozen mac and cheese from the supermarket can certainly be a convenient family favorite, it just doesn't hold the same allure for adults as for kids. And many "quick" homemade macaroni and cheese recipes are just as lackluster, involving a tasteless, lumpy mix of shredded cheese and mushy pasta. Our goal was to develop a skillet macaroni and cheese that the whole family would enjoy as a weeknight meal. We went for simplicity and convenience when developing our recipe, opting to keep the whole process on the stovetop to make it a quick-cooking dinner. Using evaporated milk in place of whole milk or heavy cream kept the sauce from curdling and from being too rich. A mix of mild cheddar and Monterey Jack cheeses provided plenty of rich flavor and gave us the right amount of meltability, and the great heat retention of the cast-iron pan kept the cheese from congealing after it was stirred in. You can substitute small shells (3 cups) for the macaroni.

3½ cups water, plus extra as needed

1 (12-ounce) can evaporated milk

12 ounces (3 cups) elbow macaroni

Salt and pepper

1 teaspoon cornstarch

½ teaspoon dry mustard

¼ teaspoon hot sauce

6 ounces mild cheddar cheese, shredded (1½ cups)

6 ounces Monterey Jack cheese, shredded (1½ cups)

3 tablespoons unsalted butter

1 Bring water, 1 cup evaporated milk, macaroni, and ½ teaspoon salt to vigorous simmer in 12-inch cast-iron skillet over medium-high heat. Cook, stirring often, until macaroni is tender and liquid has almost completely evaporated, 8 to 10 minutes.

2 Whisk remaining ½ cup evaporated milk, cornstarch, mustard, and hot sauce together in bowl, then stir into skillet. Cook until sauce is slightly thickened, about 1 minute.

3 Off heat, stir in cheddar and Monterey Jack, 1 handful at a time, until melted. Stir in extra hot water as needed to adjust consistency. Stir in butter and season with salt and pepper to taste. Serve.

VARIATIONS

Skillet Macaroni and Cheese with Broccoli
Bring 3 cups chopped broccoli florets, ½ cup water, and ¼ teaspoon salt to simmer in 12-inch cast-iron skillet over medium heat. Cover and steam broccoli until tender, about 5 minutes. Using slotted spoon, transfer broccoli to bowl; set aside. Wipe skillet clean with paper towels and proceed with recipe, stirring steamed broccoli into macaroni with butter.

Skillet Macaroni and Cheese with Ham and Peas
Stir 4 ounces diced deli ham and ½ cup frozen peas into skillet with evaporated milk mixture in step 2.

Baked Skillet Macaroni and Cheese
Adjust oven rack to middle position and heat oven to 475 degrees. Pulse 2 slices hearty white sandwich bread, torn into quarters, 2 tablespoons melted unsalted butter, ¼ teaspoon salt, and ⅛ teaspoon pepper in food processor to coarse crumbs, about 6 pulses. Before serving, sprinkle crumb mixture over macaroni and cheese and bake until topping is browned, about 10 minutes.

PAN-ROASTED CHICKEN BREASTS
WITH ROOT VEGETABLES

SERVES 4

WHY THIS RECIPE WORKS For this version of classic roast chicken and vegetables, we knew we could use our cast-iron skillet to get a great seared crust on the chicken, but could we cook the vegetables in sync—and not dry out the chicken? To get the best sear on our chicken, we preheated the skillet over medium heat for 5 minutes for the quickest, most even browning. After the initial sear, we took the chicken out of the skillet and filled the pan with potatoes, parsnips, carrots, and shallots. We then put the chicken back in the pan on top of the vegetables and moved the whole thing to the oven. The intense heat of the cast-iron pan helped cook our root vegetables quickly and evenly. Elevating the chicken on top of the vegetables allowed the meat to gently cook while the vegetables roasted against the hot surface of the pan. Once the chicken was done, we removed it and let it rest while we finished cooking our vegetables. Cutting the vegetables into bite-size pieces helped them cook faster so they were done by the time the chicken was rested and ready to serve. A simple sprinkling of chives was all that was needed to finish our dish. Use small red potatoes measuring 2 inches in diameter.

4 (12-ounce) bone-in split chicken breasts, trimmed
Salt and pepper
1 tablespoon vegetable oil
1 pound small red potatoes, unpeeled, quartered
8 ounces parsnips, peeled, halved lengthwise, and cut into 1-inch pieces
4 carrots, peeled, halved lengthwise, and cut into 1-inch pieces
4 shallots, peeled and quartered
1 teaspoon minced fresh rosemary or ¼ teaspoon dried
1 tablespoon minced fresh chives

1 Adjust oven rack to middle position and heat oven to 450 degrees. Pat chicken dry with paper towels and season with salt and pepper. Heat 12-inch cast-iron skillet over medium heat for 5 minutes. Add oil and heat until just smoking. Place chicken skin side down in skillet and cook until well browned on first side, 5 to 7 minutes. Flip chicken and continue to cook until lightly browned on second side, about 3 minutes; transfer to plate.

2 Add potatoes, parsnips, carrots, shallots, rosemary, ½ teaspoon salt, and ¼ teaspoon pepper to fat left in skillet and toss to coat. Place chicken skin side up on top of vegetables, transfer skillet to oven, and roast until chicken registers 160 degrees, 20 to 25 minutes.

3 Using potholders, remove skillet from oven. Transfer chicken to serving platter, tent loosely with aluminum foil, and let rest while finishing vegetables.

4 Being careful of hot skillet handle, stir vegetables, return skillet to oven, and roast until vegetables are tender, about 15 minutes. Stir in chives and season with salt and pepper to taste. Serve chicken with vegetables.

BRAISED CHICKEN THIGHS
WITH SWISS CHARD AND CARROTS

SERVES 4

WHY THIS RECIPE WORKS An easy one-dish meal that delivers rich, meaty chicken plus greens and carrots? Yes, please! For a simple, satisfying one-pan weeknight dinner, we started with skin-on, bone-in chicken thighs, which turn meltingly tender when braised. We browned the thighs on both sides to build flavor and help the skin crisp, then took the chicken out of the pan to build our braising liquid. We included plenty of aromatics for depth of flavor, and a slightly unusual addition— anchovies—gave the dish a savory backbone and provided even more depth without making it taste fishy. Once our braising liquid was complete, we added carrots and the browned chicken thighs to the skillet and moved the whole operation to the oven. Using a cast-iron skillet meant that the heat stayed even throughout cooking, ensuring perfectly cooked chicken. Slightly bitter Swiss chard complemented the sweetness of the carrots and added complexity to the dish. Finally, a dab of mustard contributed a punch of flavor, and lemon zest and juice added brightness. We rounded out the sauce with butter, creating a nice balance for our hearty, meaty chicken and bitter greens. Use carrots that measure ¾ inch to 1 inch at the thicker end.

8 (5- to 7-ounce) bone-in chicken thighs, trimmed
  Salt and pepper
1 tablespoon vegetable oil
1 onion, chopped fine
6 garlic cloves, minced
1 tablespoon minced fresh thyme or 1 teaspoon dried
2 anchovy fillets, rinsed and minced
2 tablespoons all-purpose flour
1 cup chicken broth
1 pound carrots, peeled and halved crosswise
1½ pounds Swiss chard, stemmed and sliced into
  ½-inch-wide strips
3 tablespoons whole-grain mustard
1 tablespoon unsalted butter
1 teaspoon grated lemon zest plus 2 teaspoons juice

1 Adjust oven rack to lower-middle position and heat oven to 325 degrees. Pat chicken dry with paper towels and season with salt and pepper. Heat 12-inch cast-iron skillet over medium heat for 5 minutes. Add oil and heat until just smoking. Brown half of chicken, about 4 minutes per side; transfer to plate. Repeat with remaining chicken; transfer to plate.

2 Pour off all but 1 tablespoon fat from skillet. Add onion and cook over medium heat until softened, about 5 minutes. Stir in garlic, thyme, and anchovies and cook until fragrant, about 30 seconds. Stir in flour and cook for 1 minute. Slowly stir in broth, scraping up any browned bits and smoothing out any lumps. Stir in carrots and bring to simmer.

3 Nestle chicken skin side up into skillet (skin should be above surface of liquid) along with any accumulated juices. Transfer skillet to oven and braise until chicken offers little resistance when poked with tip of paring knife but still clings to bones, 1 to 1¼ hours.

4 Using potholders, remove skillet from oven. Transfer chicken to serving platter, tent loosely with aluminum foil, and let rest while finishing vegetables.

5 Being careful of hot skillet handle, stir in chard, 1 handful at a time, and cook over medium heat until wilted and tender, about 5 minutes. Off heat, stir in mustard, butter, and lemon zest and juice. Season with salt and pepper to taste. Serve chicken with vegetables.

CURRIED CHICKEN AND RICE

SERVES 4

WHY THIS RECIPE WORKS For a simple, flavorful weeknight take on chicken and rice, we started with boneless, skinless chicken breasts. Dredging the chicken in flour before browning it helped develop a golden crust. We then came up with some creative ways to develop deep flavor without the need for a long simmering time. To start, after we browned the chicken we removed it from the skillet and sautéed the rice with onion, carrots, garlic, and curry powder before we added the cooking liquid. This step gave the rice more complex flavor and also kept the grains distinct and creamy without being mushy. We then added back the browned chicken breasts with the rice and the chicken broth, but to ensure that the chicken did not dry out we cooked it until just done, then set it aside while the rice finished. Once we removed the chicken, we added coconut milk to the rice to give it an additional flavor boost and complement the curry powder. Adding the coconut milk toward the end of cooking kept the flavor bright and distinct. Cilantro and almonds gave us the final freshness and crunch we wanted in this fast and flavorful dish. The spice level of curry varies from brand to brand. If your curry powder is very spicy, you may need to reduce the amount listed.

½ cup all-purpose flour

4 (6- to 8-ounce) boneless, skinless chicken breasts, trimmed

Salt and pepper

3 tablespoons vegetable oil

2 carrots, peeled and cut into ¼-inch pieces

1 onion, chopped fine

1½ cups long-grain white rice

2 garlic cloves, minced

1 tablespoon curry powder

4 cups chicken broth

½ cup canned light coconut milk

1 cup frozen peas

¼ cup minced fresh cilantro

2 tablespoons sliced almonds, toasted

1 Spread flour in shallow dish. Pound thicker ends of chicken breasts as needed to create even thickness. Pat chicken dry with paper towels and season with salt and pepper. Dredge chicken in flour to coat, shaking off excess.

2 Heat 12-inch cast-iron skillet over medium heat for 5 minutes. Add 2 tablespoons oil and heat until just smoking. Brown chicken, about 4 minutes per side; transfer to plate.

3 Heat remaining 1 tablespoon oil in now-empty skillet over medium heat until shimmering. Add carrots, onion, and ½ teaspoon salt and cook until softened, about 5 minutes. Stir in rice, garlic, and curry powder and cook until fragrant, about 30 seconds. Stir in broth, scraping up any browned bits, and bring to simmer.

4 Nestle chicken into skillet along with any accumulated juices. Reduce heat to gentle simmer, cover, and cook until chicken registers 160 degrees, about 8 minutes. Transfer chicken to serving platter, brushing any rice that sticks to chicken back into skillet, and tent loosely with aluminum foil. Let chicken rest while finishing rice.

5 Add coconut milk to skillet, cover, and cook over medium-low heat, stirring occasionally, until liquid has been absorbed and rice is tender, 12 to 15 minutes. Off heat, sprinkle peas over rice, cover, and let sit until heated through, about 2 minutes. Gently fold cilantro and almonds into rice. Season with salt and pepper to taste. Serve chicken with rice.

CHICKEN CHILAQUILES

SERVES 4

WHY THIS RECIPE WORKS *Chilaquiles* is a Mexican comfort food favorite made from fried tortilla wedges tossed in a deeply flavored chile sauce. The crisp chips soften slightly in the sauce, giving the dish a unique crunchy-chewy texture. The finished dish is usually topped with a variety of fresh garnishes along with a fried egg and served for breakfast. We decided to swap the fried egg for shredded chicken for a hearty main course. We quickly discovered that using store-bought tortilla chips led to disappointing results; they either turned completely mushy or never softened properly, so we made our own. Baking the chips kept the dish from getting too greasy. We then made a simple sauce by toasting dried guajillo chiles in our cast-iron skillet and pureeing them in a blender with tomatoes, onion, two other kinds of chile peppers, garlic, cilantro, and salt. We poached the chicken directly in the sauce to infuse both with greater depth of flavor. Shredding the chicken and stirring in the homemade chips brought the dish together. New Mexican or Anaheim chiles can be substituted for the guajillo chiles. Serve with sour cream and lime wedges.

16 (6-inch) corn tortillas, cut into 8 wedges

¼ cup vegetable oil

Salt

5 dried guajillo chiles, stemmed, seeded, and torn into ½-inch pieces (⅔ cup)

1 (28-ounce) can whole peeled tomatoes

1 cup finely chopped onion

1 poblano chile, stemmed, seeded, and chopped

1 jalapeño chile, stemmed, seeded, and chopped

3 garlic cloves, peeled and chopped

8 sprigs fresh cilantro plus 2 tablespoons minced

1½ pounds boneless, skinless chicken breasts, trimmed

1½ cups chicken broth

4 ounces queso fresco, crumbled (1 cup)

1 avocado, halved, pitted, and cut into ½-inch pieces

2 radishes, trimmed and sliced thin

1 Adjust oven racks to upper-middle and lower-middle positions and heat oven to 425 degrees. Spread tortillas evenly in 2 rimmed baking sheets. Drizzle each sheet with 2 tablespoons oil, sprinkle with ¼ teaspoon salt, and toss until evenly coated. Bake, stirring occasionally, until tortillas are golden brown and crisp, 15 to 20 minutes, switching and rotating sheets halfway through baking.

2 Toast guajillos in 12-inch cast-iron skillet over medium heat, stirring frequently, until fragrant, 2 to 6 minutes. Transfer toasted guajillos to blender and process until finely ground, 60 to 90 seconds. Add tomatoes and their juice, ¾ cup onion, poblano, jalapeño, garlic, cilantro sprigs, and ¾ teaspoon salt to blender and process until very smooth, 60 to 90 seconds.

3 Pound thicker ends of chicken breasts as needed to create even thickness. Combine guajillo-tomato mixture and broth in now-empty skillet and bring to simmer over medium-high heat. Nestle chicken into sauce. Reduce heat to gentle simmer, cover, and cook until chicken registers 160 degrees, 10 to 15 minutes, flipping chicken halfway through cooking.

4 Transfer chicken to carving board, let cool slightly, then shred into bite-size pieces using 2 forks. Meanwhile, increase heat to medium and simmer sauce until thickened and measures 4 cups, about 6 minutes.

5 Stir shredded chicken into sauce and cook until heated through, about 2 minutes. Off heat, stir in tortillas, cover, and let sit until tortillas have softened slightly, 2 to 5 minutes. Sprinkle with queso fresco, avocado, radishes, remaining ¼ cup onion, and minced cilantro. Serve immediately.

EASIER FRIED CHICKEN

SERVES 4

WHY THIS RECIPE WORKS Juicy, crisp bone-in fried chicken is a cast iron classic. We wanted to come up with a foolproof recipe that would ensure chicken with a moist, perfectly seasoned interior and a supercrunchy crust. To start, we brined the chicken in salted buttermilk to infuse it with moisture and flavor. For a perfectly crunchy coating, we combined flour with a little baking powder and some seasonings, then added more buttermilk to make a thick slurry that would cling tightly to the meat. Four cups of oil (instead of the usual 12) was all that was needed to get a perfect light brown crust on our whole batch of chicken. Then to finish cooking we moved the shallow-fried pieces to a hot oven (perched on a wire rack set in a sheet pan to prevent burnt spots and promote air circulation around the meat). This hybrid method gave us perfectly crisp, evenly cooked results that were even better than deep-fried. We got all the benefits of frying without any danger of burnt coating or undercooked chicken. Any combination of chicken pieces will work well here; just be sure the total amount equals 2½ pounds. You will need a 12-inch cast-iron skillet with at least 2-inch sides for this recipe. Don't let the chicken soak in the buttermilk brine for longer than 1 hour or it will be too salty. Covering the skillet with a splatter screen will reduce the mess that frying inevitably makes.

1¼ cups buttermilk

Salt and pepper

1¼ teaspoons garlic powder

1¼ teaspoons paprika

½ teaspoon cayenne pepper

2½ pounds bone-in chicken pieces (split breasts cut in half, drumsticks, and/or thighs), trimmed

2 cups all-purpose flour

2 teaspoons baking powder

4 cups peanut or vegetable oil

1 Whisk 1 cup buttermilk, 1 tablespoon salt, 1 teaspoon pepper, ¼ teaspoon garlic powder, ¼ teaspoon paprika, and ¼ teaspoon cayenne together in large bowl. Add chicken, cover, and refrigerate for at least 30 minutes or up to 1 hour.

2 Adjust oven rack to middle position and heat oven to 400 degrees. Whisk flour, baking powder, 2 teaspoons pepper, 1 teaspoon salt, remaining 1 teaspoon garlic powder, remaining 1 teaspoon paprika, and

remaining ¼ teaspoon cayenne together in large bowl. Add remaining ¼ cup buttermilk and rub into flour mixture using your hands until evenly incorporated and small clumps form. Working with 1 piece of chicken at a time, dredge in flour mixture, pressing gently to adhere, then transfer to large plate.

3 Set wire rack in rimmed baking sheet. Add oil to 12-inch cast-iron skillet until it measures about ¾ inch deep and heat over medium-high heat to 375 degrees.

4 Carefully place half of chicken skin side down in oil. Fry until deep golden brown, about 6 minutes, flipping chicken halfway through frying. Adjust burner, if necessary, to maintain oil temperature between 350 and 375 degrees. Transfer chicken to prepared rack. Return oil to 375 degrees and repeat with remaining chicken; transfer to prepared rack.

5 Bake chicken until breasts register 160 degrees and drumsticks/thighs register 175 degrees, 12 to 18 minutes. Serve.

SOUTHWESTERN-STYLE CHICKEN AND BISCUITS

SERVES 4 TO 6

WHY THIS RECIPE WORKS Southern chicken and biscuits is a hearty oven-to-table staple that we aimed to streamline by cooking the entire dish in a cast-iron skillet. We started by searing boneless, skinless chicken thighs in the hot skillet to give them a good crust and create some browning, or fond, in the pan. We then set the meat aside while we sautéed onion, celery, and thyme for an aromatic base of flavor. We added flour and broth and quickly poached the chicken in the sauce, then shredded it into fork-friendly pieces. To give this classic dish a modern update, we went for Southwestern flavors, stirring bell pepper and corn into the stew with the shredded chicken. Next came the biscuits. In some recipes the biscuits are cooked separately, but we wanted to stick with a one-dish preparation, which meant simply dropping spoonfuls of biscuit dough on top of the stew before sliding the skillet into the oven. Our major challenge was creating a biscuit that could sit on our brothy stew and still emerge from the oven fully cooked. The answer was making a drier biscuit that could absorb some liquid from the stew without compromising texture. Adding cheddar and scallions to the biscuit dough bumped up the flavor profile.

2 pounds boneless, skinless chicken thighs, trimmed
  Salt and pepper
3 tablespoons vegetable oil
2 celery ribs, chopped fine
1 onion, chopped fine
1 teaspoon minced fresh thyme or ¼ teaspoon dried
1½ cups (7½ ounces) plus 3 tablespoons all-purpose flour
2¾ cups chicken broth
1 red bell pepper, stemmed, seeded, and cut into ¼-inch pieces
1 cup frozen corn, thawed
3 ounces sharp cheddar cheese, shredded (¾ cup)
3 scallions, sliced thin
1½ teaspoons baking powder
⅛ teaspoon cayenne pepper
¾ cup heavy cream

1 Adjust oven rack to middle position and heat oven to 450 degrees. Pat chicken dry with paper towels and season with salt and pepper. Heat 12-inch cast-iron skillet over medium heat for 5 minutes. Add 2 tablespoons oil and heat until shimmering. Brown chicken, about 4 minutes per side; transfer to plate.

2 Heat remaining 1 tablespoon oil in now-empty skillet over medium heat until shimmering. Add celery and onion and cook until softened and lightly browned, 5 to 7 minutes. Stir in thyme and cook until fragrant, about 30 seconds. Stir in 3 tablespoons flour and cook for 1 minute. Slowly whisk in 2½ cups broth, scraping up any browned bits and smoothing out any lumps, and bring to simmer.

3 Nestle chicken into skillet along with any accumulated juices. Reduce heat to gentle simmer, cover, and cook until chicken registers 175 degrees, 12 to 15 minutes, flipping chicken halfway through cooking.

4 Transfer chicken to carving board, let cool slightly, then pull into large chunks using 2 spoons. Stir shredded chicken, bell pepper, and corn into skillet.

5 Whisk remaining 1½ cups flour, cheddar, scallions, baking powder, ¾ teaspoon salt, ½ teaspoon pepper, and cayenne together in large bowl. Stir in cream and remaining ¼ cup broth until just combined. Using greased ¼-cup dry measure, scoop out and drop 9 mounds of dough onto chicken mixture, spaced about ½ inch apart. Transfer skillet to oven and bake until biscuits are golden brown and filling is bubbling, about 20 minutes. Let casserole cool for 10 minutes before serving.

CHICKEN POT PIE

SERVES 4 TO 6

WHY THIS RECIPE WORKS The preparations required for chicken pot pie have largely relegated it to a Sunday treat, but moving this dish to a cast-iron skillet sped up the process and also improved the results. We started by parbaking the crust separately, which kept it from becoming soggy and ensured that it was done at the same time as the filling. Sautéing the vegetables and aromatics and adding broth created a rich, caramelized base in which we then poached the chicken. Next we shredded the meat and then stirred it back in with heavy cream, peas, parsley, and dry sherry. We slipped on the parbaked crust and baked the dish for a short time to bring it all together. You can use our Foolproof Single-Crust Pie Dough (page 199) or ready-made pie dough in this recipe.

1 recipe single-crust pie dough

1 large egg, lightly beaten with 2 tablespoons water

4 tablespoons unsalted butter

4 carrots, peeled and sliced ¼ inch thick

2 celery ribs, cut into ¼-inch pieces

1 onion, chopped fine

   Salt and pepper

1 teaspoon minced fresh thyme or ¼ teaspoon dried

6 tablespoons all-purpose flour

2 cups chicken broth

1½ pounds boneless, skinless chicken breasts, trimmed

½ cup frozen peas

¼ cup heavy cream

3 tablespoons minced fresh parsley

1 tablespoon dry sherry

1 Roll dough between 2 sheets of parchment paper into 11-inch circle. Remove top parchment sheet. Fold in outer ½ inch of dough to make 10-inch circle. Using index finger of one hand and thumb and index finger of other hand, crimp edge of dough to make attractive fluted rim. Using paring knife, cut 4 oval-shaped vents, each about 2 inches long and ½ inch wide, in center of dough. Transfer dough, still on parchment, to baking sheet and refrigerate until firm, about 15 minutes.

2 Adjust oven rack to middle position and heat oven to 400 degrees. Brush dough with egg mixture and bake until golden brown, 10 to 12 minutes, rotating sheet halfway through baking. Transfer crust, still on sheet, to wire rack and let cool; do not turn off oven.

3 Heat 10-inch cast-iron skillet over medium heat for 3 minutes. Melt butter in skillet. Add carrots, celery, onion, ¼ teaspoon salt, and ¼ teaspoon pepper and cook until softened and lightly browned, 5 to 7 minutes. Stir in thyme and cook until fragrant, about 30 seconds. Stir in flour and cook for 2 minutes. Slowly whisk in broth, scraping up any browned bits and smoothing out any lumps, and bring to simmer.

4 Pound thicker ends of chicken breasts as needed to create even thickness. Nestle chicken into skillet. Reduce heat to gentle simmer, cover, and cook until chicken registers 160 degrees and sauce has thickened, 10 to 15 minutes, flipping chicken halfway through.

5 Transfer chicken to carving board, let cool slightly, then shred into bite-size pieces using 2 forks. Stir shredded chicken, peas, cream, parsley, and sherry into skillet. Season with salt and pepper to taste.

6 Place parbaked pie crust on top of filling, transfer skillet to oven, and bake until crust is deep golden brown and filling is bubbling, about 10 minutes. Let pot pie cool for 10 minutes before serving.

SHAPING A POT PIE CRUST

After folding in outer ½ inch of dough, crimp edge to make attractive fluted rim using index finger of 1 hand and thumb and index finger of other hand.

BEEF POT PIE

SERVES 4 TO 6

WHY THIS RECIPE WORKS For a quick, richly flavored beef pot pie made in the skillet, picking the right cut of beef was an essential first step. We went with beefy chuck-eye roast, which turns meltingly tender when properly cooked. Searing only half the meat built plenty of rich, caramelized flavor while saving time on the stovetop. We created a rich sauce using the browned fond from the meat as a base, then added the meat back in and used the oven for a hands-off way to gently simmer the dish until the meat was tender. Parbaking the crust ensured that when we baked the topped pie, it cooked up bubbly hot and golden brown with no mushiness or scorching. You can use our Classic Single-Crust Pie Dough (page 199) or ready-made pie dough in this recipe.

1 recipe single-crust pie dough

1 large egg, lightly beaten with 2 tablespoons water

2 pounds boneless beef chuck-eye roast, pulled apart at seams, trimmed, and cut into ¾-inch pieces
  Salt and pepper

3 tablespoons vegetable oil

8 ounces cremini mushrooms, trimmed and quartered

2 carrots, peeled and cut into ½-inch pieces

1 onion, chopped fine

2 tablespoons tomato paste

4 garlic cloves, minced

3 tablespoons all-purpose flour

½ cup dry red wine

1¾ cups beef broth

1 tablespoon Worcestershire sauce

1 cup frozen peas

1 teaspoon minced fresh thyme

1 Roll dough between 2 sheets of parchment paper into 11-inch circle. Remove top parchment sheet. Fold in outer ½ inch of dough to make 10-inch circle. Using index finger of one hand and thumb and index finger of other hand, crimp edge of dough to make attractive fluted rim. Using paring knife, cut 4 oval-shaped vents, each about 2 inches long and ½ inch wide, in center of dough. Transfer dough, still on parchment, to baking sheet and refrigerate until firm, about 15 minutes.

2 Adjust oven rack to middle position and heat oven to 400 degrees. Brush dough with egg mixture and bake until golden brown, 10 to 12 minutes, rotating sheet halfway through baking. Transfer crust, still on sheet, to wire rack and let cool slightly; do not turn off oven.

3 Pat beef dry with paper towels and season with salt and pepper. Heat 10-inch cast-iron skillet over medium heat for 5 minutes. Add 2 tablespoons oil and heat until just smoking. Brown half of beef on all sides, 7 to 10 minutes; transfer to bowl.

4 Heat remaining 1 tablespoon oil in now-empty skillet over medium heat until shimmering. Add mushrooms, carrots, and onion and cook until softened and lightly browned, 5 to 7 minutes. Stir in tomato paste and garlic and cook until fragrant, about 30 seconds. Stir in flour and cook for 1 minute.

5 Stir in wine and cook until almost completely evaporated, about 2 minutes. Slowly stir in broth and Worcestershire, scraping up any browned bits and smoothing out any lumps, and bring to simmer. Stir in browned beef and any accumulated juices and remaining uncooked beef. Cover, transfer skillet to oven, and cook until beef is tender, about 1 hour, stirring halfway through cooking.

6 Using potholders, remove skillet from oven. Stir in peas and thyme and season with salt and pepper to taste. Being careful of hot skillet handle, place parbaked pie crust on top of filling, return skillet to oven, and bake until crust is deep golden brown and filling is bubbling, about 10 minutes. Let pot pie cool for 10 minutes before serving.

SHEPHERD'S PIE

SERVES 4 TO 6

WHY THIS RECIPE WORKS Despite its status as a classic comfort food, there's nothing comforting about the many steps and piles of dirty dishes that shepherd's pie usually requires. Using the cast-iron skillet as our sautéing, baking, and serving pan streamlined the process. We used ground beef as our base and added tomato paste, garlic, and thyme to bump up the flavor. Flour, chicken broth, and Worcestershire sauce were all that we needed to create a rich gravy, and a final addition of green peas added a pop of freshness. To give our potato topping needed structure, we added egg, milk, and butter. We used a zipper-lock bag to pipe the potato mixture on top of the pie and finished the dish under the broiler to give it an attractive golden crust. Don't use ground beef that's fattier than 93 percent or the dish will be greasy.

2 pounds russet potatoes, peeled and cut into 1-inch pieces

Salt and pepper

½ cup milk

1 large egg

4 tablespoons unsalted butter, melted, plus 2 tablespoons unsalted butter

2 carrots, peeled and chopped

1 onion, chopped fine

1½ pounds 93 percent lean ground beef

2 tablespoons tomato paste

2 garlic cloves, minced

2 teaspoons minced fresh thyme or ½ teaspoon dried

2 tablespoons all-purpose flour

1½ cups chicken broth

2 teaspoons Worcestershire sauce

1 cup frozen peas

1 Cover potatoes with water in large saucepan. Add 1 tablespoon salt, bring to simmer over medium-high heat, and cook until potatoes are tender, 8 to 10 minutes. Drain potatoes and return to now-empty saucepan. Using potato masher, mash potatoes until smooth. Whisk milk and egg together, then stir into potatoes along with 4 tablespoons melted butter, 1 teaspoon salt, and ½ teaspoon pepper; cover and set aside.

2 Heat 10-inch cast-iron skillet over medium heat for 3 minutes. Melt remaining 2 tablespoons butter in skillet. Add carrots, onion, and ¾ teaspoon salt and cook until softened, about 5 minutes. Add ground beef and cook, breaking up meat with wooden spoon, until no longer pink, 8 to 10 minutes.

3 Stir in tomato paste, garlic, and thyme and cook until fragrant, about 1 minute. Stir in flour and cook for 1 minute. Slowly stir in broth and Worcestershire, scraping up any browned bits and smoothing out any lumps. Bring to simmer and cook, stirring occasionally, until mixture has thickened slightly, about 10 minutes. Off heat, stir in peas and season with salt and pepper to taste.

4 Adjust oven rack 5 inches from broiler element and heat broiler. Transfer potato mixture to 1-gallon zipper-lock bag and snip off 1 corner to create 1-inch opening. Pipe mixture in even layer over filling. Smooth mixture with back of spoon, then use tines of fork to make ridges on surface. Place skillet in rimmed baking sheet and broil until topping is golden brown and crusty, 5 to 10 minutes. Let casserole cool for 10 minutes before serving.

TOPPING SHEPHERD'S PIE

Transfer potato mixture to 1-gallon zipper-lock bag and snip off 1 corner. Pipe mixture over filling, making sure to cover entire surface. Smooth with back of spoon, then make ridges with fork.

WEEKNIGHT BEEF CHILI

SERVES 4 TO 6

WHY THIS RECIPE WORKS The trouble with cooking chili in cast iron is that simmering acidic ingredients like tomatoes for a long period of time can strip away the pan's seasoning and leave a metallic off-flavor (see page 13 for more information). But we were determined to find a way to cook our chili in cast iron so we could take advantage of all the other assets the pan had to offer for this meaty dish. Our solution? Reserve the tomatoes until the very end of cooking. Instead of starting with the tomato base, we began by sweating onion and bell pepper and adding tomato paste and chili powder reinforced with cumin, oregano, coriander, red pepper flakes, and cayenne. (The tomato paste wasn't acidic enough to be problematic in this early stage.) We stirred in our beef and allowed it to brown, then we added kidney beans and chicken broth, which provided enough liquid to simmer our chili without the tomatoes. Cooking the chili with the lid off for half the simmering time resulted in a rich, thick consistency. Stirring in a can of tomato sauce at the very end of cooking and simmering for just a few minutes allowed the flavors to meld without any threat of damage to our pan or our food. Using sauce rather than crushed tomatoes helped keep this late addition from adding raw flavor to the cooked chili. For best results, serve within 15 minutes and transfer leftovers to an airtight container. Serve with your favorite chili toppings.

2 tablespoons chili powder

2¼ teaspoons minced fresh oregano or ¾ teaspoon dried

2 teaspoons ground cumin

1½ teaspoons ground coriander

⅛ teaspoon cayenne pepper

¾ teaspoon red pepper flakes

Salt and pepper

3 tablespoons vegetable oil

1 onion, chopped fine

1 red bell pepper, stemmed, seeded, and cut into ½-inch pieces

2 tablespoons tomato paste

4 garlic cloves, minced

1 pound 85 percent lean ground beef

1½ cups chicken broth

1 (15-ounce) can red kidney beans, rinsed

1 (15-ounce) can tomato sauce

1 Combine chili powder, oregano, cumin, coriander, cayenne pepper, pepper flakes, and ¼ teaspoon salt in bowl.

2 Heat 12-inch cast-iron skillet over medium heat for 3 minutes. Add oil and heat until shimmering. Add onion and bell pepper and cook until softened, about 5 minutes. Stir in spice mixture, tomato paste, and garlic and cook until fragrant, about 1 minute.

3 Add ground beef and cook, breaking up meat with wooden spoon, until no longer pink, 5 to 7 minutes. Stir in broth and beans, scraping up any browned bits, and bring to simmer. Reduce heat to gentle simmer, cover, and cook for 20 minutes.

4 Uncover and continue to cook, stirring occasionally, until beef is tender and chili is thickened, about 20 minutes. (If chili begins to stick to bottom of skillet, stir in water as needed.) Stir in tomato sauce and cook until flavors meld, about 5 minutes. Season with salt and pepper to taste. Serve.

MARINATED STEAK TIPS
WITH CHARRED PEPPERS AND ONIONS

SERVES 4

WHY THIS RECIPE WORKS Grilling might seem like the only way to get a good char on steak and vegetables at home, but you don't always have the space or the equipment (or the ideal weather conditions) for outdoor cooking. We wanted to bring all the advantages of grilling indoors by using the high heat retention of the cast-iron skillet. Steak tips are an affordable and flavorful cut of meat. For deep flavor, we marinated the meat before searing it. If the pan is too crowded, the meat steams instead of searing, so we split the steak tips into two batches and seared one batch at a time. With the meat properly charred, it was time to tackle the peppers and onions. We found that adding ⅓ cup of water to the vegetables and covering the pan released all the flavorful charred beef bits from the bottom of the pan while steaming the vegetables until perfectly tender. When the skillet was uncovered, the remaining water evaporated and the vegetables finished browning. Sirloin steak tips, also known as flap meat, can be sold as whole steaks, cubes, and strips. To ensure uniform pieces, we prefer to purchase whole steaks and cut them ourselves.

½ cup vegetable oil

6 garlic cloves, minced

2 tablespoons Worcestershire sauce

1 teaspoon grated lemon zest plus 3 tablespoons juice
  Salt and pepper

2 pounds sirloin steak tips, trimmed and cut
  into 1½-inch pieces

2 red bell peppers, stemmed, seeded, and cut
  into 1½-inch pieces

1 large onion, cut into 1½-inch pieces

1 tablespoon minced fresh parsley

1 tablespoon minced fresh oregano

1 Whisk ¼ cup oil, garlic, Worcestershire, lemon zest and juice, 1 teaspoon salt, and ½ teaspoon pepper together in bowl. Measure out and reserve 2 tablespoons marinade. Combine remaining marinade and steak tips in 1-gallon zipper-lock bag and toss to coat; press out as much air as possible and seal bag. Refrigerate for at least 30 minutes or up to 1 hour, flipping bag halfway through marinating.

2 Adjust oven rack to middle position, place 12-inch cast-iron skillet on rack, and heat oven to 500 degrees.

Meanwhile, remove steak tips from bag and pat dry with paper towels.

3 When oven reaches 500 degrees, remove skillet from oven using potholders and place over medium heat; turn off oven. Being careful of hot skillet handle, add 2 tablespoons oil and heat until just smoking. Place half of steak tips in skillet and cook until well browned on all sides and beef registers 130 to 135 degrees (for medium), 8 to 10 minutes; transfer to serving platter and tent loosely with aluminum foil. Repeat with 1 tablespoon oil and remaining steak tips; transfer to platter. Let steak tips rest while making vegetables.

4 Heat remaining 1 tablespoon oil in now-empty skillet over medium-low heat until just smoking. Add bell peppers, onion, ⅓ cup water, and ¼ teaspoon salt. Cover and cook, stirring occasionally, until vegetables are softened, about 5 minutes. Uncover and continue to cook, stirring occasionally, until water evaporates and vegetables are tender and lightly charred, 5 to 10 minutes. Off heat, stir in reserved marinade, parsley, oregano, and any accumulated meat juices. Season with salt and pepper to taste. Serve steak tips with vegetables.

PAN-SEARED FLANK STEAK
WITH CRISPY POTATOES AND CHIMICHURRI

SERVES 4

WHY THIS RECIPE WORKS Steak frites is a classic bistro dish, but cooking up a steak in one pan while simultaneously deep-frying potatoes in another is a recipe for disaster in a home kitchen. We wanted to harness the power of cast iron and make an approachable version of this meat and potatoes classic. We started with flank steak cut into quarters to increase the surface area, which helped it develop a better crust. We preheated our cast-iron skillet in the oven for a hot, even cooking surface and seared both sides of the steak before dropping the heat while it finished cooking through. While the meat was resting, we moved to the potatoes, which we had jump-started in the microwave so they could quickly brown and crisp when added to the now-empty, hot skillet. Letting the potatoes cook without stirring ensured that the exteriors became crunchy. We served our steak and potatoes with a quick *chimichurri* made with herbs, garlic, and red wine vinegar as a fresh counterpoint.

1 (1½-pound) flank steak, trimmed

Salt and pepper

3 russet potatoes, unpeeled, sliced lengthwise into 6 wedges

½ cup vegetable oil

1 cup fresh parsley leaves

2 tablespoons red wine vinegar

3 garlic cloves, minced

1 tablespoon minced fresh oregano or 1 teaspoon dried

¼ teaspoon red pepper flakes

½ cup extra-virgin olive oil

1 Adjust oven rack to middle position, place 12-inch cast-iron skillet on rack, and heat oven to 500 degrees. Meanwhile, cut steak lengthwise with grain into 2 equal pieces, then cut each piece in half crosswise to create 4 equal pieces. Season steaks with salt and let sit at room temperature.

2 Toss potatoes with 2 tablespoons vegetable oil, ¼ teaspoon salt, and ⅛ teaspoon pepper in bowl. Cover potatoes and microwave until just beginning to soften, 7 to 10 minutes, stirring halfway through microwaving; set aside.

3 Pulse parsley, vinegar, garlic, oregano, pepper flakes, and ½ teaspoon salt in food processor until coarsely chopped, about 10 pulses, scraping down sides of bowl as needed. Transfer mixture to serving bowl, stir in olive oil, and season with salt and pepper to taste; set aside for serving.

4 When oven reaches 500 degrees, pat steaks dry with paper towels and season with pepper. Using potholders, remove skillet from oven and place over medium-high heat; turn off oven. Being careful of hot skillet handle, add 2 tablespoons vegetable oil and heat until just smoking. Cook steaks, without moving, until lightly browned on first side, about 2 minutes. Flip steaks and continue to cook until lightly browned on second side, about 2 minutes.

5 Flip steaks, reduce heat to medium-low, and cook, flipping every 2 minutes, until steaks are well browned and meat registers 120 to 125 degrees (for medium-rare), 4 to 8 minutes. Transfer steaks to serving platter, tent loosely with aluminum foil, and let rest while finishing potatoes.

6 Drain potatoes well. Heat remaining ¼ cup vegetable oil in now-empty skillet over medium heat until shimmering. Place potatoes cut side down in skillet in even layer and cook, without moving, until golden brown on first side, about 5 minutes. Flip potatoes and continue to cook, without moving, until golden brown on second side, about 5 minutes; transfer to serving platter. Serve steaks with potatoes and chimichurri.

STIR-FRIED BEEF AND BROCCOLI

SERVES 4

WHY THIS RECIPE WORKS Chinese beef and broccoli seems to have fallen on hard times: Tough meat, overcooked vegetables, and a thick brown sauce are all too common. We set out to rescue this takeout staple for home cooks. Our cast-iron skillet was a surprisingly perfect tool for stir-frying; when we got it ripping hot, we could sear the meat and vegetables quickly without overcooking them. For the meat, flank steak offered the best beefy taste, and slicing it thin against the grain made it tender. We cooked the beef in two batches over medium heat to make sure it browned and didn't steam. Then we cooked the broccoli until crisp-tender using a combination of methods—sautéing and steaming—and added some red bell pepper for sweetness and color. For the sauce, a flavorful combination of oyster sauce, chicken broth, dry sherry, brown sugar, and toasted sesame oil, lightly thickened with cornstarch, clung to the beef and vegetables without getting gloppy. To make slicing the flank steak easier, freeze it for 15 minutes. Serve with white rice.

SAUCE

- 5 tablespoons oyster sauce
- 2 tablespoons chicken broth
- 1 tablespoon dry sherry
- 1 tablespoon packed light brown sugar
- 1 teaspoon toasted sesame oil
- 1 teaspoon cornstarch

STIR-FRY

- 1 (1-pound) flank steak, trimmed and sliced thin against grain into 2-inch-long pieces
- 3 tablespoons soy sauce
- 6 garlic cloves, minced
- 1 tablespoon grated fresh ginger
- ¼ cup vegetable oil
- 1¼ pounds broccoli, florets cut into bite-size pieces, stalks peeled and cut ⅛ inch thick on bias
- 1 small red bell pepper, stemmed, seeded, and cut into ½-inch pieces
- 3 scallions, sliced ½ inch thick on bias

1 FOR THE SAUCE Whisk all ingredients together in bowl.

2 FOR THE STIR-FRY Combine beef and soy sauce in bowl, cover, refrigerate, and let marinate for at least 10 minutes or up to 1 hour. Drain beef and discard liquid. In separate bowl combine garlic, ginger, and 1 teaspoon oil.

3 Heat 12-inch cast-iron skillet over medium heat for 5 minutes. Add 1 tablespoon oil and heat until just smoking. Add half of beef, break up any clumps, and cook, without stirring, for 1 minute. Stir beef and continue to cook until browned, about 2 minutes; transfer to bowl. Repeat with 1 tablespoon oil and remaining beef; transfer to bowl.

4 Heat 1 tablespoon oil in now-empty skillet over medium-high heat until just smoking. Add broccoli and cook for 30 seconds. Add ⅓ cup water, cover, and reduce heat to medium. Steam broccoli until crisp-tender, about 2 minutes; transfer to paper towel–lined plate.

5 Wipe skillet clean with paper towels. Heat remaining 2 teaspoons oil in now-empty skillet over medium-high heat until just smoking. Add bell pepper and cook, stirring often, until spotty brown, about 1½ minutes.

6 Clear center of skillet, add garlic mixture, and cook, mashing mixture into skillet, until fragrant, about 30 seconds. Add broccoli, beef, and any accumulated beef juices and toss to combine. Whisk sauce to recombine, then add to skillet. Cook, stirring constantly, until sauce is thickened, about 30 seconds. Transfer to platter, sprinkle with scallions, and serve.

PAN-SEARED PORK CUTLETS
WITH HORSERADISH AND HERBED GREEN BEANS

SERVES 4

WHY THIS RECIPE WORKS Simple sautéed pork cutlets and green beans make an easy, fresh weeknight meal, but if you don't pay proper attention to the quick-cooking ingredients, the thin cutlets can turn out dry and rubbery and the green beans mushy and bland. Getting a good sear on the cutlets and blistering the green beans with our cast-iron skillet were crucial for quickly developing flavor without risk of overcooking. We made our own tender cutlets by gently pounding pieces of pork tenderloin to an even ½-inch thickness. These cutlets then were seared in our piping-hot cast-iron skillet until they were dark golden brown on the exterior but still moist and juicy inside. To serve with our pork, we wanted lightly browned, crisp-tender green beans that we could cook right in the same pan. We first sautéed the beans until spotty brown but not yet cooked through before a short stint of steaming in the covered pan. We then uncovered the skillet to quickly evaporate the water and finish browning the beans. The addition of horseradish, lemon juice, and parsley brightened up the flavor profile. To finish our dish with zesty flavor, we made a compound butter of garlic and herbs to divide between the green beans and pork. Buy refrigerated prepared horseradish, not the shelf-stable kind, which contains preservatives and additives and isn't as flavorful.

4 tablespoons unsalted butter, softened

3 garlic cloves, minced

2 teaspoons minced fresh thyme

2 teaspoons minced fresh chives

2 (1-pound) pork tenderloins, trimmed and each
    cut on angle into 4 equal pieces
    Salt and pepper

2 tablespoons vegetable oil

1 pound green beans, trimmed and cut
    into 2-inch lengths

1 tablespoon prepared horseradish, drained

1 tablespoon minced fresh parsley
    Lemon wedges

1 Adjust oven rack to middle position, place 12-inch cast-iron skillet on rack, and heat oven to 500 degrees. Meanwhile, combine 3 tablespoons butter, garlic, thyme, and chives in bowl; set aside.

2 Working with 1 piece at a time, place pork cut side down between 2 sheets of parchment paper or plastic wrap and gently pound to even ½-inch thickness. Pat pork dry with paper towels and season with salt and pepper.

3 When oven reaches 500 degrees, remove skillet from oven using potholders and place over medium-high heat; turn off oven. Being careful of hot skillet handle, add 1 tablespoon oil and heat until just smoking. Brown 4 cutlets, about 2 minutes per side; transfer to serving platter. Repeat with remaining 1 tablespoon oil and remaining 4 cutlets; transfer to platter. Dollop 3 tablespoons herb butter over cutlets, tent loosely with aluminum foil, and let rest while making green beans.

4 Melt remaining 1 tablespoon butter in now-empty skillet over medium heat. Add green beans, ¼ teaspoon salt, and ⅛ teaspoon pepper and cook, stirring occasionally, until spotty brown, 3 to 5 minutes. Add ¼ cup water, cover, and cook until green beans are bright green and still crisp, about 2 minutes. Uncover and continue to cook until water evaporates, 30 to 60 seconds. Stir in horseradish and remaining herb butter and cook until green beans are crisp-tender and beginning to wrinkle, 1 to 3 minutes. Off heat, stir in parsley and season with salt and pepper to taste. Serve cutlets with green beans and lemon wedges.

CRISPY PAN-FRIED PORK CHOPS WITH SUCCOTASH

SERVES 4

WHY THIS RECIPE WORKS When they're done right, pan-fried pork chops feature a crisp exterior and moist, juicy meat. When handled poorly, you get a soggy, messy coating and bland, overcooked pork. Pan frying in a cast-iron skillet helps solve these problems because the heavy pan helps maintain a constant frying temperature for even cooking. To fix the breading, we used buttermilk for a light texture and tangy flavor, plus garlic and mustard. Crushed cornflakes added a desirable cragginess. To ensure that the breading adhered to the chops, we lightly scored the meat before breading and gave it a short rest before adding the chops to the pan. Succotash, the classic American vegetable blend of lima beans, corn, and bell pepper, was the perfect complement for our pork chops. Zucchini added an extra layer of freshness. You can substitute ¾ cup of store-bought cornflake crumbs for the whole cornflakes. If using store-bought crumbs, omit the processing step and mix the crumbs with the cornstarch, salt, and pepper. Serve with lemon wedges.

3 cups (3 ounces) cornflakes
⅔ cup cornstarch
1 teaspoon minced fresh thyme
Salt and pepper
¼ teaspoon cayenne pepper
1 cup buttermilk
2 tablespoons Dijon mustard
2 garlic cloves, minced
4 (6- to 8-ounce) boneless pork chops,
   ¾ to 1 inch thick
½ cup vegetable oil
2 tablespoons unsalted butter
1 zucchini, cut into ½-inch pieces
1 red bell pepper, stemmed, seeded, and cut
   into ½-inch pieces
1 small onion, chopped fine
1½ cups frozen baby lima beans, thawed
1½ cups frozen corn, thawed
1 tablespoon minced fresh tarragon

1 Process cornflakes, ⅓ cup cornstarch, thyme, ½ teaspoon salt, ½ teaspoon pepper, and cayenne in food processor until cornflakes are finely ground, about 10 seconds; transfer to shallow dish. Spread remaining ⅓ cup cornstarch in second shallow dish. In third shallow dish whisk buttermilk, mustard, and half of garlic together until combined.

2 Adjust oven rack to middle position and heat oven to 200 degrees. With sharp knife, cut 1/16-inch-deep slits on both sides of chops, spaced ½ inch apart, in cross-hatch pattern. Season chops with salt and pepper. Working with 1 chop at a time, dredge chops in cornstarch, dip in buttermilk mixture, then coat with cornflake mixture, pressing gently to adhere. Transfer coated chops to plate and let sit for 10 minutes.

3 Set wire rack in rimmed baking sheet and line with triple layer of paper towels. Heat oil in 12-inch cast-iron skillet over medium heat until shimmering. Place chops in skillet and cook until golden brown and crisp on first side, about 5 minutes. Carefully flip chops, reduce heat to medium-low, and continue to cook until golden brown and crisp on second side and pork registers 145 degrees, about 5 minutes. Transfer chops to prepared rack and keep warm in oven.

4 Discard oil and wipe skillet clean with paper towels. Melt 1 tablespoon butter in now-empty skillet over medium heat. Add zucchini, bell pepper, onion, ½ teaspoon salt, and ¼ teaspoon pepper and cook until softened, about 5 minutes. Stir in lima beans, corn, and remaining garlic and cook until heated through, about 5 minutes. Off heat, stir in remaining 1 tablespoon butter and tarragon and season with salt and pepper to taste. Serve chops with succotash.

PORK CHOPS AND DIRTY RICE

SERVES 4

WHY THIS RECIPE WORKS To spice up a simple weeknight dinner, we looked to the South for inspiration, where seared pork chops and rice spiked with sausage, aromatics, and Cajun seasoning (called dirty rice) is a classic supper. Using a cast-iron skillet meant that the whole dish could be cooked in one pan, saving on time and cleanup. We started by using our preheated skillet to get an even sear on the chops. We then removed them from the pan and cooked the "dirty" flavor foundation for the rice—spicy chorizo, red bell pepper, and onion—before adding rice, garlic, thyme, and Cajun seasoning. Blooming the aromatics with the rice before adding the chicken broth boosted the zesty flavor profile of the dish. We then nestled the seared chops browned side up into the rice to maintain the flavorful crust while the pork finished cooking. With everything in the skillet, we simply covered the pan and cooked until the pork was done, then removed the chops to rest and continued to simmer the rice until tender and fluffy. The heat retention of the skillet ensured even cooking of both elements of this easy, flavorful supper. If you can't find chorizo sausage, use andouille or linguiça. Chili powder may be substituted for Cajun seasoning.

4 (8- to 10-ounce) bone-in pork rib chops,
  ¾ to 1 inch thick, trimmed
  Salt and pepper
1 tablespoon vegetable oil
4 ounces Spanish-style chorizo sausage, cut into
  ¼-inch pieces
1 red bell pepper, stemmed, seeded, and chopped fine
1 small onion, chopped fine
1 cup long-grain white rice, rinsed
6 garlic cloves, minced
1 teaspoon minced fresh thyme or ½ teaspoon dried
¾ teaspoon Cajun seasoning
2 cups chicken broth
3 scallions, sliced thin

1 Cut 2 slits about 2 inches apart through fat on edges of each pork chop. Pat chops dry with paper towels and season with salt and pepper. Heat 12-inch cast-iron skillet over medium heat for 5 minutes. Add oil and heat until just smoking. Place chops in skillet and cook until well browned on one side, about 5 minutes; transfer to plate.

2 Pour off all but 1 tablespoon fat from skillet. Add chorizo, bell pepper, and onion and cook over medium heat until vegetables are softened, about 5 minutes.

Stir in rice, garlic, thyme, and Cajun seasoning and cook until fragrant, about 30 seconds. Stir in broth, scraping up any browned bits, and bring to simmer.

3 Nestle chops browned side up into skillet along with any accumulated juices. Reduce heat to gentle simmer, cover, and cook until pork registers 145 degrees, 6 to 8 minutes. Transfer chops to serving platter, brushing any rice that sticks to pork back into skillet, and tent loosely with aluminum foil. Let chops rest while finishing rice.

4 Cover skillet and continue to cook over low heat, stirring occasionally, until liquid has been absorbed and rice is tender, 12 to 15 minutes. Sprinkle with scallions and season with salt and pepper to taste. Serve chops with rice.

PREVENTING CURLED CHOPS

To keep thin-cut pork chops from buckling or curling as they cook, cut 2 small slits, about 2 inches apart, into fat and connective tissue on edges of each chop.

PORK TAMALE PIE

SERVES 4 TO 6

WHY THIS RECIPE WORKS Inspired by Mexican tamales but a lot less labor intensive, a good tamale pie is loaded with a juicy, spicy mixture of meat and vegetables and topped with a golden cornmeal crust. Bad tamale pies, however, are dry and bland and usually have too little filling. We wanted to develop a tamale pie with plenty of rich, well-seasoned filling and a flavorful but not overwhelming cornmeal crust. The cast-iron skillet's deep, straight sides made it an excellent cooking vessel for our pie's hearty layers, and the skillet's superior heat retention offered even, steady cooking, guaranteeing that our filling remained moist while the topping cooked to a perfect golden brown. We started with ground pork as our base for a good balance of richness and flavor without too much grease or heaviness. We then bloomed chili powder and oregano with scallion whites to intensify their flavor and aromatic appeal. Convenient canned black beans made our pie heartier, and corn and canned diced tomatoes provided additional texture and a fresh flavor profile. We stirred pepper Jack cheese into the filling to add another layer of spice and cheesy richness. To finish our pie, we made a simple cornbread batter that we spread over the filling before baking. The slightly sweet cornbread topping relies on pantry staples, is a cinch to mix, and emerges from the oven with a golden brown crust and tender crumb. Do not use coarse-ground cornmeal in this recipe.

¼ cup vegetable oil

1 pound ground pork

6 scallions, white and green parts separated and sliced thin

2 tablespoons chili powder

1 tablespoon minced fresh oregano or 1 teaspoon dried

Salt and pepper

1 (15-ounce) can black beans, rinsed

1 (14.5-ounce) can diced tomatoes

1 cup frozen corn

½ cup chicken broth

4 ounces pepper Jack cheese, shredded (1 cup)

¾ cup (3¾ ounces) all-purpose flour

¾ cup (3¾ ounces) cornmeal

¾ teaspoon baking powder

¼ teaspoon baking soda

¾ cup buttermilk

1 large egg

1 Adjust oven rack to middle position and heat oven to 400 degrees. Heat 10-inch cast-iron skillet over medium heat for 5 minutes. Add 1 tablespoon oil and heat until just smoking. Add pork and cook, breaking up meat with wooden spoon, until just beginning to brown, about 5 minutes.

2 Stir in scallion whites, chili powder, oregano, and ¼ teaspoon salt and cook until fragrant, about 1 minute. Stir in beans, tomatoes and their juice, corn, and broth. Bring to simmer and cook until mixture has thickened slightly, 5 to 7 minutes. Off heat, stir in pepper Jack until well combined. Season with salt and pepper to taste.

3 Whisk flour, cornmeal, baking powder, baking soda, scallion greens, and ¾ teaspoon salt together in large bowl. In separate bowl, whisk buttermilk, egg, and remaining 3 tablespoons oil together until smooth. Stir buttermilk mixture into flour mixture until just combined. Pour batter over meat mixture and smooth into even layer. Transfer skillet to oven and bake until topping is golden brown and toothpick inserted into center comes out clean, 15 to 20 minutes, rotating skillet halfway through baking. Let casserole cool for 10 minutes before serving.

PAN-ROASTED COD AND POTATOES WITH ORANGE-PARSLEY SALAD

SERVES 4

WHY THIS RECIPE WORKS This dish features flaky, moist fish atop a bed of crisp, creamy potatoes for a fresh take on a classic flavor combination. Cooking the fish and potatoes together in one skillet had the benefit of melding the flavors and limiting the number of pans that needed to be washed. We started with the potatoes, which we knew would need plenty of time to cook through. After slicing the potatoes thin and shingling them around the skillet, we gave them a head start by cooking them briefly on the stove and then moving them to the oven for 15 minutes. Only then did we add the quick-cooking fish fillets on top of the potatoes for the last 15 minutes of cooking so both parts of the dish would finish at the same time without any risk of the fish overcooking. The hot cast-iron skillet created a layer of very crisp potatoes on the bottom and soft, creamy potatoes on top. A simple, robust salad of oranges with fresh parsley leaves and capers was the ideal complement to our hearty dish. Halibut and haddock are good substitutes for cod in this recipe.

2 oranges

½ cup fresh parsley leaves

1 shallot, minced

2 tablespoons capers, rinsed

2 tablespoons red wine vinegar

5 tablespoons extra-virgin olive oil

Salt and pepper

1½ pounds russet potatoes, peeled and sliced ⅛ inch thick

4 (6- to 8-ounce) skinless cod fillets, 1 to 1½ inches thick

1 Adjust oven rack to lowest position and heat oven to 450 degrees. Cut away peel and pith from oranges. Quarter oranges, then slice crosswise into ½-inch-thick pieces. Combine oranges, parsley, shallot, capers, vinegar, 1 tablespoon oil, ¼ teaspoon salt, and ⅛ teaspoon pepper in bowl; set aside for serving.

2 Toss potatoes with 2 tablespoons oil, 1 teaspoon salt, and ¼ teaspoon pepper in bowl. Grease 12-inch cast-iron skillet with remaining 2 tablespoons oil. Shingle potatoes into even layer on bottom of skillet. Place skillet over medium-high heat and cook until potatoes begin to sizzle and turn translucent near sides of skillet, about

5 minutes. Transfer skillet to oven and bake until potatoes are tender and beginning to brown, about 15 minutes.

3 Season cod with salt and pepper and arrange skinned side down on top of potatoes. Bake until potatoes are tender and fish flakes apart when gently prodded with paring knife and registers 140 degrees, about 15 minutes. Slide spatula under potatoes and fish and transfer to individual plates. Serve with salad.

CUTTING ORANGES INTO PIECES

1 Using paring knife, cut away peel and pith from orange.

2 Quarter orange, then slice crosswise into pieces as directed.

CLAMS WITH ISRAELI COUSCOUS AND CHORIZO

SERVES 4

WHY THIS RECIPE WORKS To infuse this simple seafood dish with big flavors, we added chorizo, leeks, garlic, and thyme to white wine and broth for a potent and flavorful base that we could use to steam our shellfish. Thinly sliced half-moons of chorizo contributed richness and savory, spicy notes to the broth, and aromatics gave the dish a vibrant backbone. To keep it simple, we cooked the couscous right in the skillet with our clams, infusing the grains with the flavor of the seafood and letting them soak in the strong flavor base of our broth. We used larger-grained Israeli couscous instead of traditional small-grain couscous—it made the perfect vehicle to soak up the dish's flavors and added textural appeal. Minced parsley added at the very end before serving lent an element of freshness to our salty, briny dish. Israeli couscous, also known as pearl couscous, has grains about the size of capers and is not precooked, unlike traditional couscous. It has a unique, nutty flavor and satisfying chew. Be sure to use Israeli couscous; regular (or fine-grain) couscous won't work here. Small quahogs or cherrystones are good alternatives to the littleneck clams in this dish. If you can't find chorizo sausage, use andouille or linguiça.

1 tablespoon vegetable oil

6 ounces Spanish-style chorizo sausage, halved lengthwise and sliced ¼ inch thick

1 pound leeks, white and light green parts only, halved lengthwise, sliced thin, and washed thoroughly

3 garlic cloves, minced

1 tablespoon minced fresh thyme or 1 teaspoon dried

1 cup dry white wine

2 cups Israeli couscous

1½ cups chicken broth

3 pounds littleneck clams, scrubbed

2 tablespoons minced fresh parsley

Pepper

1 Heat 12-inch cast-iron skillet over medium heat for 5 minutes. Add oil and heat until just smoking. Add chorizo and cook until well browned and fat begins to render, about 5 minutes. Stir in leeks and cook until softened, about 3 minutes. Stir in garlic and thyme and cook until fragrant, about 30 seconds. Stir in wine, scraping up any browned bits. Bring to simmer and cook until slightly reduced, about 1 minute. Stir in couscous and broth and return to simmer.

2 Nestle clams into skillet. Reduce heat to gentle simmer, cover, and cook until clams have opened and couscous is al dente, 10 to 12 minutes. Off heat, discard any clams that refuse to open. Sprinkle with parsley and season with pepper to taste. Serve immediately.

PAELLA

SERVES 4 TO 6

WHY THIS RECIPE WORKS Saffron-infused paella is a popular Spanish rice and seafood dish that's packed with flavor, but unusual ingredients and complicated preparations can make it intimidating to tackle at home. We translated this Spanish classic for American kitchens by taking advantage of the inherent benefits of the cast-iron skillet. We started by browning chicken, then sautéing vegetables and aromatics with flavorful chorizo. Next, we added rice, along with saffron and a whopping hit of garlic. Tomatoes cooked until they darkened created deep flavor in a short amount of time. When the rice reached al dente, we added our seafood and let it finish cooking. The briny mussels and shrimp released their juices, flavoring the rice even more. A simple sprinkling of peas brightened the flavor of the dish. One of the key elements of paella is the *soccarat*, a crusty brown layer of rice that develops on the bottom of the dish. A traditional stainless-steel pan would have to sit over high heat for the last 5 minutes of cooking to develop this crust, which creates a high risk of the more delicate ingredients overcooking, but the cast-iron pan, with its high heat retention, naturally created the crust during the course of cooking the recipe without any extra steps. If you can't find chorizo sausage, use andouille or linguiça.

12 ounces extra-large shrimp (21 to 25 per pound), peeled and deveined

9 garlic cloves, minced

3 tablespoons vegetable oil

Salt and pepper

12 ounces boneless, skinless chicken thighs, trimmed and cut crosswise into thirds

8 ounces Spanish-style chorizo sausage, halved lengthwise and sliced ¼ inch thick

1 red bell pepper, stemmed, seeded, and chopped fine

1 onion, chopped fine

1¼ cups Valencia or Arborio rice

½ teaspoon saffron threads, crumbled

1 (14.5-ounce) can diced tomatoes, drained

2¼ cups chicken broth

¼ cup dry white wine

12 mussels, scrubbed and debearded

½ cup frozen peas

Lemon wedges

1 Toss shrimp with 1 teaspoon garlic and 1 tablespoon oil and season with salt and pepper; set aside. Pat chicken dry with paper towels and season with salt and pepper. Heat 12-inch cast-iron skillet over medium heat for 5 minutes. Add 1 tablespoon oil and heat until just smoking. Brown chicken on all sides, about 6 minutes; transfer to bowl.

2 Heat remaining 1 tablespoon oil in now-empty skillet until shimmering. Add chorizo, bell pepper, onion, and ¼ teaspoon salt and cook until vegetables are softened, about 5 minutes. Stir in rice, saffron, and remaining garlic and cook until fragrant, about 30 seconds. Stir in tomatoes and cook until mixture begins to darken and thicken slightly, about 3 minutes. Stir in broth and wine, scraping up any browned bits, and bring to simmer.

3 Nestle chicken into skillet. Reduce heat to gentle simmer, cover, and cook until most of liquid is absorbed and rice is al dente, about 15 minutes.

4 Insert mussels hinged side down into rice (so they stand upright) and scatter shrimp over top. Cover and cook until shrimp are opaque throughout and mussels have opened, 6 to 8 minutes.

5 Off heat, discard any mussels that refuse to open. Scatter peas over rice, cover, and let sit until heated through, about 5 minutes. Serve immediately with lemon wedges.

SANDWICHES, BURGERS, AND PIZZAS

Skillet Pizza Margherita

GROWN-UP GRILLED CHEESE SANDWICHES WITH CHEDDAR AND SHALLOTS

SERVES 4

WHY THIS RECIPE WORKS In an attempt to liven up grilled cheese, some cooks add so many ingredients that the cheese becomes an afterthought. For a sandwich with more robust flavor and personality without going overboard on the toppings, we focused on the cheese. Inspired by fondue, our grown-up grilled cheese sandwiches started with flavorful aged cheddar, to which we added a small amount of wine and Brie. These two ingredients helped the aged cheddar melt evenly without becoming greasy. A little bit of shallot increased the sandwiches' complexity without detracting from the cheese. A smear of mustard butter on the bread added a shot of hot tang and helped it toast evenly while cooking in the steady heat of the cast-iron skillet. Look for a cheddar aged for about one year (avoid cheddar aged for longer; it won't melt well). To quickly bring the cheddar to room temperature, microwave the pieces until warm, about 30 seconds.

7 ounces aged cheddar cheese, cut into 24 equal pieces, room temperature (1¾ cups)

2 ounces Brie cheese, rind removed

2 tablespoons dry white wine

4 teaspoons minced shallot

3 tablespoons unsalted butter, softened

1 teaspoon Dijon mustard

8 slices hearty white sandwich bread

1 Adjust oven rack to middle position and heat oven to 200 degrees. Set wire rack in rimmed baking sheet. Process cheddar, Brie, and wine in food processor until mixture forms smooth paste, 20 to 30 seconds. Add shallot and pulse to combine, 3 to 5 pulses; transfer to bowl. In separate bowl, combine softened butter and mustard.

2 Spread butter-mustard mixture on 1 side of bread slices. Flip 4 slices over and spread cheese mixture on second side. Top with remaining 4 slices bread, buttered sides up, and press gently to set.

3 Heat 12-inch cast-iron skillet over medium heat for 3 minutes. Place 2 sandwiches in skillet, reduce heat to medium-low, and cook until bread is golden and crisp, 2 to 4 minutes per side, redistributing sandwiches as needed to ensure even browning.

4 Transfer sandwiches to prepared rack and keep warm in oven. Wipe skillet clean with paper towels and repeat with remaining 2 sandwiches. Serve.

VARIATIONS

Grown-Up Grilled Cheese Sandwiches with Gruyère and Chives
Substitute 1¾ cups Gruyère cheese for cheddar, 4 teaspoons minced fresh chives for shallot, and 8 slices rye sandwich bread for hearty white sandwich bread.

Grown-Up Grilled Cheese Sandwiches with Robiola and Chipotle
Substitute 1¾ cups Robiola cheese for cheddar, ¼ teaspoon minced canned chipotle chile in adobo sauce for shallot, and 8 slices hearty oatmeal sandwich bread for hearty white sandwich bread.

SMOKED TURKEY CLUB PANINI

SERVES 4

WHY THIS RECIPE WORKS Italians have it right when it comes to sandwiches: They load meat, cheese, and flavorful condiments between slices of crusty bread and then compact the whole thing in a heated, ridged press for dense, melty grilled packages called panini. We wanted a smoked turkey panini recipe that we could make without a fancy press, so we turned to our trusty cast-iron skillet, which can produce steady, even heat just like that specialized appliance. To build the sandwich, we used bold, zesty sun-dried tomatoes mixed into mayonnaise for a deeply flavored condiment that perfectly complemented the smokiness of the turkey. We also brushed some of the oil from the tomatoes on the bread for an additional flavor boost and a crisp, golden exterior. Bacon, crisped in the skillet, gave the sandwich additional smokiness and crunch, and Swiss cheese and arugula added flavorful depth. Cooking the sandwiches in the skillet under a heavy Dutch oven created perfectly pressed panini. We like to use rustic artisanal bread for this recipe; do not use a baguette, but rather look for a wide loaf that will yield big slices.

8 slices bacon

⅓ cup mayonnaise

⅓ cup oil-packed sun-dried tomatoes, rinsed, patted dry, and minced, plus ¼ cup tomato packing oil

8 (½-inch-thick) slices crusty bread

8 ounces thinly sliced Swiss cheese

8 ounces thinly sliced smoked turkey

2 ounces (2 cups) baby arugula

1 Adjust oven rack to middle position and heat oven to 200 degrees. Set wire rack in rimmed baking sheet. Cook bacon in 12-inch cast-iron skillet over medium heat until crisp, 12 to 15 minutes. Transfer bacon to paper towel–lined plate. Pour off fat from skillet, then wipe skillet clean with paper towels.

2 Combine mayonnaise and tomatoes in bowl. Brush tomato oil on 1 side of bread slices. Flip slices over and spread mayonnaise mixture on second side. Assemble 4 sandwiches by layering ingredients as follows between prepared slices (with mayonnaise mixture inside sandwiches): half of Swiss, turkey, bacon, arugula, and remaining Swiss. Press gently on sandwiches to set.

3 Heat now-empty skillet over medium heat for 3 minutes. Place 2 sandwiches in skillet, reduce heat to medium-low, and set Dutch oven on top. Cook until bread is golden and crisp, 4 to 6 minutes per side, redistributing sandwiches as needed to ensure even browning.

4 Transfer sandwiches to prepared rack and keep warm in oven. Wipe skillet clean with paper towels and repeat with remaining 2 sandwiches. Serve.

MAKING PANINI

Place 2 sandwiches in skillet and set Dutch oven on top. Cook until bread is golden and crisp, flipping sandwiches and replacing Dutch oven halfway through cooking.

FRIED CHICKEN SANDWICHES

SERVES 4

WHY THIS RECIPE WORKS Fried chicken sandwiches look appealing, but too often they fail to deliver on flavor, leaving you with an overcooked chicken breast and a greasy, bland crust. To create a sandwich with all the crunchy appeal of fried chicken, we needed to start with the right piece of meat; boneless breasts halved crosswise proved to be ideal. We created a simple craggy coating with flour and water plus baking powder for an extra-crisp crust. Dipping the pieces of chicken in egg white first helped the coating adhere without making the chicken taste eggy. Letting the dredged chicken chill for at least 30 minutes before frying helped the coating set up and enabled our salty spice rub—a combination of paprika, garlic powder, dried sage, and cayenne pepper—to season the meat throughout. A mayo-based sauce spiked with mustard and pickles proved to be the perfect condiment to spread on the buns and accent our well-seasoned, crunchy fried chicken. With its high sides and great heat retention, our cast-iron skillet was the perfect frying vessel; we needed only 1 quart of oil to fry all the chicken. You will need a 12-inch cast-iron skillet with at least 2-inch sides for this recipe. Covering the skillet with a splatter screen will reduce the mess that frying inevitably makes. Serve with shredded iceberg lettuce and sliced tomato.

Kosher salt and pepper

1 teaspoon paprika

1 teaspoon garlic powder

½ teaspoon dried sage

¼ teaspoon cayenne pepper

2 (6- to 8-ounce) boneless, skinless chicken breasts, trimmed and halved crosswise

1½ cups all-purpose flour

1 teaspoon baking powder

3 tablespoons water

2 large egg whites

4 cups peanut or vegetable oil

¼ cup mayonnaise

¼ cup dill pickle chips, patted dry and chopped fine, plus ½ teaspoon brine

2 teaspoons yellow mustard

4 hamburger buns

1 Combine 1½ teaspoons salt, 1 teaspoon pepper, paprika, garlic powder, sage, and cayenne in bowl. Measure out and reserve 1 tablespoon spice mixture. Cover chicken with plastic wrap and pound to even ½-inch thickness. Pat chicken dry with paper towels and sprinkle with remaining spice mixture.

2 Whisk flour, baking powder, and reserved spice mixture together in large bowl. Add water and rub into flour mixture using your hands until evenly incorporated and small clumps form. Lightly beat egg whites in shallow dish.

3 Working with 1 piece of chicken at a time, dip chicken in egg whites, then dredge in flour mixture, pressing gently to adhere. Transfer chicken to plate and refrigerate for at least 30 minutes or up to 1 hour.

4 Set wire rack in rimmed baking sheet. Add oil to 12-inch cast-iron skillet until it measures about ¾ inch deep and heat over medium-high heat to 375 degrees. Carefully place chicken in oil. Fry, stirring gently to prevent pieces from sticking together, until chicken is golden brown and registers 160 degrees, 4 to 6 minutes, flipping chicken halfway through frying. Adjust burner, if necessary, to maintain oil temperature between 350 and 375 degrees. Transfer chicken to prepared rack and let rest while making sauce.

5 Combine mayonnaise, pickles and brine, mustard, and ½ teaspoon pepper in bowl. Serve chicken with buns and sauce.

ULTIMATE INDOOR BURGERS

SERVES 4

WHY THIS RECIPE WORKS The ultimate indoor burger should be a juicy patty with a crisp crust. Typically, for a great charred exterior we turn to the grill, but we knew our cast-iron skillet was up to the challenge. To control the texture and fat content of the beef, we ground it at home: We partially froze chunks of sirloin steak tips before pulsing them in the food processor, then tossed the meat with melted butter to add juiciness and promote browning. Chilling the formed patties in the refrigerator while the skillet preheated in the oven improved their structure. We used a preheated skillet on the stove to sear the burgers on both sides before letting the cooked burgers rest for 5 minutes so the juices redistributed evenly. A quick, tangy sauce was the perfect accent for the burgers. Sirloin steak tips, also known as flap meat, can be sold as whole steaks, cubes, and strips. To ensure uniform pieces, we prefer to purchase whole steaks and cut them ourselves. While you'll get much better results with home-ground meat, it is possible to substitute 1½ pounds 85 percent lean ground beef for the steak tips; skip steps 2 and 3 and proceed with the recipe as directed.

SAUCE

¾ cup mayonnaise

2 tablespoons soy sauce

1 tablespoon packed dark brown sugar

1 tablespoon Worcestershire sauce

1 tablespoon minced fresh chives

1 garlic clove, minced

¾ teaspoon pepper

BURGERS

1½ pounds sirloin steak tips, trimmed and cut into ½-inch pieces

4 tablespoons unsalted butter, melted and cooled
Kosher salt and pepper

1 tablespoon vegetable oil

4 hamburger buns, toasted

1 FOR THE SAUCE Whisk all ingredients together in bowl; refrigerate until ready to serve.

2 FOR THE BURGERS Place beef pieces in rimmed baking sheet in single layer. Freeze until meat is very firm and starting to harden around edges but still pliable, about 35 minutes.

3 Working with one-quarter of meat at a time, pulse in food processor until finely ground into rice grain–size pieces (about 1⁄16 inch), 15 to 20 pulses, stopping and redistributing meat around bowl as necessary to ensure that beef is evenly ground. Transfer meat to sheet and inspect carefully, discarding any long strands of gristle or large chunks of hard meat or fat. Drizzle with melted butter and sprinkle with 1 teaspoon pepper and ¾ teaspoon salt. Gently toss meat with fork to combine.

4 Divide meat into 4 balls. Toss each between your hands until uniformly but lightly packed, then gently flatten into 1-inch-thick patties. Cover patties and refrigerate for at least 30 minutes or up to 24 hours.

5 While patties chill, adjust oven rack to middle position, place 12-inch cast-iron skillet on rack, and heat oven to 500 degrees. Season 1 side of patties with salt and pepper, then, using spatula, flip patties and season second side.

6 When oven reaches 500 degrees, remove skillet from oven using potholders and place over medium-high heat; turn off oven. Being careful of hot skillet handle, add oil and heat until just smoking. Cook patties until well browned on first side, about 3 minutes.

7 Flip burgers and continue to cook until well browned on second side and burgers register 120 to 125 degrees (for medium-rare), about 3 minutes. Transfer burgers to plate and let rest for 5 minutes. Serve burgers with buns and sauce.

FRIED ONION CHEESEBURGERS

SERVES 4

WHY THIS RECIPE WORKS During the Depression, enterprising cooks in Oklahoma discovered they could use less meat without reducing portion size by mashing thinly sliced onions into beef patties. This trick not only bulked up the patties, it created a delicious layer of caramelized onions on the outside that infused the meat with extra richness. We wanted to adapt this technique for the home cook for juicy and tender burgers that focused on flavor, not thrift. To make these enhanced burgers, we first sliced an onion as thin as possible and then salted the slices to draw out all the extra moisture so they'd brown and caramelize fully. To further reduce the moisture content, we squeezed the salted onion in a dish towel. We then formed the patties by making a small mound of onion, placing a loosely formed ball of ground beef on top, and pressing the beef into the onion. We cooked the patties, onion side down, over gentle and steady heat provided by our cast-iron skillet until the onion layer developed a deep golden-brown color and began to crisp. To finish the burgers, we simply flipped them and turned up the heat to develop light browning on the second side. Layering the finished burgers on top of—rather than beneath—a slice of American cheese kept the onion crisp. These burgers are traditionally served with yellow mustard and slices of dill pickle.

1 onion, halved and sliced thin
Salt and pepper
12 ounces 85 percent lean ground beef
1 tablespoon unsalted butter
1 teaspoon vegetable oil
4 slices American cheese (4 ounces)
4 hamburger buns, toasted

1 Combine onion slices and 1 teaspoon salt in colander and let sit for 30 minutes, tossing occasionally. Transfer to clean dish towel, gather edges, and squeeze onion slices dry.

2 Spread onion slices on rimmed baking sheet, sprinkle with ½ teaspoon pepper, and toss to combine. Divide onion mixture into four 2-inch mounds. Divide ground beef into 4 lightly packed balls. Place balls on top of onion mounds and flatten beef firmly so onion adheres and patties measure 4 inches in diameter.

3 Heat 12-inch cast-iron skillet over medium heat for 5 minutes. Add butter and oil and heat until butter is melted. Using spatula, place patties onion side down in skillet. Reduce heat to medium-low and cook until onion is deep golden brown and beginning to crisp around edges, 5 to 7 minutes.

4 Flip burgers and continue to cook until lightly browned on second side, about 2 minutes. Place 1 slice American cheese on each bun bottom and top with burgers and bun tops. Serve.

MAKING FRIED ONION CHEESEBURGERS

After dividing salted onion slices into mounds, place beef balls on top and flatten firmly until patties measure 4 inches in diameter.

CHICAGO-STYLE ITALIAN BEEF SANDWICHES

SERVES 4

WHY THIS RECIPE WORKS At first glance, the spicy Italian beef sandwich that is popular in Chicago looks similar to a French dip sandwich, but this midwestern favorite takes the flavors to another level. Not only is the Chicago-style smothered in the flavorful beef jus, the meat is topped with spicy pickled vegetables, called *giardiniera*, which add a delicious tangy bite to the rich beef. Typical Chicago-style Italian beef sandwich recipes call for using leftover roast beef, but sometimes we crave this hearty sandwich when we don't have any roast beef on hand. To get our sandwich fix fast, we turned to shaved steak, which generally comes from a tougher cut of meat such as top round that turns tender when cut extra-thin. We tossed these paper-thin slices of meat with a combination of garlic powder and pepper to mimic the slow-cooked flavors of an actual beef roast. Using a cast-iron skillet was crucial: The heat retention of the pan ensured that it stayed hot when we added the beef, allowing us to get great browning quickly without overcooking the delicate slices of meat. After searing the meat, we made a quick jus in the same pan using a combination of beef broth, aromatics, and herbs. We included a touch of flour, which gave the jus some extra clinging power. To finish the beef, we tossed it back into the jus to reheat it and meld all the flavors. For an authentic giardiniera topping, we chopped the pickled vegetables quickly in a food processor with a little mayonnaise and some red pepper flakes, which made a cohesive spread for our sandwiches and gave us the classic Chicago-style flavor. You can find shaved steak in the meat section of your grocery store; do not use packaged frozen shaved steak.

2 cups giardiniera pickled vegetables, plus 1 tablespoon brine
¼ cup mayonnaise
¼ teaspoon red pepper flakes
1½ pounds shaved steak
1 teaspoon garlic powder
Salt and pepper
2 tablespoons plus 1 teaspoon vegetable oil
¼ cup finely chopped onion
2 teaspoons minced fresh oregano or ½ teaspoon dried
2 garlic cloves, minced
1 teaspoon all-purpose flour
2 cups beef broth
4 (8-inch) Italian sub rolls, split lengthwise and toasted

1 Pulse giardiniera, mayonnaise, and pepper flakes in food processor until finely ground, about 10 pulses, scraping down sides of bowl as needed; transfer to bowl and set aside.

2 Season beef with garlic powder and ½ teaspoon pepper. Heat 12-inch cast-iron skillet over medium heat for 5 minutes. Add 1 tablespoon oil and heat until just smoking. Add half of beef, break up any clumps, and cook, without stirring, for about 2 minutes. Stir beef and continue to cook until lightly browned, about 1 minute; transfer to bowl. Repeat with 1 tablespoon oil and remaining beef; transfer to bowl.

3 Add remaining 1 teaspoon oil and onion to now-empty skillet and cook over medium heat until softened, about 1 minute. Stir in oregano, garlic, and flour and cook until fragrant, about 30 seconds. Whisk in broth and brine, scraping up any browned bits. Bring to simmer and cook until broth mixture is reduced to 1 cup, 6 to 8 minutes.

4 Off heat, stir beef and any accumulated juices into jus and let sit until heated through, about 1 minute. Spread giardiniera mixture on rolls, then top with beef. Serve, passing remaining jus separately.

BALTIMORE PIT BEEF SANDWICHES

SERVES 6 TO 8

WHY THIS RECIPE WORKS Baltimore pit beef traditionally starts as a massive spice-rubbed beef roast that's grilled over a hot fire until it's thoroughly charred on the outside and a juicy medium-rare on the inside. The meat is then shaved paper thin, piled on a kaiser roll, topped with a horseradish mayo known as tiger sauce, and finally covered with sliced onions. For our cast-iron skillet version of this regional classic, we started by coating the meat with a bold spice rub of salt, pepper, paprika, oregano, garlic powder, and cayenne, reserving some extra rub to coat the meat just before searing. After letting the spice-rubbed meat rest for at least an hour to become well seasoned, we added the remaining rub to the beef, got our cast-iron skillet ripping hot, and seared all sides of the roast to develop a charred crust to rival the one usually achieved on a grill. We then transferred the skillet, meat and all, to a low-temperature oven where the meat gently finished cooking through to a perfect medium-rare while we prepared the tiger sauce. Buy refrigerated prepared horseradish, not the shelf-stable kind, which contains preservatives and additives. Look for an evenly shaped roast with a ¼-inch fat cap.

Kosher salt and pepper
1 tablespoon paprika
1 tablespoon minced fresh oregano
  or 1 teaspoon dried
1 teaspoon garlic powder
¼ teaspoon cayenne pepper
1 (3-pound) boneless top sirloin roast, trimmed
1 tablespoon vegetable oil
⅓ cup mayonnaise
⅓ cup prepared horseradish
¾ teaspoon lemon juice
1 small garlic clove, minced
6-8 kaiser rolls
1 small onion, halved and sliced thin

1 Combine 4 teaspoons salt, 1 tablespoon pepper, paprika, oregano, garlic powder, and cayenne in bowl. Rub 2 tablespoons spice mixture over roast, wrap tightly with plastic wrap, and refrigerate for at least 1 hour or up to 24 hours.

2 Adjust oven rack to middle position and heat oven to 225 degrees. Pat roast dry with paper towels and rub with remaining spice mixture. Heat 12-inch cast-iron skillet over medium heat for 5 minutes. Add oil and heat until just smoking. Brown roast on all sides, 8 to 12 minutes.

3 Flip roast fat side up, transfer skillet to oven, and roast until meat registers 120 to 125 degrees (for medium-rare), 1 to 1½ hours.

4 Using potholders, remove skillet from oven. Transfer roast to carving board, tent loosely with aluminum foil, and let rest for 20 minutes.

5 Meanwhile, combine mayonnaise, horseradish, lemon juice, and garlic in bowl. Season with salt and pepper to taste. Slice roast thin against grain. Transfer sliced beef to rolls, top with onion slices, and drizzle with sauce. Serve.

MIDDLE EASTERN–STYLE LAMB PITA SANDWICHES

SERVES 4

WHY THIS RECIPE WORKS The traditional method for cooking the meat in a restaurant-style Greek gyro sandwich employs an electric vertical rotisserie, on which layers of sliced and marinated leg of lamb are stacked. After cooking for hours, the meat is shaved with a long slicing knife, revealing pieces with crisp crusts and moist interiors infused with herbs and garlic. Since most home cooks don't have access to a rotisserie, we wanted a home-style lamb sandwich recipe that would give us the same flavors and textures in a simple patty. We started with ground lamb. Using onion and pita bread, as well as add-ins such as oregano and garlic, we created a panade that we mixed with the lamb to ensure that each patty was moist and juicy. We seared the patties in our hot cast-iron skillet to develop a flavorful crust on both sides. To accompany the lamb, we made a quick cucumber-yogurt sauce with rich Greek yogurt, cooling cucumber, tangy lemon juice, bold garlic, and bright fresh herbs.

¾ cup plain Greek yogurt

½ cucumber, peeled, halved lengthwise, seeded, and chopped fine

2 tablespoons lemon juice

3 garlic cloves, minced

1 tablespoon minced fresh mint or dill

Salt and pepper

4 (8-inch) pita breads

½ onion, chopped coarse

1 tablespoon minced fresh oregano or 1 teaspoon dried

1 teaspoon ground cumin

1 pound ground lamb

1 teaspoon vegetable oil

1 large tomato, sliced thin

2 cups shredded lettuce

2 ounces feta cheese, crumbled (½ cup)

1 Combine yogurt, cucumber, 1 tablespoon lemon juice, ½ teaspoon garlic, mint, and ¼ teaspoon salt in bowl; set aside for serving.

2 Adjust oven rack to middle position and heat oven to 350 degrees. Cut top quarter off each pita bread. Tear 1 quarter into 1-inch pieces and discard remaining 3 top quarters. (You should have about ¼ cup pita pieces.) Stack trimmed pitas and wrap tightly with aluminum foil; set aside.

3 Process pita bread pieces, onion, oregano, cumin, ½ teaspoon salt, ¼ teaspoon pepper, remaining 1 tablespoon lemon juice, and remaining garlic in food processor to smooth paste, about 20 seconds, scraping down sides of bowl as needed; transfer to large bowl. Add lamb and gently knead with hands until uniformly combined. Divide meat mixture into 12 lightly packed balls, then flatten into ½-inch-thick patties.

4 Heat 12-inch cast-iron skillet over medium heat for 5 minutes. Add oil and heat until just smoking. Cook patties, without moving, until well browned on first side, about 5 minutes. Flip patties and continue to cook until well browned on second side, about 5 minutes.

5 Meanwhile, place foil-wrapped pitas directly on oven rack and heat for 10 minutes. Serve patties with pitas, sauce, tomato, lettuce, and feta.

MAKING PITA POCKETS

To make sandwich pocket, cut top quarter off each pita bread. Reserve 1 trimmed piece to use as binder in lamb patties.

ITALIAN-STYLE SAUSAGE AND PEPPER SUBS

SERVES 4

WHY THIS RECIPE WORKS A submarine sandwich filled with sausages and peppers is most familiar as the stuff of street festivals and ball games, but it also makes a perfect quick weeknight meal at the dinner table or a gathering around the TV on game day, no grill or griddle required. We started by browning the sausages in a hot cast-iron skillet, which gave us a great sear and plenty of flavor. We then added the peppers, onions, and a little water, covered the pan, and cooked the sausages through. Next, we pulled the sausages out and browned our peppers and onions in all the delicious bits the sausages left behind. For even more complex flavor, we added some tomato paste, Worcestershire sauce, oregano, and garlic. This savory combination coated the peppers and onions and gave each bite a burst of flavor.

1 tablespoon vegetable oil

1½ pounds hot or sweet Italian sausage (8 sausages)

3 red or green bell peppers, stemmed, seeded, and cut into ¼-inch-wide strips

1 large onion, halved and sliced thin

1 tablespoon tomato paste

1 tablespoon Worcestershire sauce

1 tablespoon minced fresh oregano or 1 teaspoon dried

2 garlic cloves, minced

4 (8-inch) Italian sub rolls, split lengthwise

1 Heat 12-inch cast-iron skillet over medium heat for 5 minutes. Add oil and heat until just smoking. Cook sausages until browned on both sides, about 5 minutes, flipping sausages halfway through cooking.

2 Distribute bell peppers and onion around sausages. Add ⅓ cup water, cover, and cook until sausages register 160 to 165 degrees and vegetables are softened, 7 to 9 minutes, flipping sausages halfway through cooking.

3 Transfer sausages to cutting board, tent loosely with aluminum foil, and let rest while finishing vegetables.

Increase heat to medium-high and cook without stirring until liquid has evaporated and vegetables are lightly browned, 5 to 7 minutes. Stir in tomato paste, Worcestershire, oregano, and garlic and cook until fragrant, about 1 minute. Halve sausages crosswise and serve with rolls and pepper-onion mixture.

PREPARING BELL PEPPERS

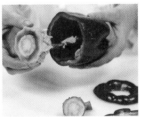

1 Slice off top and bottom of pepper and remove seeds and stem.

2 Slice down through sides of pepper and lay flat. Trim away remaining ribs and seeds, then cut pepper into strips or pieces as directed.

CHIPOTLE CHICKEN TACOS

SERVES 4

WHY THIS RECIPE WORKS While we love braised, slow-cooked taco fillings when time isn't an issue, weeknights are reserved for simple, relatively quick fillings. Building flavor is still important, however, and we had a few tricks in mind. Boneless, skinless chicken breasts were a convenient place to start. We first seared the breasts quickly in our piping-hot cast-iron skillet to create savory browning, then built a flavorful poaching liquid and cooked the browned chicken through gently to imbue it with flavor. For our poaching liquid, we started by sautéing chipotle chile in adobo and garlic for a smoky, aromatic flavor base. We then added orange juice for citrusy freshness, cilantro for a pleasant herbal note, and Worcestershire for savory depth. Once the chicken was finished cooking, our poaching liquid pulled double duty: We reduced it to a sauce, which took only a minute with our heat-retaining cast-iron skillet. A bit of mustard thickened the sauce and provided a sharp counterpoint to the sweet orange juice. Finally, we shredded and sauced the chicken, which was then ready to be spooned into warm tortillas. Serve with your favorite taco toppings. For more information on warming tortillas in the microwave, see page 175.

1½ pounds boneless, skinless chicken breasts, trimmed
    Salt and pepper
2 tablespoons vegetable oil
4 garlic cloves, minced
2 teaspoons minced canned chipotle chile in adobo sauce
¾ cup orange juice (2 oranges)
¾ cup chopped fresh cilantro
1 tablespoon Worcestershire sauce
1 teaspoon yellow mustard
12 (6-inch) corn tortillas, warmed

1 Pound thicker ends of chicken breasts as needed to create even thickness. Pat chicken dry with paper towels and season with salt and pepper. Heat 12-inch cast-iron skillet over medium heat for 5 minutes. Add oil and heat until just smoking. Brown chicken, about 4 minutes per side; transfer to plate.

2 Add garlic and chipotle to now-empty skillet and cook over medium heat until fragrant, about 30 seconds. Stir in orange juice, ½ cup cilantro, and Worcestershire and bring to simmer. Nestle chicken into skillet along with any accumulated juices. Reduce heat to gentle simmer, cover, and cook until chicken registers 160 degrees, 4 to 8 minutes, flipping chicken halfway through cooking.

3 Transfer chicken to carving board, let cool slightly, then shred into bite-size pieces using 2 forks. Meanwhile, increase heat to medium-high and simmer cooking liquid until reduced to ½ cup, about 1 minute. Off heat, whisk in mustard.

4 Stir shredded chicken into sauce and let sit until heated through, about 5 minutes. Stir in remaining ¼ cup cilantro and season with salt and pepper to taste. Serve with warm tortillas.

POUNDING CHICKEN BREASTS

To create chicken breasts of even thickness, pound thicker ends of breasts until all are uniform in thickness. Though some breasts will still be larger, they will cook at the same rate.

FLANK STEAK TACOS WITH CHARRED CORN SALSA

SERVES 4

WHY THIS RECIPE WORKS Charred corn salsa combined with cumin-scented flank steak is a winning match. We wanted all the char and perfectly seared steak without having to step outside to grill, so we turned to our cast-iron skillet. We cut the steak into fourths to increase its surface area and seasoned it with ground cumin, salt, and pepper so that when we seared it, it developed a great crust. After cooking the steak, we took it out to rest and added the corn to the skillet. We let the corn cook without disturbing it to create a flavorful char. We then built our salsa: We added the corn to a lively combination of red onion, spicy jalapeño, lime juice, and cilantro. Finally, we cut the meat thin against the grain, ensuring that each bite was as tender as it was flavorful. Serve with your favorite taco toppings.

1 teaspoon ground cumin
Salt and pepper
1 (1½-pound) flank steak, trimmed
2 tablespoons vegetable oil
1½ cups fresh or thawed frozen corn
¼ cup finely chopped red onion
1 jalapeño chile, stemmed, seeded, and minced
2 tablespoons lime juice
1 tablespoon minced fresh cilantro
12 (6-inch) corn tortillas, warmed

1 Adjust oven rack to middle position, place 12-inch cast-iron skillet on rack, and heat oven to 500 degrees. Meanwhile, combine cumin, ¾ teaspoon salt, and ½ teaspoon pepper in bowl. Cut steak lengthwise with grain into 2 equal pieces, then cut each piece in half crosswise to create 4 equal pieces. Season steaks with spice mixture and let sit at room temperature.

2 When oven reaches 500 degrees, pat steaks dry with paper towels. Using potholders, remove skillet from oven and place over medium-high heat; turn off oven. Being careful of hot skillet handle, add oil and heat until just smoking. Cook steaks, without moving, until lightly browned on first side, about 2 minutes. Flip steaks and continue to cook until lightly browned on second side, about 2 minutes.

3 Flip steaks, reduce heat to medium-low, and cook, flipping every 2 minutes, until steaks are well browned and meat registers 120 to 125 degrees (for medium-rare), 4 to 8 minutes. Transfer steaks to carving board, tent loosely with aluminum foil, and let rest while making salsa.

4 Add corn to now-empty skillet and cook over medium heat, without stirring, until lightly charred, about 4 minutes. Stir corn and continue to cook until tender, about 1 minute; transfer to medium bowl. Stir in onion, jalapeño, lime juice, cilantro, ¼ teaspoon salt, and ¼ teaspoon pepper. Season with additional salt and pepper to taste. Slice steak thin against grain and serve with tortillas and corn salsa.

WARMING TORTILLAS

Stack tortillas on plate, cover with damp dish towel, and microwave for 60 to 90 seconds.

SKILLET PIZZA MARGHERITA

SERVES 4

WHY THIS RECIPE WORKS Getting crisp pizza crust from your oven can be a challenge, but with just a few tweaks and the right tools, you'll have homemade pizza that's miles better than offerings from the freezer case or the delivery guy. We started by rolling out pizza dough thinly and then gently pressing it into our cast-iron skillet. Heating the pizza dough in the skillet on the stove gave our crust a jump start before going into the oven. Once in the oven, the skillet functioned like a pizza stone and crisped up our crust perfectly in just minutes. Our simple, classic pizza toppings—pizza sauce, mozzarella cheese, and basil—allowed our crust to really shine. We like to use our Classic Pizza Dough (page 43) and No-Cook Pizza Sauce; however, you can use ready-made pizza dough and sauce from the local pizzeria or supermarket.

¼ cup extra-virgin olive oil

1 pound pizza dough, room temperature

1 cup pizza sauce

12 ounces fresh mozzarella cheese, sliced ¼ inch thick

2 tablespoons chopped fresh basil

1 Adjust oven rack to upper-middle position and heat oven to 500 degrees. Grease 12-inch cast-iron skillet with 2 tablespoons oil.

2 Place dough on lightly floured counter, divide in half, and cover with greased plastic wrap. Press and roll 1 piece of dough (keeping remaining dough covered) into 11-inch round. Transfer dough to prepared skillet and gently push it to corners of pan. Spread ½ cup sauce over surface of dough, leaving ½-inch border around edge. Top with half of mozzarella.

3 Set skillet over medium-high heat and cook until outside edge of dough is set, pizza is lightly puffed, and bottom crust is spotty brown when gently lifted with spatula, 2 to 4 minutes. Transfer skillet to oven and bake until edge of pizza is golden brown and cheese is melted, 7 to 10 minutes.

4 Using potholders, remove skillet from oven and slide pizza onto wire rack using spatula; let cool slightly. Sprinkle with 1 tablespoon basil, cut into wedges, and serve. Being careful of hot skillet, repeat with remaining 2 tablespoons oil, dough, sauce, mozzarella, and 1 tablespoon basil. Cut into wedges and serve.

NO-COOK PIZZA SAUCE
MAKES 2 CUPS

While it is convenient to use ready-made pizza sauce, we think it is almost as easy, and a lot tastier, to make your own.

1 (28-ounce) can whole peeled tomatoes, drained with juice reserved

1 tablespoon extra-virgin olive oil

1 teaspoon red wine vinegar

2 garlic cloves, minced

1 teaspoon dried oregano

Salt and pepper

Process tomatoes with oil, vinegar, garlic, and oregano in food processor until smooth, about 30 seconds. Transfer mixture to 2-cup liquid measuring cup and add tomato juice until sauce measures 2 cups. Season with salt and pepper to taste. (Sauce can be refrigerated for up to 1 week or frozen for up to 1 month.)

CHICAGO-STYLE PEPPERONI PAN PIZZA

SERVES 4

WHY THIS RECIPE WORKS Chicago-style deep-dish pizza is known for its special tender crust, which is crisp on the bottom and chewy in the middle. To make a dough with just the right consistency, we used milk instead of water, which also gave the crust a richer flavor. While whole milk is fine, we found that skim milk helped the dough rise better and bake up especially soft and light. Kneading the dough in a stand mixer also helped it attain a perfect chewy-yet-plush texture. A cast-iron skillet was the perfect cooking vessel for our deep-dish pizza: It evenly distributed heat from the oven to the dough, producing a browned and crisp crust across the bottom and edges, and its tall sides made it the ideal vessel for this thick, layered type of pizza. For the toppings, we precooked the pepperoni in our skillet to drive off excess grease. We followed Chicago tradition and layered the cheese underneath the sauce and pepperoni, with an added sprinkle of Parmesan on top of the pie for even more pronounced cheesy flavor. For the pizza sauce, consider using our No-Cook Pizza Sauce (page 176).

3 ounces thinly sliced pepperoni

½ cup plus 2 tablespoons warm skim milk (110 degrees)

1½ tablespoons extra-virgin olive oil

1¾ teaspoons instant or rapid-rise yeast

1¾ cups (8¾ ounces) all-purpose flour

1½ teaspoons sugar

¼ teaspoon salt

8 ounces mozzarella cheese, shredded (2 cups)

1½ cups pizza sauce

¼ cup grated Parmesan cheese

1 Cook pepperoni in 12-inch cast-iron skillet over medium heat until rendered and beginning to crisp, 3 to 5 minutes. Using slotted spoon, transfer pepperoni to paper towel–lined plate; set aside. Wipe skillet clean with paper towels.

2 Whisk milk, oil, and yeast together in 2-cup liquid measuring cup until yeast is dissolved. Combine flour, sugar, and salt in bowl of stand mixer. Using dough hook on low speed, slowly add milk mixture and mix until dough comes together, about 2 minutes. Increase speed to medium-low and continue to mix until dough is smooth and pulls away from sides of bowl, 3 to 5 minutes.

3 Transfer dough to lightly floured counter and knead by hand to form smooth, round ball, about 1 minute. Place dough in large, lightly greased bowl, cover tightly with greased plastic wrap, and let rise until doubled in size, 1 to 1½ hours.

4 Adjust oven rack to middle position and heat oven to 400 degrees. Press and roll dough into 12-inch round on lightly floured counter. Loosely roll dough around rolling pin and gently unroll it onto now-empty skillet. Ease dough into skillet by gently lifting and supporting edge of dough with your hand while pressing into corners and 1 inch up sides with your other hand. Cover with plastic and let rest until dough is puffy and slightly risen, 20 to 30 minutes.

5 Sprinkle mozzarella over surface of dough and top with pepperoni. Spread sauce over pepperoni, then sprinkle with Parmesan. Set skillet over medium-high heat and cook until outside edge of dough is slightly puffed, about 3 minutes. Transfer skillet to oven and bake until crust is golden brown, 20 to 30 minutes, rotating skillet halfway through baking.

6 Using potholders, transfer skillet to wire rack and let pizza cool for 10 minutes. Being careful of hot skillet handle, slide pizza onto cutting board using spatula and cut into wedges. Serve.

CAST-IRON SKILLET CALZONE

SERVES 6 TO 8

WHY THIS RECIPE WORKS We reimagined a calzone as a pie with a top and bottom crust for a crowd-size version of this party favorite with a hefty dose of savory filling. The high sides of our cast-iron skillet made assembly easy: We lined the pan with dough and added layers of cheese, meat, and sauce. We like to use our Classic Pizza Dough (page 43); however, you can use ready-made pizza dough from the local pizzeria or supermarket. Use low-sodium marinara sauce to prevent the calzone from becoming overly salty. Serve with extra marinara sauce, if desired.

2 teaspoons extra-virgin olive oil

1 pound hot or sweet Italian sausage, casings removed

4 ounces thinly sliced pepperoni, quartered

2 garlic cloves, minced

2 pounds pizza dough

8 ounces (1 cup) whole-milk ricotta cheese

2 tablespoons chopped fresh basil

1 teaspoon pepper

1 pound mozzarella cheese, shredded (4 cups)

1 cup low-sodium marinara sauce

1 large egg, lightly beaten with 2 tablespoons water

2 teaspoons toasted sesame seeds (optional)

1 Adjust oven rack to lower-middle position and heat oven to 450 degrees. Heat 12-inch cast-iron skillet over medium heat for 3 minutes. Add oil and heat until shimmering. Add sausage and pepperoni and cook, breaking up pieces of meat with wooden spoon, until sausage is no longer pink, 5 to 7 minutes. Stir in garlic and cook until fragrant, about 30 seconds. Using slotted spoon, transfer meat mixture to paper towel–lined plate. Wipe skillet clean with paper towels.

2 Place dough on lightly floured counter, divide into two-thirds and one-third (one 22-ounce piece and one 10-ounce piece). Press and roll larger piece of dough (keeping remaining dough covered with greased plastic wrap) into 16-inch round. Loosely roll dough around rolling pin and gently unroll it onto now-empty skillet, letting excess dough hang over edge. Ease dough into skillet by gently lifting and supporting edge of dough with your hand while pressing into skillet bottom and corners with your other hand. Some dough will overhang edge of skillet; leave in place.

3 Combine meat mixture, ricotta, basil, and pepper in bowl. Sprinkle 2 cups mozzarella over surface of dough. Dollop meat mixture over mozzarella and press into even layer. Spread sauce over top, then sprinkle with remaining 2 cups mozzarella.

4 Brush overhanging dough of bottom crust with egg wash. Press and roll remaining dough into 14-inch circle, then loosely roll dough around rolling pin and gently unroll it over filling. Trim overhanging dough to ½ inch beyond edge of skillet. Pinch edges of top and bottom crusts firmly together. Roll overhang to be flush with edge of skillet, then crimp with tines of fork.

5 Brush top of calzone with egg wash and sprinkle with sesame seeds, if using. Using paring knife, cut eight 1-inch vents in top of dough in circular pattern. Transfer skillet to oven and bake until crust is golden brown, about 30 minutes, rotating skillet halfway through baking.

6 Using potholders, transfer skillet to wire rack and let calzone cool for 30 minutes. Being careful of hot skillet handle, slide calzone onto cutting board using spatula and slice into wedges. Serve.

MAKING A CAST-IRON SKILLET CALZONE

After unrolling dough onto skillet, ease it into skillet by gently lifting and supporting edge of dough with your hand while pressing into skillet bottom and corners with your other hand.

EGGS AND BREAKFAST

Fried Eggs

BEST SCRAMBLED EGGS

SERVES 4

WHY THIS RECIPE WORKS A well-seasoned cast-iron skillet has great nonstick properties, making it ideal for cooking scrambled eggs. For perfectly cooked, fluffy scrambled eggs, we started by using eight whole eggs plus two additional yolks. The extra yolks not only enriched the egg flavor, but the extra fat and emulsifiers also helped stave off overcooking. To ensure that the eggs would come out of the skillet easily, we greased the pan with a little vegetable oil. A small amount of butter acted in concert with the oil to prevent sticking and helped to make the eggs even more flavorful. Starting the egg mixture in a preheated skillet produced puffy curds; turning the heat to low once the eggs began to coagulate ensured that they didn't overcook. Using a 10-inch skillet kept the eggs in a thicker layer, thereby producing larger, soft curds. You can substitute 8 teaspoons of whole milk plus 4 teaspoons of heavy cream for the half-and-half. The eggs can overcook quickly, especially if they are allowed to sit in the hot skillet past the cooking time. To avoid overcooking, have serving plates ready before starting the recipe. To dress up the dish, consider adding 2 tablespoons of chopped parsley, chives, basil, or cilantro or 1 tablespoon of dill or tarragon to the eggs after reducing the heat to low.

1 tablespoon vegetable oil

8 large eggs plus 2 large yolks

¼ cup half-and-half

Salt and pepper

1 tablespoon unsalted butter

1 Grease 10-inch cast-iron skillet with oil and heat over medium heat for 3 minutes. Beat eggs and yolks, half-and-half, ¼ teaspoon salt, and ¼ teaspoon pepper together with fork in bowl until thoroughly combined and mixture is pure yellow; do not overbeat.

2 Add butter to skillet and quickly swirl to coat. Add egg mixture and, using heat-resistant rubber spatula, constantly and firmly scrape along bottom and sides of skillet until eggs begin to clump and spatula just leaves trail on bottom of skillet, about 1 minute.

3 Reduce heat to low and gently but constantly fold eggs until clumped and just slightly wet, 1 to 4 minutes. Transfer eggs to plates and season with salt and pepper to taste. Serve immediately.

SCRAMBLING EGGS

1 Add egg mixture and, using rubber spatula, constantly and firmly scrape bottom and sides of skillet until eggs begin to clump and spatula just leaves trail.

2 Reduce heat to low and gently but constantly fold eggs until clumped and just slightly wet.

FRIED EGGS

SERVES 2

WHY THIS RECIPE WORKS A classic fried egg features a tender white with crisp, lacy brown edges and a fluid but lightly thickened yolk. When you're working with a hot cast-iron skillet, all you need is a touch of butter and a lid to produce perfectly cooked fried eggs in just a few minutes. Preheating the skillet for 3 minutes guaranteed a skillet free from hot spots, which gave us eggs that cooked evenly throughout. We gave the eggs diner-style richness by adding butter to the skillet just before the eggs went in to fry. Cracking the four eggs into two small bowls made it possible to add them to the skillet all at once so they cooked at the same rate. Adding a lid to the skillet during cooking was necessary to trap heat and steam so the eggs cooked from above as well as below, firming up the white before the yolk overcooked. After 1 minute, we moved the pan off the heat, allowing the whites to finish cooking gently using the residual heat from the cast iron while keeping the yolks fluid. You will need a 12-inch skillet with a tight-fitting lid for this recipe. When checking the eggs for doneness, lift the lid just a crack to prevent loss of steam should they need further cooking. When cooked, the thin layer of white surrounding the yolk will turn opaque, but the yolk should remain runny. To cook two eggs, use a 10-inch cast-iron skillet and halve the amount of butter. You can use this method with extra-large or jumbo eggs without altering the timing.

1 tablespoon vegetable oil

4 large eggs

Salt and pepper

1 tablespoon unsalted butter

1 Grease 12-inch cast-iron skillet with oil and heat over medium heat for 3 minutes. Crack 2 eggs into small bowl and season with salt and pepper. Repeat with remaining 2 eggs and second small bowl.

2 Add butter to skillet and quickly swirl to coat. Working quickly, pour 1 bowl of eggs in 1 side of skillet and second bowl of eggs in other side. Cover and cook for 1 minute.

3 Remove skillet from heat and let sit, covered, 15 to 45 seconds for runny yolks (white around edge of yolk will be barely opaque), 45 to 60 seconds for soft but set yolks, and about 2 minutes for medium-set yolks. Transfer eggs to plates and serve immediately.

MAKING FRIED EGGS

1 To quickly add 4 eggs to skillet all at once, crack them into 2 small bowls.

2 Working quickly, position bowls on either side of skillet and add eggs simultaneously.

DENVER OMELET

SERVES 2

WHY THIS RECIPE WORKS The Denver omelet has become a breakfast staple in American restaurants and diners. Filled with ham and vegetables in addition to cheese, it's a meal in itself. For our version, we found that cooking the filling separately, before the eggs, was the best way to avoid undercooked vegetables. We chopped the bell pepper and onion fine to make our filling easier to eat. Deli ham was readily available in small amounts and easy to dice. Using a well-seasoned 10-inch cast-iron skillet, we sautéed the ham to create some browning and begin developing flavor for our omelet filling. Chopped pepper and onion were then added to the browned ham to gain some color of their own. For an omelet that was moist, tender, and sturdy, we focused on both the temperature at which the omelet cooked and the treatment of the eggs while they were in the pan. We cooked the omelet over medium-low heat until it was partway done, then we took it off the heat and sprinkled the filling and cheese over the top. After the omelet sat covered for about 5 minutes, the cheese was melted and the eggs were perfectly set but still tender. Gently tilting the pan made it easy to fold the omelet over as we slid it out of the skillet. You will need a 10-inch skillet with a tight-fitting lid for this recipe. It is important to lift the edges of the omelet when cooking the eggs, rather than pushing them toward the center. This recipe can be easily doubled to make two omelets; make a doubled batch of filling and then use half for each omelet.

2 tablespoons unsalted butter

1 (¼-inch-thick) slice deli ham (2 ounces), cut into ¼-inch pieces

½ red bell pepper, chopped fine

¼ cup finely chopped onion

6 large eggs

Salt and pepper

1½ ounces Monterey Jack cheese, shredded (⅓ cup)

1 Heat 10-inch cast-iron skillet over medium heat for 5 minutes. Melt 1 tablespoon butter in skillet. Add ham and cook until lightly browned, about 3 minutes. Stir in bell pepper and onion and cook until softened and lightly browned, about 5 minutes; transfer to bowl.

2 Beat eggs, ¼ teaspoon salt, and ¼ teaspoon pepper together with fork in bowl until thoroughly combined and mixture is pure yellow; do not overbeat. Melt remaining 1 tablespoon butter in now-empty skillet over medium-low heat and swirl to coat. Add egg mixture and cook, without stirring, until eggs begin to set, about 1 minute.

3 Using heat-resistant rubber spatula, lift edge of cooked eggs, then tilt skillet to 1 side so that uncooked eggs run underneath. Repeat process, working around edge of skillet. Using spatula, gently scrape any remaining uncooked eggs toward edge of skillet until top is just slightly wet. Entire process should take about 2 minutes.

4 Off heat, sprinkle ham mixture and Monterey Jack evenly over omelet. Cover and let sit until eggs no longer appear wet, about 5 minutes. Run spatula around edge of skillet to loosen omelet. Slide omelet halfway out of skillet onto cutting board, then tilt skillet so top of omelet folds over itself. Cut omelet in half and serve immediately.

REMOVING OMELET FROM SKILLET

Run spatula around edge of skillet to loosen omelet. Slide omelet halfway out of skillet onto cutting board, then tilt skillet so top of omelet folds over itself.

HUEVOS RANCHEROS

SERVES 2 TO 4

WHY THIS RECIPE WORKS This spicy dish of eggs, salsa, and tortillas makes for an eye-opening breakfast. We took advantage of the powerful searing properties of our cast-iron skillet to get great charring on the vegetables in the flavorful salsa base of the dish. Our vegetable mixture was chopped in a food processor to the perfect consistency before getting simmered in the skillet to develop even more flavor. We then cracked our eggs into small wells in the simmering salsa and covered the skillet to allow the eggs to gently poach and absorb flavor from the zesty vegetables. You will need a 12-inch skillet with a tight-fitting lid for this recipe. For more heat, add the jalapeño ribs and seeds in step 3. Serve with refried beans, diced avocados, and chopped scallions.

1½ pounds grape tomatoes

3 tablespoons vegetable oil

Salt and pepper

2 jalapeño chiles, halved, seeds and ribs removed

½ onion, cut into 1-inch pieces

1 tablespoon tomato paste

2 garlic cloves, lightly crushed and peeled

½ teaspoon ground cumin

3 tablespoons minced fresh cilantro

1 tablespoon lime juice, plus lime wedges for serving

4 large eggs

4 (6-inch) corn tortillas, warmed

1 Heat 12-inch cast-iron skillet over medium heat for 5 minutes. Toss tomatoes with 1 tablespoon oil and 1 teaspoon salt. Add tomatoes to skillet and cook, stirring occasionally, until lightly charred and blistered, about 10 minutes; transfer to bowl.

2 Heat remaining 2 tablespoons oil in now-empty skillet over medium heat until shimmering. Add jalapeños and onion and cook until lightly charred, about 8 minutes. Stir in tomato paste, garlic, 1 teaspoon salt, and cumin and cook until fragrant, about 30 seconds.

3 Process jalapeño-onion mixture in food processor until finely ground, about 15 seconds, scraping down sides of bowl as needed. Add tomatoes and pulse until coarsely chopped, about 10 pulses. (Salsa can be refrigerated for up to 24 hours.)

4 Bring salsa to simmer in now-empty skillet over medium heat. Cook, stirring occasionally, until thickened slightly, about 10 minutes. Off heat, stir in 2 tablespoons cilantro and lime juice and season with salt and pepper to taste.

5 Using back of large spoon, make 4 shallow indentations (about 3 inches wide) in salsa. Crack 1 egg into each indentation and season with salt and pepper. Cover and cook over medium-low heat, 4 to 5 minutes for runny yolks (white around edge of yolk will be barely opaque), 5 to 6 minutes for soft but set yolks, or 6 to 7 minutes for medium-set yolks. Sprinkle with remaining 1 tablespoon cilantro. Serve immediately with warm tortillas and lime wedges.

POACHING EGGS IN SALSA

1 Off heat, use back of large spoon to make 4 shallow indentations (about 3 inches wide) in salsa.

2 Crack 1 egg into each indentation and season with salt and pepper. Cover and cook over medium-low heat to desired doneness.

SPINACH AND FETA FRITTATA

SERVES 4 TO 6

WHY THIS RECIPE WORKS Frittatas are similar to omelets, but much easier to make: All of the ingredients are combined at once so you need much less hands-on time during cooking. For a perfect, tender frittata packed with flavor, we started with 10 large eggs mixed with half-and-half. The water in the dairy helped create steam so that the eggs puffed up, and the fat kept the frittata tender. We used the microwave to quickly wilt fresh spinach and then drained it to keep the frittata from becoming waterlogged. Feta cheese and oregano added great savory flavor. Actively stirring and scraping the egg mixture during cooking kept the eggs from becoming tough and ensured quicker cooking. Shaking the skillet helped the eggs distribute properly, and cooking the frittata on the stovetop created some nice browning on the bottom. We then transferred the skillet to the broiler, where the high heat helped the frittata puff slightly and set without overcooking the bottom. The cast iron was perfectly at home under the broiler, unlike nonstick pans with plastic handles and coatings that shouldn't be exposed to intense heat. Once we moved the skillet from the broiler to a wire rack, the residual heat from the cast iron helped the frittata finish cooking.

11 ounces (11 cups) baby spinach

10 large eggs

3 tablespoons half-and-half

    Salt and pepper

3 ounces feta cheese, crumbled (¾ cup)

2 tablespoons vegetable oil

1 onion, chopped fine

2 garlic cloves, minced

1 teaspoon minced fresh oregano
    or ¼ teaspoon dried

1 Adjust oven rack 6 inches from broiler element and heat broiler. Microwave spinach and ½ cup water in large covered bowl until spinach is wilted and decreased in volume by half, about 4 minutes. Remove bowl from microwave and keep covered for 1 minute. Carefully remove cover, allowing steam to escape away from you, and transfer spinach to colander set in sink. Using back of rubber spatula, gently press spinach against colander to release excess liquid. Transfer spinach to cutting board and coarsely chop. Return spinach to colander and press a second time.

2 Beat eggs, half-and-half, ¾ teaspoon salt, and ½ teaspoon pepper together with fork in bowl until thoroughly combined and mixture is pure yellow; do not overbeat. Stir in ½ cup feta.

3 Heat 10-inch cast-iron skillet over medium heat for 3 minutes. Add oil and heat until shimmering. Add onion and cook until softened, about 5 minutes. Stir in garlic and oregano and cook until fragrant, about 30 seconds. Stir in spinach and cook until uniformly wilted and glossy, about 2 minutes.

4 Add egg mixture and, using heat-resistant rubber spatula, constantly and firmly scrape along bottom and sides of skillet until eggs form large curds and spatula leaves trail on bottom of skillet but eggs are still moist, 1 to 2 minutes. Shake skillet to distribute eggs evenly. Sprinkle with remaining ¼ cup feta and gently press into eggs with spatula.

5 Transfer skillet to oven and broil until center of frittata is puffed and surface is just beginning to brown, 3 to 5 minutes; when cut into with paring knife, eggs should be slightly wet and runny.

6 Using potholders, transfer skillet to wire rack and let frittata rest for 5 minutes. Being careful of hot skillet handle, run spatula around edge of skillet to loosen frittata, then slide frittata out of skillet onto cutting board. Cut frittata into wedges and serve warm or at room temperature.

HASH BROWN PIE

SERVES 4 TO 6

WHY THIS RECIPE WORKS For a light-on-effort, big-on-flavor breakfast casserole, we started by cooking sausage in our cast-iron skillet. Next we fried shredded potatoes in the sausage fat. We added eggs, cheese, and scallions to the sausage and potatoes, periodically shaking the pan to distribute the mixture until the bottom was golden brown. Then, instead of flipping the hot, heavy cast-iron skillet, we simply ran a rubber spatula around the edge of the pan to loosen the pie, slid it onto a plate, and then used a second plate to invert the pie and slide it back into the skillet to brown the second side. You will need a 10-inch skillet with a tight-fitting lid for this recipe. To thaw the potatoes quickly, microwave them in a covered bowl for about 4 minutes, tossing occasionally.

¼ cup vegetable oil

8 ounces breakfast sausage, casings removed

1 pound (5 cups) frozen shredded hash browns, thawed and squeezed dry

6 large eggs

4 scallions, sliced thin

¼ teaspoon pepper

6 ounces cheddar cheese, shredded (1½ cups)

1 Heat 10-inch cast-iron skillet over medium heat for 5 minutes. Add 3 tablespoons oil and heat until shimmering. Add sausage and cook, breaking up meat with wooden spoon, until no longer pink, about 3 minutes. Add hash browns and cook, turning occasionally, until lightly browned and crisp, about 15 minutes.

2 Beat eggs, scallions, and pepper together with fork in large bowl until thoroughly combined and mixture is pure yellow; do not overbeat. Gently fold in potato mixture and cheddar.

3 Heat remaining 1 tablespoon oil in now-empty skillet over medium heat until shimmering. Add egg mixture and cook, shaking skillet and folding mixture constantly for 15 seconds. Smooth top of egg mixture, cover, and cook, gently shaking skillet occasionally, until bottom is golden brown and top is lightly set, about 4 minutes.

4 Off heat, run heat-resistant rubber spatula around edge of skillet to loosen pie. Slide pie onto large plate, then invert onto second large plate and slide back into skillet with browned side up. Tuck edges of pie

into skillet with spatula. Continue to cook over medium heat until second side is golden and eggs are cooked through, about 2 minutes. Using spatula, slide pie onto cutting board and let cool slightly. Cut pie into wedges and serve warm or at room temperature.

FLIPPING HASH BROWN PIE

1 After browning first side, loosen pie with spatula and slide onto large plate.

2 Place second large plate face down over pie. Invert pie onto second plate so that browned side faces up.

3 Slide pie back into skillet, browned side up, then tuck edges into skillet with spatula.

SKILLET STRATA WITH BACON AND SCALLIONS

SERVES 4 TO 6

WHY THIS RECIPE WORKS A strata is a layered dish of bread, eggs, cheese, and milk that bakes up into a hearty, savory bread pudding that can be served for breakfast or brunch. We wanted a simplified version for the cast-iron skillet that would deliver the same cheesy richness as a layered casserole but could be made with less fuss. We were after a balance between bread and custard, with a flavorful filling chosen to complement the main ingredients. Our tasters preferred sliced white bread for its neutral flavor and convenience. We decided to toast the bread in the skillet and leave the crusts on, which helped our bread hold up during the cooking process and gave the strata more structure. Whole milk combined in almost equal amounts with the eggs for our custard base provided an even but not overwhelming richness. Five slices of bread cut into small pieces filled the skillet for the perfect balance of craggy crust and soft interior. A full cup of cheddar cheese mixed into the eggs added sharpness, and scallions lent a welcome fresh note. Bacon contributed some smokiness, and its rendered fat helped to toast the bread. After sautéing the onions and toasting the bread, we folded in the custard-cheese mixture and moved the skillet to the oven. Finishing the strata in a 425-degree oven helped produce a delicate, soufflé-like texture.

6 large eggs

1½ cups whole milk

3 scallions, sliced thin

Salt and pepper

4 ounces cheddar cheese, shredded (1 cup)

4 slices bacon, chopped

1 onion, chopped fine

5 slices hearty white sandwich bread,
    cut into 1-inch pieces

1 Adjust oven rack to middle position and heat oven to 425 degrees. Beat eggs, milk, scallions, and ¼ teaspoon pepper together with fork in large bowl until thoroughly combined and mixture is pure yellow; do not overbeat. Stir in cheddar.

2 Cook bacon in 10-inch cast-iron skillet over medium heat until crisp, 5 to 7 minutes. Add onion and ½ teaspoon salt and cook until softened and lightly browned, about 5 minutes. Add bread and, using heat-resistant rubber spatula, carefully fold into bacon-onion mixture until evenly coated. Cook bread, folding occasionally, until lightly toasted, about 3 minutes.

3 Off heat, fold in egg mixture until slightly thickened and well combined with bread. Gently press on top of strata to help bread soak up egg mixture. Transfer skillet to oven and bake until center of strata is puffed and set and edges have browned and pulled away slightly from sides of skillet, 12 to 15 minutes, rotating skillet halfway through baking. Let strata cool for 5 minutes before serving.

SIMPLE CHEESE QUICHE

SERVES 6 TO 8

WHY THIS RECIPE WORKS The ideal quiche has tender, flaky pastry and velvety custard. Parbaking the crust in our cast-iron skillet ensured it wouldn't be soggy or underbaked. Pulling the dish out of the oven when the filling was still slightly soft and letting it set up as it cooled guaranteed perfectly baked custard every time. You can substitute other fresh herbs such as tarragon or parsley for the chives. You can use our Foolproof Single-Crust Pie Dough or store-bought pie dough in this recipe.

1 recipe single-crust pie dough, rolled into 12-inch round

5 large eggs

2 cups half-and-half

1 tablespoon minced fresh chives

¼ teaspoon salt

¼ teaspoon pepper

4 ounces cheddar cheese, shredded (1 cup)

1 Adjust oven rack to middle position and heat oven to 375 degrees. Grease 10-inch cast-iron skillet. Loosely roll crust around rolling pin and gently unroll it onto prepared skillet. Ease crust into skillet by gently lifting and supporting edge of dough with your hand while pressing into skillet bottom and corners with your other hand. Tuck ½ inch of dough underneath itself to form tidy, even edge that lies against sides of skillet. Press tucked edge against sides of skillet using index finger to create attractive fluted rim. Wrap skillet loosely in plastic wrap and freeze until dough is firm, about 30 minutes.

2 Line pie crust with double layer of aluminum foil, covering edges, and fill with pie weights. Transfer skillet to oven and bake until pie dough looks dry and is pale in color, 25 to 30 minutes. Using potholders, transfer skillet to wire rack and remove weights and foil. Reduce oven temperature to 350 degrees.

3 Beat eggs, half-and-half, salt, and pepper with fork in 4-cup liquid measuring cup. Stir in cheddar. Being careful of hot skillet handle, return skillet to oven. Carefully pour egg mixture into shell until it reaches about ½ inch from top edge of crust (you may have extra egg mixture).

4 Bake quiche until center is set and knife inserted 1 inch from edge comes out clean, about 30 minutes. Let quiche cool for at least 1 hour before sprinkling with chives and serving.

FOOLPROOF SINGLE-CRUST PIE DOUGH

MAKES ENOUGH FOR ONE 10-INCH PIE

This recipe can be easily doubled to make double-crust pie dough; divide dough in half before refrigerating.

1¼ cups (6¼ ounces) all-purpose flour

1 tablespoon sugar

½ teaspoon salt

6 tablespoons unsalted butter, cut into ¼-inch pieces and chilled

4 tablespoons vegetable shortening, cut into 2 pieces and chilled

2 tablespoons vodka, chilled

2 tablespoons ice water

1 Process ¾ cup flour, sugar, and salt in food processor until combined, about 5 seconds. Scatter butter and shortening over top and process until mixture forms uneven clumps with no floury bits, about 10 seconds.

2 Scrape down sides of bowl and redistribute dough around processor blade. Sprinkle remaining ½ cup flour over dough and pulse until mixture has broken up into pieces and is evenly distributed around bowl, 4 to 6 pulses.

3 Transfer mixture to large bowl and sprinkle with vodka and ice water. Stir and press dough together, using stiff rubber spatula, until dough sticks together. Turn dough onto sheet of plastic wrap and flatten into 4-inch disk. Wrap tightly and refrigerate for 1 hour. Before rolling out dough, let it sit on counter to soften slightly, about 10 minutes. (Dough can be refrigerated for up to 2 days.)

HOME FRIES

SERVES 4

WHY THIS RECIPE WORKS A diner-style breakfast simply isn't complete without a side of crusty, deeply browned home fries. Diner cooks start off with roasted or boiled potatoes and use plenty of fat on a broad griddle to generate those great-tasting spuds. To replicate these perfectly crisp, fluffy fries at home, we replaced the griddle with our cast-iron skillet. Its unique properties encourage effective heat retention, which made getting a great sear easy even without a powerful restaurant griddle. We used Yukon Gold potatoes, which retain their shape through cooking. We tossed the potatoes with oil and parcooked them in the microwave before frying them, then sautéed the onion and garlic separately and stirred them into the potatoes just before serving. This kept the moist onions from compromising the crust on the potatoes and ensured that the garlic didn't burn. Chives sprinkled over the dish right before serving added a little freshness and enhanced the flavor profile. Although we prefer the sweetness of Yukon Gold potatoes, other medium-starch or waxy potatoes, such as red-skinned potatoes, can be substituted.

1½ pounds Yukon Gold potatoes, unpeeled, cut into ¾-inch pieces
5 tablespoons vegetable oil
Salt and pepper
1 onion, chopped fine
1 garlic clove, minced
1½ tablespoons minced fresh chives

1 Microwave potatoes, 1 tablespoon oil, ½ teaspoon salt, and ½ teaspoon pepper in covered bowl, stirring occasionally, until potatoes begin to soften, 7 to 10 minutes; drain well.

2 Heat 12-inch cast-iron skillet over medium heat for 3 minutes. Add 2 tablespoons oil and heat until shimmering. Add onion and cook until softened and lightly browned, about 5 minutes. Stir in garlic and cook until fragrant, about 30 seconds; transfer to bowl.

3 Heat remaining 2 tablespoons oil in now-empty skillet over medium heat until shimmering. Add potatoes and gently pack into skillet using back of spatula. Cook, without moving, until potatoes begin to brown, 5 to 7 minutes.

4 Flip potatoes, 1 portion at a time, and lightly repack into skillet. Repeat flipping process every few minutes until potatoes are tender, well browned, and crisp, 12 to 16 minutes. Stir in onion mixture and chives. Season with salt and pepper to taste. Serve.

CUTTING POTATOES INTO EVENLY SIZED PIECES

1 Using chef's knife, cut 1 thin sliver from 1 side of potato. Set potato on cut side and slice crosswise into even planks.

2 Stack several planks and cut crosswise, then rotate 90 degrees and cut crosswise again to create evenly sized pieces as directed in recipe.

CORNED BEEF HASH

WHY THIS RECIPE WORKS It can be a challenge to attain the holy grail of hash—crisp texture, perfect browning, and great flavor—when you're working with starchy, sticky ingredients. The nonstick surface of a well-seasoned cast-iron skillet is the perfect tool to make classic corned beef hash without sticking and burning while at the same time creating an ideal consistency. Using meat from a boiled dinner is traditional for this dish, but we found that deli-style corned beef worked great and allowed us to make this recipe anytime, regardless of leftovers status. Cutting the thinly sliced corned beef into ½-inch pieces gave us perfectly tender meat that held up in the hash. Stirring the meat in toward the end of cooking ensured that it would not dry out. Russet potatoes were our top choice for their starch content, which meant they would retain some character but also soften to help bind the hash together. To speed things along, we parcooked the potatoes in the microwave until tender, then moved them to the skillet. Heavy cream kept our hash moist and rich, and a little hot sauce added with the cream brought a touch of spice to the dish. The flavors of our hash came together with the final addition of bacon and onion. Cutting the bacon slightly smaller than the corned beef allowed the beef to take center stage while the bacon played a supporting role. We found that it was detrimental to stir our corned beef hash too often, so we allowed it to develop a good browned crust in the skillet before flipping it to brown the rest. Thyme added at the end lent a fresh, earthy note.

1½ pounds russet potatoes, peeled and cut into ½-inch pieces

1 tablespoon vegetable oil

Salt and pepper

4 slices bacon, chopped

1 onion, chopped fine

2 garlic cloves, minced

⅓ cup heavy cream

¼ teaspoon hot sauce

8 ounces thinly sliced deli corned beef, cut into ½-inch pieces

½ teaspoon minced fresh thyme

1 Microwave potatoes, oil, ¼ teaspoon salt, and ¼ teaspoon pepper in covered bowl, stirring occasionally, until potatoes begin to soften, 7 to 10 minutes; drain well.

2 Cook bacon in 12-inch cast-iron skillet over medium heat until fat begins to render, about 2 minutes. Stir in onion and cook until softened and lightly browned, about 5 minutes. Stir in garlic and cook until fragrant, about 30 seconds.

3 Stir in potatoes, cream, and hot sauce. Using back of spatula, gently pack potatoes into skillet and cook, without moving, for 2 minutes. Flip hash, 1 portion at a time, and lightly repack into skillet. Repeat flipping process every few minutes until potatoes are tender and well browned, 8 to 10 minutes.

4 Stir in corned beef and thyme and cook until corned beef is heated through, about 5 minutes. Season with pepper to taste. Serve.

HOMEMADE BREAKFAST SAUSAGE

SERVES 6 TO 8

WHY THIS RECIPE WORKS Premade frozen store-bought breakfast sausage patties commit a multitude of sins: too sweet or too salty, too bland or too highly seasoned, too greasy. Not to mention most varieties contain a number of additives, fillers, and preservatives. By making our own, we could ensure great flavor and use high-quality ingredients. We started by flavoring ground pork with classic breakfast sausage flavors: garlic, thyme, and sage, plus cayenne for a touch of heat. One tablespoon of maple syrup gently sweetened the patties. Just a single tablespoon of oil added to a preheated cast-iron skillet ensured that our breakfast sausage would develop a nice crust and also helped avoid burning and sticking. (After getting a great sear, the last thing we wanted was to leave that good flavor stuck to the pan.) Avoid lean or extra-lean ground pork; it makes the sausage dry, crumbly, and less flavorful.

2 pounds ground pork

2 tablespoons minced fresh sage or 2 teaspoons dried

1 tablespoon maple syrup

1½ teaspoons minced fresh thyme or ½ teaspoon dried

1½ teaspoons pepper

1 teaspoon salt

1 garlic clove, minced

⅛ teaspoon cayenne pepper

2 tablespoons vegetable oil

1 Gently mix pork, sage, maple syrup, thyme, pepper, salt, garlic, and cayenne together in bowl with hands until well combined. Divide meat mixture into 12 lightly packed balls, then gently flatten into 3-inch patties, about ½ inch thick. (Patties can be refrigerated for up to 24 hours.)

2 Heat 12-inch cast-iron skillet over medium heat for 5 minutes. Add 1 tablespoon oil and heat until just smoking. Brown half of patties, 3 to 5 minutes per side. Transfer patties to paper towel–lined plate and tent loosely with aluminum foil.

3 Wipe skillet clean with paper towels. Repeat with remaining 1 tablespoon oil and patties. Serve.

VARIATION

Homemade Apple-Fennel Breakfast Sausage
Substitute 2½ teaspoons ground fennel for sage. Mix 1 peeled, cored, and grated Golden Delicious apple into meat mixture before forming into patties.

FORMING SAUSAGE PATTIES

1 Use greased ⅓-cup dry measuring cup to easily make 12 uniform patties with minimum mess.

2 Cover patties with plastic wrap, then use your palm to gently flatten each sausage patty.

FLUFFY CORNMEAL PANCAKES

SERVES 6

WHY THIS RECIPE WORKS A cast-iron skillet is great for mimicking the properties of a commercial griddle. Both excel when it comes to retaining and using heat effectively on a well-seasoned surface. We set out to achieve the height and lightness of traditional pancakes with the more robust flavor and texture of cornmeal griddle cakes, but we came up against a few challenges: Coarsely ground cornmeal can impart an unpleasant sandy texture, and unlike pancakes made with regular flour, cornmeal cakes lack the gluten necessary to support a fluffy internal structure. We found that we could neutralize the texture problems by heating the cornmeal with some buttermilk to soften it. This allowed us to add more cornmeal for a boost of sweet, nutty flavor. Soaking the cornmeal also thickened the batter, helping the cakes maintain structure in the pan instead of spreading out. Using a 12-inch cast-iron skillet allowed us to get a nice crisp, golden-brown exterior on three pancakes at once without crowding the pan. Letting the batter sit for a few minutes before cooking the cakes allowed the buttermilk to react with the baking soda, making the batter foamy, which resulted in fluffier, airier pancakes.

1¾ cups buttermilk

1¼ cups (6¼ ounces) cornmeal

2 tablespoons unsalted butter, cut into ¼-inch pieces

2 large eggs, lightly beaten

¾ cup (3¾ ounces) all-purpose flour

2 tablespoons sugar

1¾ teaspoons baking powder

½ teaspoon baking soda

½ teaspoon salt

1 tablespoon vegetable oil

1 Adjust oven rack to middle position and heat oven to 200 degrees. Spray wire rack set in rimmed baking sheet with vegetable oil spray. Whisk 1¼ cups buttermilk and cornmeal together in medium bowl. Stir in butter, cover, and microwave until thickened slightly around edges, 60 to 90 seconds, stirring halfway through microwaving. Let mixture sit, covered, for 5 minutes, then whisk in eggs and remaining ½ cup buttermilk.

2 Whisk flour, sugar, baking powder, baking soda, and salt together in large bowl. Whisk cornmeal mixture into flour mixture and let sit for 10 minutes.

3 Grease 12-inch cast-iron skillet with oil and heat over medium heat for 3 minutes. Using paper towels, carefully wipe out oil, leaving thin film on bottom and sides of skillet. Reduce heat to medium-low. Using ¼-cup dry measuring cup, portion batter into skillet in 3 places. Cook until edges are set and bubbles begin to form on tops of pancakes, 1 to 2 minutes.

4 Flip pancakes and continue to cook until second side is golden brown, 1 to 2 minutes. Serve immediately or transfer to prepared rack, cover loosely with aluminum foil, and keep warm in oven. Repeat with remaining batter, adjusting heat as needed to maintain even browning. Serve.

DUTCH BABY

SERVES 4

WHY THIS RECIPE WORKS A Dutch baby is a not-too-sweet cross between a popover and a giant, eggy pancake. We wanted a puffy, well-risen Dutch baby with crisp sides and a tender bottom, but achieving that contrast did not come easily. Where ordinary pancakes call for baking soda and baking powder, Dutch babies rely on the conversion of water to steam for their lift—the milk, eggs, and butter in the batter all contain substantial amounts of water to help with that. To create a Dutch baby substantial enough to serve four, we turned to our 12-inch cast-iron skillet. Using a 450-degree oven allowed the Dutch baby to puff up spectacularly without burning. Our next goal was creating perfectly crisp sides. Since we knew that fat makes baked goods tender, we replaced the whole milk in the recipe with skim milk. Less fat translated to more crispness. To get a head start on this process, we greased and preheated the skillet. This simple step made all the difference in attaining crisp sides to go along with the custardy bottom; the lean batter cooked up quickly along the sides of the hot skillet. For even more crispness, we replaced some of the flour in the batter with cornstarch. To give the dish a flavor boost, we whisked a little vanilla extract and lemon zest into the batter. A generous dusting of confectioners' sugar provided the final touch. You can use whole or low-fat milk instead of skim, but the Dutch baby won't be as crisp. For a real treat, serve with an assortment of berries and lightly sweetened whipped cream.

2 tablespoons vegetable oil

1 cup (5 ounces) all-purpose flour

¼ cup (1 ounce) cornstarch

2 teaspoons grated lemon zest,
   plus lemon wedges for serving

1 teaspoon salt

3 large eggs

1¼ cups skim milk

1 tablespoon unsalted butter, melted and cooled

1 teaspoon vanilla extract

Confectioners' sugar

1 Adjust oven rack to middle position and heat oven to 450 degrees. Grease 12-inch cast-iron skillet with oil, place skillet in oven, and heat until oil is shimmering, about 10 minutes.

2 Meanwhile, whisk flour, cornstarch, lemon zest, and salt together in large bowl. In separate bowl, whisk eggs until frothy, then whisk in milk, melted butter, and vanilla until incorporated. Whisk one-third of milk mixture into flour mixture until no lumps remain. Slowly whisk in remaining milk mixture until smooth.

3 Quickly pour batter into skillet and bake until Dutch baby puffs and turns golden brown (edges will be dark brown), about 20 minutes, rotating skillet halfway through baking.

4 Using potholders, remove skillet from oven. Being careful of hot skillet handle, transfer Dutch baby to cutting board using spatula. Dust with sugar and slice into wedges. Serve with lemon wedges.

FRENCH TOAST CASSEROLE

SERVES 4 TO 6

WHY THIS RECIPE WORKS French toast is a delicious, easy-to-make breakfast favorite, but could we make it even easier—and more crowd friendly? To meet our goal, we translated the concept of French toast into a casserole. No more standing at the stove, flipping slice after slice, dripping egg wash on the counter, or serving one person at a time: Our French toast casserole is an ideal family breakfast. It takes full advantage of the cast-iron skillet's heat-retaining ability to replicate the crisp-crusted texture of conventional French toast in a simple, family-size dish. Potato bread, with its sturdy slices, was the perfect choice for the base of our casserole. To ensure that the bread would fit easily in a skillet, we halved the slices and layered them in the pan with a brown sugar–cinnamon mixture and butter. Repeating this process to create a double stack, we then poured egg custard over the top so it could soak through the layers of bread. For a satisfying crunch, we topped the casserole with sliced almonds before putting it into the oven and finished the baked casserole with a light dusting of confectioners' sugar. The result? A cast-iron skillet filled with layers of tender, sweet French toast—ready all at once.

1 tablespoon unsalted butter, softened, plus 4 tablespoons melted
6 tablespoons packed (2⅔ ounces) brown sugar
1½ teaspoons ground cinnamon
¼ teaspoon ground nutmeg
Pinch salt
10 slices potato sandwich bread, halved diagonally
1⅔ cups whole milk
4 large eggs
3 tablespoons sliced almonds, toasted
Confectioners' sugar

1 Adjust oven rack to middle position and heat oven to 350 degrees. Grease 12-inch cast-iron skillet with softened butter. Mix brown sugar, cinnamon, nutmeg, and salt together in bowl.

2 Sprinkle 2 tablespoons brown sugar mixture over bottom of prepared skillet. Arrange half of bread pieces in even layer in skillet. Drizzle with 1½ tablespoons melted butter and sprinkle with 2 tablespoons brown sugar mixture. Repeat layering with remaining bread pieces, 1½ tablespoons melted butter, and 2 tablespoons brown sugar mixture.

3 Whisk milk and eggs together until well combined, then pour mixture over bread and press gently to help bread soak up egg mixture. Sprinkle with almonds and remaining brown sugar mixture.

4 Transfer skillet to oven and bake until casserole is slightly puffed and golden brown and bubbling around edges, about 30 minutes, rotating skillet halfway through baking.

5 Using potholders, transfer skillet to wire rack, brush casserole with remaining 1 tablespoon melted butter, and let cool for 15 minutes. Sprinkle with confectioners' sugar and serve.

DROP DOUGHNUTS

MAKES 24 DOUGHNUTS

WHY THIS RECIPE WORKS The excellent heat retention of cast iron makes it the ideal vessel for frying, since it can keep the oil nice and hot, so we naturally turned to our 12-inch skillet for our simple drop doughnut recipe. For quick, tender, cake-style doughnuts, we first did away with rolling and stamping out the dough into rings. Instead, we merely dropped generous spoonfuls of batter into hot oil, creating round doughnut "holes." Many doughnut recipes we found called for generous amounts of oil, which is messy, wasteful, and not practical for frying in a skillet. We decided to shallow-fry our doughnuts to minimize the amount of oil needed. This method did require us to turn the doughnuts to ensure doneness, but the benefits of using less oil were well worth it. The perfect ratio of flour to baking powder produced batter that was light but not the least bit bitter—a problem with many chemically leavened baked goods. All-purpose flour gave these doughnuts the right amount of structure, and just 2 tablespoons of butter and a small amount of milk added richness and tenderness without weighing the batter down. The most important factor in preventing greasy doughnuts was making sure we fried them at the right temperature; we were careful to keep the oil between 350 and 375 degrees while cooking each batch. A dusting of confectioners' sugar made a nice final touch. You will need a 12-inch cast-iron skillet with at least 2-inch sides for this recipe.

2 cups (10 ounces) all-purpose flour

2 teaspoons baking powder

1 teaspoon ground nutmeg

¼ teaspoon salt

½ cup (3½ ounces) granulated sugar

2 large eggs

½ cup whole milk

2 tablespoons unsalted butter, melted and cooled

½ teaspoon vanilla extract

4 cups peanut or vegetable oil

Confectioners' sugar

1 Adjust oven rack to middle position and heat oven to 200 degrees. Whisk flour, baking powder, nutmeg, and salt together in medium bowl. In separate bowl, whisk granulated sugar and eggs together until smooth, then whisk in milk, melted butter, and vanilla until incorporated. Stir egg mixture into flour mixture with rubber spatula until just combined.

2 Set wire rack in rimmed baking sheet and line with triple layer of paper towels. Add oil to 12-inch cast-iron skillet until it measures about ¾ inch deep and heat over medium-high heat to 375 degrees.

3 Carefully drop one-third of batter, 1 heaping tablespoon at a time, into oil. Fry until deep golden brown, 3 to 6 minutes, flipping doughnuts halfway through frying. Adjust burner, if necessary, to maintain oil temperature between 350 and 375 degrees. Transfer doughnuts to prepared rack and keep warm in oven. (Doughnuts can be kept warm in oven for up to 30 minutes.)

4 Return oil to 375 degrees and repeat with remaining batter in 2 batches. Dust with confectioners' sugar and serve warm.

VARIATION

Orange Drop Doughnuts

Omit confectioners' sugar. Pulse ½ cup granulated sugar and 1 teaspoon grated orange zest in food processor until blended, about 5 pulses; transfer coating to bowl and set aside. Substitute 1 tablespoon grated orange zest for nutmeg and ½ cup orange juice for milk. Toss doughnuts with coating before serving.

CINNAMON BUNS

MAKES 8 BUNS

WHY THIS RECIPE WORKS Fluffy, golden-brown cinnamon buns with sweet filling and gooey icing are the ultimate treat, but between mixing, kneading, rising, shaping, rising again, baking, and icing, they can take a whole lot of effort and time—usually more than 3 hours for a batch. To make this recipe more accessible, we reevaluated the leaveners. For a quicker rise, we supplemented the yeast in the dough with baking powder. A mere 2 minutes of hand kneading and a single 30-minute rise were enough to give the extra-leavened dough long-risen flavor and texture. Our cast-iron skillet guaranteed a perfectly browned exterior on the rolls without any risk of overcooking the centers. Brown sugar and butter in the filling and a touch of vanilla in our tangy cream cheese glaze made these buns ultrarich and indulgent despite the accelerated prep time.

CINNAMON BUNS

- ¾ cup packed (5¼ ounces) dark brown sugar
- 8 tablespoons unsalted butter, melted
- 6 tablespoons (2⅔ ounces) granulated sugar
- 2 teaspoons ground cinnamon
- ⅛ teaspoon ground cloves
- Salt
- 2¾ cups (13¾ ounces) all-purpose flour
- 2½ teaspoons baking powder
- 1¼ cups warm whole milk (110 degrees)
- 4 teaspoons instant or rapid-rise yeast

GLAZE

- 3 ounces cream cheese, softened
- 1 cup (4 ounces) confectioners' sugar
- 2 tablespoons unsalted butter, melted
- 2 tablespoons whole milk
- ½ teaspoon vanilla extract
- ⅛ teaspoon salt

1 FOR THE CINNAMON BUNS Combine brown sugar, 1 tablespoon melted butter, ¼ cup granulated sugar, cinnamon, cloves, and ⅛ teaspoon salt in bowl; set aside.

2 Whisk flour, baking powder, and ¾ teaspoon salt together in large bowl. In separate bowl, whisk together milk, yeast, 2 tablespoons melted butter, and remaining 2 tablespoons granulated sugar until yeast dissolves.

Stir yeast mixture into flour mixture with rubber spatula until dough comes together (dough will be sticky).

3 Transfer dough to lightly floured counter and knead to form smooth, round ball, about 2 minutes. Roll dough into 12 by 9-inch rectangle with long side facing you. Brush 2 tablespoons melted butter over dough, leaving ½-inch border at edges. Sprinkle sugar mixture over butter, leaving ¾-inch border at top edge, and press lightly to adhere. Roll dough away from you into firm cylinder, keeping roll taut by tucking it under itself as you go. Pinch seam and ends closed. If necessary, gently reshape log to be 12 inches in length with even diameter.

4 Grease 10-inch cast-iron skillet with 1 tablespoon melted butter. Using serrated knife, cut cylinder into 8 pieces and arrange cut side down in prepared skillet. Cover buns loosely with plastic wrap and let rise for 30 minutes.

5 Adjust oven rack to middle position and heat oven to 350 degrees. Brush tops of buns with remaining 2 tablespoons melted butter, transfer skillet to oven, and bake until buns are well browned and filling is melted, 25 to 30 minutes, rotating skillet halfway through baking. Using potholders, transfer skillet to wire rack and let buns cool for 10 minutes.

6 FOR THE GLAZE Whisk all ingredients together in bowl until smooth. Being careful of hot skillet handle, spread glaze evenly over buns. Serve.

BISCUITS AND BREADS

Cinnamon Swirl Bread

BIG AND FLUFFY LEMON-DILL BISCUITS

MAKES 8 BISCUITS

WHY THIS RECIPE WORKS A good biscuit should be easy to make and able to hold its own alongside a bowl of stew or a plate of eggs. For simplicity, we aimed to go from one bowl to one pan, no fussy rolling or cutting required. We started with a simple ingredient list, with one unusual detail: We used both butter and shortening in our biscuits. The butter was important because it imparted flavor, plus as it melted during baking, it created small pockets of air in the biscuits, leading to a light, fluffy texture. Shortening helped make the dough cohesive and tender. These big biscuits were dropped right into a greased cast-iron skillet, which distributed the heat of the oven evenly to ensure a crisp bottom and nicely browned crust. A little butter brushed on the tops of the unbaked biscuits really brought out their rich flavor. To elevate these biscuits beyond basic breadbasket fare, we incorporated a mixture of light herbs and fresh citrus zest for two flavor options: lemon and dill or orange and tarragon.

3 cups (15 ounces) all-purpose flour

⅓ cup minced fresh dill

1 tablespoon grated lemon zest

1 tablespoon baking powder

½ teaspoon baking soda

1 teaspoon salt

8 tablespoons unsalted butter, cut into ½-inch
   pieces and softened, plus 1 tablespoon melted

4 tablespoons vegetable shortening,
   cut into ½-inch pieces

1¼ cups buttermilk

1 Adjust oven rack to upper-middle position and heat oven to 425 degrees. Grease 12-inch cast-iron skillet. Whisk flour, dill, lemon zest, baking powder, baking soda, and salt together in large bowl. Using your hands, rub butter and shortening into flour until mixture resembles coarse meal. Stir buttermilk into flour mixture until just combined.

2 Using greased ⅓-cup dry measuring cup, scoop out and drop 8 mounds of dough evenly into prepared skillet. Brush biscuits with 1 tablespoon melted butter.

3 Transfer skillet to oven and bake until biscuits are puffed and golden brown, 20 to 25 minutes, rotating skillet halfway through baking. Using potholders, transfer skillet to wire rack and let biscuits cool for at least 15 minutes before serving.

VARIATION

Big and Fluffy Orange-Tarragon Biscuits
Substitute ⅓ cup minced fresh tarragon for dill and 1 tablespoon grated orange zest for lemon zest.

MAKING BIG AND FLUFFY BISCUITS

Using greased ⅓-cup dry measuring cup, scoop out and drop 8 mounds of dough evenly into prepared skillet, placing 6 around skillet's perimeter and 2 in center.

SOUTHERN-STYLE CORNBREAD

MAKES 1 LOAF

WHY THIS RECIPE WORKS Unlike its sweet, cakey Northern counterpart, Southern cornbread is thin, crusty, and decidedly savory. It is traditionally made with cornmeal and no flour or sugar. We used yellow cornmeal for potent corn flavor, and we toasted it in our cast-iron skillet to bring out its flavor even more. Veering from tradition, we added a small amount of sugar to enhance the natural sweetness of the cornmeal. A cornmeal mush created by moistening the toasted cornmeal with sour cream and milk produced a fine, moist crumb. Baking the cornbread in a greased, preheated cast-iron skillet gave it a seriously crunchy, golden crust. A combination of oil and butter for greasing the skillet (as well as in the batter) struck the perfect balance in the flavor and structure of the bread—the butter added richness, and the oil raised the smoke point so the butter wouldn't burn. You can substitute any type of fine- or medium-ground cornmeal here; do not use coarse-ground cornmeal.

2¼ cups (11¼ ounces) stone-ground cornmeal

1½ cups sour cream

½ cup whole milk

¼ cup vegetable oil

5 tablespoons unsalted butter

2 tablespoons sugar

1 teaspoon baking powder

1 teaspoon baking soda

¾ teaspoon salt

2 large eggs

1 Adjust oven rack to middle position and heat oven to 450 degrees. Toast cornmeal in 10-inch cast-iron skillet over medium heat, stirring frequently, until fragrant, about 3 minutes. Transfer cornmeal to large bowl, whisk in sour cream and milk, and set aside.

2 Wipe skillet clean with paper towels. Add oil to now-empty skillet, place skillet in oven, and heat until oil is shimmering, about 10 minutes. Using potholders, remove skillet from oven, carefully add butter, and gently swirl to incorporate. Being careful of hot skillet handle, pour all but 1 tablespoon oil-butter mixture into cornmeal mixture and whisk to incorporate. Whisk sugar, baking powder, baking soda, and salt into cornmeal mixture until combined, then whisk in eggs.

3 Quickly scrape batter into skillet with remaining fat and smooth top. Transfer skillet to oven and bake until top begins to crack and sides are golden brown, 12 to 15 minutes, rotating skillet halfway through baking. Using potholders, transfer skillet to wire rack and let cornbread cool for at least 15 minutes before serving.

VARIATION

Southern-Style Jalapeño-Lime Cornbread

Whisk 2 minced jalapeño chiles and 2 teaspoons grated lime zest into cornmeal mixture with eggs.

BEER-BATTER CHEESE BREAD

MAKES 1 LOAF

WHY THIS RECIPE WORKS The beauty of a quick bread is that it can be on the table in less than an hour, but that convenience isn't worth it if the final product doesn't taste good. Recipes for beer-batter cheese bread that we tried produced loaves that tasted sour, like stale beer, or had weak, negligible cheese flavor. Still other attempts at this bread were so greasy that we had to pass out extra napkins. We wanted a lighter loaf enhanced with the yeasty flavor of beer and a rich hit of cheese—and it still had to be quick and easy. Limiting the butter in the batter to just 3 tablespoons imparted enough richness without going overboard. We put a moderate amount of cheese into the batter itself and then sprinkled some extra on top of the loaf to create a beautiful, craggy crust. Making the bread in our cast-iron skillet gave it a great bottom crust and helped it bake through quickly and evenly. It was also key to choose the right beer for clean, subtle flavor without any sourness. We prefer to use a mild American lager, such as Budweiser, here; strongly flavored beers will make this bread bitter.

2½ cups (12½ ounces) all-purpose flour
½ cup minced fresh chives
2 tablespoons sugar
4 teaspoons baking powder
1 teaspoon salt
½ teaspoon pepper
8 ounces Gruyère cheese, shredded (2 cups)
1¼ cups mild lager, such as Budweiser
3 tablespoons unsalted butter, melted

1 Adjust oven rack to middle position and heat oven to 450 degrees. Grease 10-inch cast-iron skillet.

2 Whisk flour, chives, sugar, baking powder, salt, and pepper together in large bowl. Stir in 1½ cups Gruyère, breaking up any clumps, until coated with flour. Stir beer and melted butter into flour mixture until just combined. Batter will be heavy and thick; do not overmix.

3 Scrape batter into prepared skillet and smooth top. Sprinkle with remaining ½ cup Gruyère. Transfer skillet to oven and bake until loaf is golden brown and toothpick inserted into center comes out clean, 20 to 25 minutes, rotating skillet halfway through baking.

4 Using potholders, transfer skillet to wire rack and let loaf cool for 10 minutes. Being careful of hot skillet handle, remove loaf from skillet, return to rack, and let cool for at least 20 minutes before serving.

FLIPPING OUT SKILLET BREADS

Let loaf cool in skillet for 10 minutes, then gently flip loaf onto wire rack. If you try to flip loaf out of skillet before letting it cool slightly, it will crumble.

OLIVE BREAD

MAKES 1 LOAF

WHY THIS RECIPE WORKS For a quick bread that was supersimple in method but sophisticated in flavor, we turned to a classic Italian combination of olives, cheese, and basil for an easy weeknight batter bread. We started by making a potent garlic oil that permeated the bread with garlic essence. A combination of whole milk and sour cream gave this bread extra richness and a great moist crumb. A generous amount of briny kalamata olives, which we halved to help them evenly disperse throughout the batter, gave this bread good texture and Mediterranean flavor. Coarsely grated Parmesan both in the batter and on top of the bread contributed to the savory flavor profile and helped create a crisp, golden crust. The cast-iron skillet gave us an evenly browned loaf that was almost fried around the edges where the rich batter touched the hot pan. Use the large holes of a box grater to grate the Parmesan. Do not substitute finely grated or pregrated Parmesan.

2½ cups (12½ ounces) all-purpose flour

¼ cup chopped fresh basil

1 tablespoon baking powder

½ teaspoon salt

4½ ounces Parmesan cheese, grated coarse (1½ cups)

1 cup whole milk

½ cup sour cream

1 large egg

5 tablespoons extra-virgin olive oil

3 garlic cloves, minced

1 cup pitted kalamata olives, halved

1 Adjust oven rack to middle position and heat oven to 450 degrees. Grease 10-inch cast-iron skillet.

2 Whisk flour, basil, baking powder, and salt together in large bowl. Stir in 1 cup Parmesan, breaking up any clumps, until coated with flour. In separate bowl, whisk milk, sour cream, and egg together until smooth.

3 Cook oil and garlic in 10-inch cast-iron skillet over medium heat until fragrant, about 3 minutes. Pour oil mixture into milk mixture and whisk to combine.

Stir milk mixture into flour mixture until just combined, then fold in olives. Batter will be heavy and thick; do not overmix.

4 Scrape batter into prepared skillet and smooth top. Sprinkle with remaining ½ cup Parmesan. Transfer skillet to oven and bake until loaf is golden brown and toothpick inserted into center comes out clean, 20 to 25 minutes, rotating skillet halfway through baking.

5 Using potholders, transfer skillet to wire rack and let loaf cool for 10 minutes. Being careful of hot skillet handle, remove loaf from skillet, return to rack, and let cool for at least 20 minutes before serving.

PITTING OLIVES

Place olive on cutting board and hold flat edge of knife over olive. Press blade firmly with hand to loosen olive meat from pit, then remove pit with fingers and repeat with remaining olives.

BROWN SODA BREAD

MAKES 1 LOAF

WHY THIS RECIPE WORKS For our version of hearty brown soda bread, we wanted a loaf that had good wheaty flavor, was quick to make, and featured a nicely browned crust, courtesy of our cast-iron pan. We started by finding the right ratio of whole-wheat to all-purpose flour in our bread. While we wanted the deep flavor of whole wheat, bread made with only whole-wheat flour was dense and gummy. Using almost equal amounts of whole-wheat and all-purpose flours gave us the rustic flavor we were after as well as the structure we needed. To complement the whole-wheat flour, we added toasted wheat germ, which bumped up the sweet, nutty flavor of the bread and added texture. Since our bread was still slightly dense and gummy, we turned to baking powder, an unusual ingredient in soda bread, to help lift the batter and create an airier texture. In combination with baking soda, which is a traditional soda bread ingredient, the baking powder guaranteed a loaf that was hearty but not heavy. A touch of sugar and a few tablespoons of butter added flavor without compromising the bread's wholesome roots, and brushing a portion of the melted butter on the loaf after baking gave it a rich-tasting crust.

2 cups (10 ounces) all-purpose flour
1½ cups (8¼ ounces) whole-wheat flour
½ cup toasted wheat germ
3 tablespoons sugar
1½ teaspoons salt
1 teaspoon baking powder
1 teaspoon baking soda
1¾ cups buttermilk
3 tablespoons unsalted butter, melted

1 Adjust oven rack to middle position and heat oven to 400 degrees. Grease 10-inch cast-iron skillet.

2 Whisk all-purpose flour, whole-wheat flour, wheat germ, sugar, salt, baking powder, and baking soda together in large bowl. In separate bowl, combine buttermilk and 2 tablespoons melted butter. Stir buttermilk mixture into flour mixture until dough comes together.

3 Transfer dough to lightly floured counter and knead until cohesive mass forms, about 1 minute. Pat dough into 7-inch round and transfer to prepared skillet. Using sharp serrated knife, make ¼-inch-deep cross about 5 inches long on top of loaf.

4 Transfer skillet to oven and bake until toothpick inserted into center comes out clean and internal temperature registers 195 degrees, 40 to 45 minutes, rotating skillet halfway through baking.

5 Using potholders, transfer skillet to wire rack. Brush loaf with remaining 1 tablespoon melted butter and let cool for 5 minutes. Being careful of hot skillet handle, remove loaf from skillet, return to rack, and let cool to room temperature, about 1 hour, before serving.

SLASHING SODA BREAD

After transferring loaf to prepared skillet, use sharp serrated knife to make ¼-inch-deep cross about 5 inches long on top of loaf.

ENGLISH MUFFINS

MAKES 12 MUFFINS

WHY THIS RECIPE WORKS Packaged English muffins are a fine way to start the day, but our from-scratch version is truly a breakfast treat—and easy to make. For our skillet muffins, we started with bread flour, which gave the crumb a lighter, airier texture than all-purpose. To enrich the dough, we used a combination of milk and water and added butter and honey for sweetness. Taking advantage of the great heat retention of our cast-iron skillet, we browned the muffins on both sides in the pan, then transferred them to the oven to bake through. This ensured a golden-brown exterior without any risk of burning. A sprinkle of cornmeal on the surface of the muffins helped with sticking and added an extra crunch. Pushing down on the muffins while they were in the hot skillet developed the trademark interior nooks and crannies that perfectly capture melted butter or jam.

1 cup warm whole milk (110 degrees)
⅓ cup warm water (110 degrees)
3 tablespoons unsalted butter, melted
3 tablespoons honey
2¼ teaspoons instant or rapid-rise yeast
3½ cups (19¼ ounces) bread flour, plus extra as needed
2 teaspoons salt
¾ cup (3¾ ounces) cornmeal

1 Whisk milk, water, melted butter, honey, and yeast together in 2-cup liquid measuring cup until yeast dissolves. Whisk flour and salt together in bowl of stand mixer. Using dough hook with mixer on low speed, slowly add milk mixture and mix until dough comes together, about 2 minutes. Increase speed to medium and continue to mix until dough is smooth and elastic, about 8 minutes. (If after 4 minutes dough is still very sticky, add 1 to 2 tablespoons extra flour; dough should clear sides of bowl but stick to bottom.)

2 Transfer dough to lightly floured counter and knead by hand to form smooth, round ball, about 1 minute. Place dough in large, lightly greased bowl, cover tightly with greased plastic wrap, and let rise until doubled in size, 1 to 1½ hours.

3 Sprinkle ½ cup cornmeal in rimmed baking sheet. Transfer dough to clean counter and shape into 12-inch log. Divide log into 12 equal pieces and cover with greased plastic. Working with 1 piece of dough at a time (keep other pieces covered), round dough into smooth, taut balls. Arrange dough balls on prepared sheet, spaced about 1½ inches apart. Cover dough balls with plastic and let rise until nearly doubled in size, 45 to 75 minutes.

4 Adjust oven rack to lower-middle position and heat oven to 350 degrees. Line second rimmed baking sheet with parchment paper. Using greased metal spatula, press dough balls into flat, ¾-inch-thick rounds (about 3 inches in diameter). Dust tops of muffins with remaining ¼ cup cornmeal.

5 Heat 12-inch cast-iron skillet over medium heat for 3 minutes. Place 4 muffins in skillet and cook until deep golden brown on first side, 1 to 3 minutes, occasionally pressing down on muffins with spatula to prevent doming.

6 Flip muffins, reduce heat to medium-low, and continue to cook until well browned on second side, 1 to 2 minutes. Transfer muffins to parchment paper–lined baking sheet. Repeat with remaining muffins in 2 batches, wiping skillet clean before each batch; transfer to sheet.

7 Bake until muffins are fully set and register 210 degrees, 15 to 20 minutes. Transfer muffins to wire rack and let cool for 20 minutes before splitting with fork and toasting. Serve. (Cooled, unsplit English muffins can be stored in zipper-lock bag for up to 2 days.)

PULL-APART GARLIC ROLLS

MAKES 12 ROLLS

WHY THIS RECIPE WORKS For a flavorful take on basic dinner rolls, we wanted to develop a version with a rich, buttery, garlicky profile. Our inspiration came from garlic knots, a popular pizzeria treat, but we were looking for something that would be more at home on a Sunday dinner table. To that end, we started with a tried-and-true pizza dough recipe but tweaked the ingredients slightly and changed the mixing method for a fluffier, chewier result. We ran some tests to figure out how to get just the right balance of powerful bite and mellow sweetness in the bread's garlic flavor. Garlic powder tasted musty, and fresh garlic either burned or stayed raw. Our solution was to use minced garlic sautéed in a little butter. Adding a small amount of water allowed the garlic to brown before the butter burned. We then strained the garlic butter and incorporated the solids back into the dough for an extra punch of flavor. Brushing the rolls with the garlic butter before and after baking reinforced the flavor even more. Baking the rolls in our cast-iron skillet ensured a chewy, browned crust and soft, fluffy interiors.

10 garlic cloves, minced

6 tablespoons unsalted butter, cut into 6 pieces

1 teaspoon plus ¾ cup warm water (110 degrees)

1⅛ teaspoons instant or rapid-rise yeast

2 cups (10 ounces) all-purpose flour,
plus extra as needed

1 teaspoon salt

1 Cook garlic, 1 tablespoon butter, and 1 teaspoon water in 12-inch cast-iron skillet over medium heat, stirring occasionally, until garlic is straw colored, about 2 minutes. Add remaining 5 tablespoons butter, swirling to incorporate. Remove from heat and let mixture sit for 10 minutes. Strain garlic butter through fine-mesh strainer into small bowl, reserving solids; do not clean skillet.

2 Whisk remaining ¾ cup water, yeast, 1 tablespoon garlic butter, and reserved garlic solids together in liquid measuring cup until yeast dissolves. Whisk flour and salt together in bowl of stand mixer. Using dough hook with mixer on low speed, slowly add water mixture and mix until dough comes together, about 2 minutes. Increase speed to medium and continue to mix until dough is smooth and elastic, about 8 minutes. (If after

4 minutes dough is still very sticky, add 1 to 2 tablespoons extra flour; dough should clear sides of bowl but stick to bottom.)

3 Transfer dough to lightly floured counter and knead by hand to form smooth, round ball, about 1 minute. Place dough in large, lightly greased bowl, cover tightly with greased plastic wrap, and let rise until doubled in size, about 1 hour.

4 Transfer dough to lightly floured counter and shape into 12-inch log. Divide log into 12 equal pieces and cover with greased plastic. Working with 1 piece of dough at a time (keep other pieces covered), round dough into smooth, taut balls and arrange in now-empty skillet. Cover rolls loosely with greased plastic and let rise until nearly doubled in size, about 1 hour.

5 Adjust oven rack to middle position and heat oven to 500 degrees. Brush tops of rolls with half of garlic butter, transfer skillet to oven, and bake until rolls are golden brown, about 12 minutes, rotating skillet halfway through baking.

6 Using potholders, transfer skillet to wire rack. Being careful of hot skillet handle, brush rolls with remaining garlic butter and let cool for at least 5 minutes before serving.

ROSEMARY FOCACCIA

MAKES 1 LOAF

WHY THIS RECIPE WORKS Good focaccia should have soft, chewy insides and a crisp exterior. Instead of using a starter "sponge" made of flour, water, and yeast that has been fermented overnight, which is a common but time-intensive way to build flavor and texture, we added more yeast than usual and used high-protein bread flour to give our bread more chew. This saved us from the overnight rest usually needed for a sponge. Letting the dough rise three times before pushing it into the skillet developed enough gluten to create the signature airy holes in the focaccia. Greasing the skillet with oil created a perfect, slightly fried crust when the cast iron heated up in the oven. We started the oven at 500 degrees and then lowered the temperature to 450 when the bread went in, which improved the texture of the loaf, allowing it to rise even more during baking.

1 cup plus 2 tablespoons warm water (110 degrees)

5 tablespoons extra-virgin olive oil

1⅛ teaspoons instant or rapid-rise yeast

2 cups (11 ounces) plus 2 tablespoons bread flour, plus extra as needed

1 tablespoon kosher salt

1 tablespoon minced fresh rosemary

1 Whisk water, 2 tablespoons oil, and yeast together in liquid measuring cup until yeast dissolves. Whisk flour and 2 teaspoons salt together in bowl of stand mixer. Using dough hook with mixer on low speed, slowly add water mixture and mix until dough comes together, about 2 minutes. Increase speed to medium and continue to mix until dough is smooth and elastic, about 8 minutes. (If after 4 minutes dough is still very sticky, add 1 to 2 tablespoons extra flour; dough should clear sides of bowl but stick to bottom.) Transfer dough to lightly greased bowl, cover tightly with greased plastic wrap, and let rise for 30 minutes.

2 Gently press center of dough to deflate. Using greased bowl scraper (or rubber spatula), fold partially risen dough over itself by gently lifting and folding edge of dough toward middle. Turn bowl 90 degrees and fold dough again; repeat turning bowl and folding dough 1 more time. Cover with plastic and let rise for 30 minutes.

3 Grease 12-inch cast-iron skillet with 2 tablespoons oil. Transfer dough to prepared skillet, top side down, sliding dough around skillet to coat with oil. Cover with plastic and let rise for 30 minutes.

4 Adjust oven rack to middle position and heat oven to 500 degrees. Using fingertips, press dough out toward edges of skillet. Using fork, poke entire surface of dough 25 to 30 times. Drizzle with remaining 1 tablespoon oil and sprinkle with rosemary and remaining 1 teaspoon salt. Let dough rest for 10 minutes.

5 Transfer skillet to oven and reduce oven temperature to 450 degrees. Bake until top of loaf is golden brown, 23 to 26 minutes, rotating skillet halfway through baking.

6 Using potholders, transfer skillet to wire rack and let loaf cool for 10 minutes. Being careful of hot skillet handle, remove loaf from skillet, return to rack, and let cool for at least 20 minutes before serving.

TURNING DOUGH

Slide bowl scraper or spatula under 1 side of dough. Gently lift and fold about one-third of dough toward center. Turn bowl 90 degrees and fold dough again; repeat 1 more time.

RUSTIC ITALIAN LOAF

MAKES 1 LOAF

WHY THIS RECIPE WORKS You might assume that you have to make a special trip to a bakery for good Italian bread, or else settle for the pale, doughy loaves at the average supermarket, but making your own from scratch isn't as hard as you think. For a rustic Italian loaf with a chewy but tender crumb that was crusty without being tough, we used bread flour, which gave our bread voluminous height and a thick crust. We wanted to shorten the rising time for the bread, but that meant we were cutting out a step that usually provides a lot of flavor. To make up for this, we added a shot of yeasty tang by using a 5-to-1 ratio of beer to water as the liquid in our dough. Our cast-iron skillet played the role of a baking stone, giving us a nicely browned and even crust, and it also helped shape the loaf. Once the dough rose in a bowl for an hour, we transferred it to the skillet and let it rise again, which gave the loaf a nice round, even shape. Last, to ensure a good rise and a nice crust, we added water to the oven during baking to create steam, an element that helped the bread stay supple and encouraged a light, tender crumb. We prefer to use a mild American lager, such as Budweiser, here; strongly flavored beers will make this bread bitter.

1¼ cups mild lager, such as Budweiser

¼ cup water

2 tablespoons extra-virgin olive oil

2¼ teaspoons instant or rapid-rise yeast

3 cups (16½ ounces) bread flour, plus extra as needed

2 teaspoons salt

1 Microwave beer, water, and oil in 2-cup liquid measuring cup, stirring occasionally, until mixture registers 110 degrees, about 1 minute. Whisk in yeast until dissolved.

2 Whisk flour and salt together in bowl of stand mixer. Using dough hook with mixer on low speed, slowly add beer mixture and mix until dough comes together, about 2 minutes. Increase speed to medium and continue to mix until dough is smooth and elastic, about 10 minutes. (If after 5 minutes dough is still very sticky, add 1 to 2 tablespoons extra flour; dough should clear sides of bowl but stick to bottom.)

3 Transfer dough to lightly floured counter and knead by hand to form smooth, round ball, about 1 minute. Place dough in large, lightly greased bowl, cover tightly with greased plastic wrap, and let rise until doubled in size, about 1 hour.

4 Transfer dough to lightly floured counter and loosely reshape into ball. Cup hands slightly around dough and drag it over the counter in circular motion, forming dough into round loaf with smooth, taut surface. Pinch bottom seam closed and transfer loaf seam side down to 10-inch cast-iron skillet. Cover loosely with greased plastic and let rise until dough has doubled in size, about 1 hour.

5 Adjust oven rack to lower-middle position, place empty loaf pan (or other ovensafe pan) on rack, and heat oven to 450 degrees. Bring 2 cups water to boil.

6 Sprinkle flour lightly over top of loaf. Using sharp serrated knife, make ½-inch-deep cross about 5 inches long on top of loaf. Working quickly, carefully pour boiling water into hot loaf pan, then transfer skillet to oven. Bake until crust is deep golden brown and internal temperature registers 210 degrees, about 45 minutes, rotating skillet halfway through baking.

7 Using potholders, transfer skillet to wire rack and let loaf cool for 10 minutes. Being careful of hot skillet handle, remove loaf from skillet, return to rack, and let cool to room temperature, about 2 hours, before serving.

CINNAMON SWIRL BREAD

MAKES 1 LOAF

WHY THIS RECIPE WORKS For a bread that was reminiscent of cinnamon buns but more elegant in presentation, we started with a slightly sweet base that was rich enough to stand up to a hearty filling. Getting the filling to stay put and not ooze out of the loaf required a special braiding technique that produced a beautiful loaf with deep golden swirls of cinnamon in every bite.

1 cup warm whole milk (110 degrees)

8 tablespoons unsalted butter, melted

¼ cup (1¾ ounces) granulated sugar

2 tablespoons warm tap water

2¼ teaspoons instant or rapid-rise yeast

3¼ cups (16¼ ounces) all-purpose flour, plus extra as needed

2 teaspoons salt

2 teaspoons ground cinnamon

½ cup packed (3½ ounces) light brown sugar

1 large egg, lightly beaten

1 Whisk milk, 6 tablespoons melted butter, granulated sugar, water, and yeast together in 2-cup liquid measuring cup until yeast dissolves. Whisk flour, salt, and 1 teaspoon cinnamon together in bowl of stand mixer. Using dough hook with mixer on low speed, slowly add milk mixture and mix until dough comes together, about 2 minutes. Increase speed to medium and continue to mix until dough is smooth and elastic, about 10 minutes. (If after 5 minutes dough is still very sticky, add 1 to 2 tablespoons extra flour; dough should clear sides of bowl but stick to bottom.)

2 Transfer dough to lightly floured counter and knead by hand to form smooth, round ball, about 1 minute. Place dough in large, lightly greased bowl, cover tightly with greased plastic wrap, and let rise until doubled in size, about 1 hour.

3 Combine brown sugar and remaining 1 teaspoon cinnamon in bowl. Transfer dough to lightly floured counter and roll into 16 by 12-inch rectangle with long side facing you. Brush remaining 2 tablespoons melted butter over dough, leaving ½-inch border at edges. Sprinkle cinnamon-sugar mixture over butter, leaving

¾-inch border at top edge, and press lightly to adhere. Roll dough away from you into firm cylinder, keeping roll taut by tucking it under itself as you go. Pinch seam and ends closed. If necessary, gently reshape log to be 16 inches in length with even diameter.

4 Grease 10-inch cast-iron skillet. With short side of dough log facing you, cut log in half lengthwise, using bench scraper. Turn dough halves cut sides up and arrange side by side. Pinch top ends together. Lift and place 1 dough half on opposite side of second half. Repeat, keeping cut sides up, until dough halves are tightly braided. Pinch remaining ends together. Twist braided dough into spiral and tuck end underneath. Transfer loaf to prepared skillet, cover with greased plastic, and let rise until doubled in size, 45 to 60 minutes.

5 Adjust oven rack to lower-middle position and heat oven to 325 degrees. Brush loaf with beaten egg, transfer skillet to oven, and bake until loaf is deep golden brown and filling is melted, 45 to 55 minutes, rotating skillet halfway through baking.

6 Using potholders, transfer skillet to wire rack and let loaf cool for 10 minutes. Being careful of hot skillet handle, remove loaf from skillet, return to rack, and let cool to room temperature, about 2 hours, before serving.

BRAIDING CINNAMON SWIRL BREAD

After pinching top ends of dough halves together, lift and place 1 dough half on opposite side of second half. Repeat, keeping cut sides up, until dough halves are tightly braided.

CORN TORTILLAS

MAKES TWELVE 6-INCH TORTILLAS

WHY THIS RECIPE WORKS Once you've tried homemade corn tortillas, you'll never want to buy the grocery store kind again. Fresh corn tortillas have a lightly sweet flavor and a soft, springy texture. Surprisingly, making tortillas is far easier than most people realize. Most of the recipes we researched were similar—masa harina and water are kneaded together to form a dough, then pressed into thin tortillas (either by hand or with a tortilla press) and toasted in a hot, dry pan (a well-seasoned cast-iron skillet is the perfect tool for the job). We tested a few variables, including whether to add salt (yes) and how long to rest the dough before pressing the tortillas (5 minutes so the masa is fully hydrated). Although you can press the dough into tortillas by hand or with a pie plate, we found it difficult to get the tortillas uniformly thin without lots of practice, so we prefer to use a tortilla press. The dough was still a little finicky to work with, but the addition of vegetable oil (a nontraditional ingredient) made it much easier to handle. The oil also gave the cooked tortillas a softer texture that our tasters liked. When the tortillas puff in the cast-iron skillet after flipping, you know that you've done it right: that's a sign that distinct layers are forming, and the finished product will be soft and tender. For efficiency, press the next ball of dough while each tortilla is cooking.

2 cups (8 ounces) masa harina
1 teaspoon vegetable oil
¼ teaspoon salt
1¼ cups warm tap water, plus extra as needed

1 Mix masa harina, oil, and salt together in medium bowl, then fold in water with rubber spatula. Using your hands, knead mixture in bowl, adding extra water 1 tablespoon at a time as needed, until dough is soft and tacky but not sticky and has texture of Play-Doh. Cover dough with damp dish towel and let sit for 5 minutes.

2 Cut sides of 1-quart zipper-lock bag, leaving bottom seam intact. Line large plate with 2 damp dish towels. Divide dough into 12 equal pieces (1½ ounces each); keep covered. Working with 1 piece of dough at a time, roll into ball, place on 1 side of zipper-lock bag, and fold other side over top. Press dough flat into 6½-inch-wide tortilla(about ¹⁄₁₆ inch thick) using tortilla press or pie plate; leave tortilla in plastic until skillet is hot.

3 Heat 10-inch cast-iron skillet over medium heat for 5 minutes. Remove plastic on top of tortilla, flip tortilla into your palm, then remove plastic on bottom and lay tortilla in skillet. Cook tortilla, without moving it, until it moves freely when skillet is shaken and has shrunk slightly in size, about 45 seconds.

4 Flip tortilla over and cook until edges curl and bottom is spotty brown, about 1 minute. Flip tortilla back over and continue to cook until first side is spotty brown and puffs up slightly in center, 30 to 60 seconds. Lay toasted tortilla between damp dish towels. Repeat with remaining dough. Serve. (Cooled tortillas can be layered between sheets of clean parchment paper, wrapped in plastic wrap, and refrigerated for up to 5 days.)

PRESSING CORN TORTILLAS

Place ball in center of split-open zipper-lock bag. Using tortilla press or pie plate, press ball gently and evenly into 6½-inch tortilla.

FLOUR TORTILLAS

MAKES TWELVE 8-INCH TORTILLAS

WHY THIS RECIPE WORKS Supple and flavorful, homemade flour tortillas far surpass store-bought versions. Although we tried using a tortilla press to make even disks, a rolling pin worked better with this elastic dough. While testing recipes for our flour tortillas, we learned that too little fat produced brittle results, too little salt yielded tasteless ones, and baking powder made them doughy and thick. Adding warm water to the dough melted the shortening, which then coated the flour and prevented it from absorbing excess moisture. This resulted in less gluten development and yielded more tender tortillas. A brief rest in the refrigerator firmed up the shortening again so that the dough wasn't too sticky to roll. One minute per side in a preheated cast-iron skillet was all the tortillas needed before they were ready to eat. For ten 10-inch tortillas, double the recipe, divide the dough evenly into 10 pieces, and roll each into a 10-inch round; cook as directed.

2¾ cups (13¾ ounces) all-purpose flour

1½ teaspoons salt

6 tablespoons vegetable shortening, cut into 6 pieces

¾ cup plus 2 tablespoons warm tap water

1 Combine flour and salt in large bowl. Using your hands, rub shortening into flour until mixture resembles coarse meal. Stir in water with wooden spoon until incorporated and dough comes together. Turn dough out onto counter and knead briefly to form smooth, cohesive ball. Divide dough into 12 pieces (1½ ounces each), roll into balls, and transfer to plate. Cover with plastic wrap and refrigerate until dough is firm, at least 30 minutes or up to 3 days.

2 Working with 1 piece of dough at a time, roll dough into 8-inch tortilla between two 12-inch squares of greased parchment paper. Remove top piece of parchment and gently reshape edges of tortilla as needed.

3 Heat 12-inch cast-iron skillet over medium heat for 3 minutes. Flip tortilla onto your palm, then remove parchment on bottom and lay tortilla in skillet. Reduce heat to medium-low and cook until surface of tortilla begins to bubble and it moves freely when skillet is shaken, about 1 minute.

4 Flip tortilla over and cook until puffed and bottom is spotty brown, about 1 minute. Transfer to plate and cover with dish towel. Repeat with remaining dough. Serve. (Cooled tortillas can be layered between sheets of clean parchment paper, wrapped in plastic, and refrigerated for up to 3 days.)

SHAPING FLOUR TORTILLAS

1 Divide dough into 12 pieces. Roll pieces into balls, cover with plastic, and refrigerate until dough is firm.

2 Using rolling pin, roll dough balls between sheets of greased parchment into 8-inch tortillas.

GRIDDLED FLATBREADS

MAKES FOUR 9-INCH FLATBREADS

WHY THIS RECIPE WORKS We set out to make flavorful, rustic flatbreads that were tender yet chewy, and easy enough to make while a curry or stew was cooking for dinner. We knew we wanted hearty wheat flavor along with great texture, so we added a small amount of whole-wheat flour to high-protein bread flour for the perfect balance between wheatiness and chew. We enriched the dough with oil and yogurt. To keep the rising short and simple, we used a generous amount of yeast so the dough required only short rests between periods of kneading. A hot cast-iron pan mimicked the tandoor or brick oven often used to bake similar breads around the world; its great heat retention helped create the signature spotty brown flecks covering these breads. For efficiency, stretch the next ball of dough while each bread is cooking.

---

1 cup warm water (110 degrees), plus extra as needed
¼ cup plain yogurt
2 tablespoons extra-virgin olive oil
2¼ teaspoons instant or rapid-rise yeast
2 teaspoons sugar
2½ cups (13¾ ounces) bread flour, plus extra as needed
¼ cup (1⅓ ounces) whole-wheat flour
1½ teaspoons salt
1½ tablespoons unsalted butter, melted
   Coarse sea salt

1 Whisk water, yogurt, 1 tablespoon oil, yeast, and sugar together in 2-cup liquid measuring cup until yeast dissolves. Whisk bread flour, whole-wheat flour, and salt together in bowl of stand mixer. Using dough hook with mixer on low speed, slowly add water mixture and mix until dough comes together, about 2 minutes. Increase speed to medium and continue to mix until dough is smooth and elastic, about 8 minutes. (If after 4 minutes dough is still very sticky, add 1 to 2 tablespoons extra flour; dough should clear sides of bowl but stick to bottom.)

2 Transfer dough to lightly floured counter and knead by hand to form smooth, round ball, about 1 minute. Place dough in large, lightly greased bowl, cover tightly with greased plastic wrap, and let rise until doubled in size, 1 to 1½ hours.

3 Adjust oven rack to middle position and heat oven to 200 degrees. Transfer dough to lightly floured counter, divide into 4 pieces, and cover with greased plastic. Working with 1 piece of dough at a time (keep other pieces covered), round dough into smooth, taut balls. Let balls rest, covered, for 10 minutes.

4 Grease 12-inch cast-iron skillet with remaining 1 tablespoon oil and heat over medium heat for 5 minutes. Meanwhile, press and roll 1 dough ball into 9-inch round of even thickness, sprinkling dough and counter with flour as needed to prevent sticking. Using fork, poke entire surface of round 20 to 25 times.

5 Using paper towels, carefully wipe out oil in skillet, leaving thin film on bottom and sides. Mist top of dough lightly with water. Place dough in skillet, moistened side down, then mist top surface of dough with water. Cover and cook until bottom of bread is browned in spots across surface, 2 to 4 minutes. Flip bread, cover, and continue to cook until lightly browned on second side, 2 to 3 minutes. (If bread puffs up, gently poke with fork to deflate.)

6 Brush 1 side of bread with about 1 teaspoon melted butter and sprinkle with sea salt. Serve immediately or transfer to ovensafe plate, cover loosely with aluminum foil, and keep warm in oven. Repeat with remaining 3 dough balls, melted butter, and sea salt. Serve.

DESSERTS

Blueberry Pie

SKILLET-ROASTED PEARS WITH CARAMEL SAUCE

SERVES 2 TO 4

WHY THIS RECIPE WORKS Pears tend to take a back seat in the dessert world, frequently getting passed over in favor of colorful berries or reliable apples. However, when given the proper treatment, these sweet, juicy fruits have a unique texture and flavor all their own. Paired with the power of a cast-iron skillet, pears become the base for a simple yet elegant dessert. Bartlett and Bosc varieties were the clear winners for our recipe as both became sweeter when cooked and retained their texture instead of becoming mushy. We started by roasting the pears in boiling sugar and water until they softened and became golden, which developed a complex sweetness in the fruit and also created the base for an accompanying caramel sauce, turning this rich dessert into a simple one-skillet dish. We cut out the need for an intimidating candy thermometer by relying on visual cues to tell us when the caramel was ready and the pears were properly cooked. To finish the sauce, we added heavy cream to the skillet toward the end of cooking and gently shook the pan to help give the sauce a rich, glossy consistency. For the best texture, try to buy pears that are neither fully ripe nor rock hard; choose fruit that yields slightly when pressed.

⅓ cup water

⅔ cup sugar

2 ripe but firm Bartlett or Bosc pears (8 ounces each), peeled, halved, and cored

⅔ cup heavy cream

Salt

1 Add water to 12-inch cast-iron skillet, then pour sugar into center of skillet (don't let it hit skillet's sides). Gently stir sugar with clean spatula to moisten it thoroughly. Bring to boil over medium heat and cook, stirring occasionally, until sugar is completely dissolved and liquid is bubbling, about 2 minutes.

2 Add pears to skillet cut side down, cover, and cook until almost tender (a fork inserted into center of pears meets slight resistance), 10 to 15 minutes, reducing heat as needed to prevent caramel from getting too dark.

3 Uncover, reduce heat to medium-low, and continue to cook until sauce is golden brown and cut sides of pears are beginning to brown, about 3 minutes. Pour cream around pears and cook, shaking skillet occasionally, until sauce is smooth and deep caramel color and cut sides of pears are golden brown, 3 to 5 minutes.

4 Transfer pears cut side up to serving platter and season sauce with salt to taste. Spoon sauce over pears. Serve.

CORING PEARS

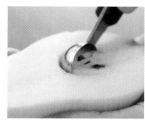

1 Halve pear from stem to blossom end, then remove core using melon baller.

2 Use edge of melon baller to scrape away interior stem of pear from core to stem.

GLAZED PEACHES WITH PISTACHIOS

SERVES 6

WHY THIS RECIPE WORKS It's hard to improve upon a perfectly ripe peach, but with the help of our cast-iron skillet we aimed to enhance the fruit's natural sweetness and create a fresh, light dessert. Many recipes for glazed peaches do nothing but drown the star of the show in cloyingly sweet syrup, when what you really want is to emphasize the fruit's flavor. We started by cooking peach halves cut side down in water, lemon juice, sugar, and salt in a covered skillet to tenderize the fruit. Next we uncovered the skillet to let the excess water evaporate so the sugar would start browning the peaches. Red currant jelly and a little butter added toward the end of cooking created a lightly sweet, syrupy glaze that perfectly complemented the peaches without overwhelming them. A sprinkling of toasted pistachios on top added a flavorful crunch. We kept all the cooking in one skillet on the stovetop, which made this dessert quick and easy, with no need to heat up the oven or broiler. Occasionally shaking the skillet to shift the peaches while cooking helped prevent them from sticking to the bottom of the pan. For the best texture, try to buy peaches that are neither fully ripe nor rock hard; choose fruit that yields slightly when pressed. A serrated peeler makes easy work of peeling the peaches. Serve with vanilla ice cream.

⅓ cup water

2 tablespoons lemon juice

1½ tablespoons sugar

¼ teaspoon salt

6 ripe but firm peaches, peeled, halved, and pitted

¼ cup red currant jelly

1 tablespoon unsalted butter, cut into 4 pieces

¼ cup shelled pistachios, toasted and chopped coarse

1 Bring water, lemon juice, sugar, and salt to boil in 12-inch cast-iron skillet over medium heat. Add peaches to skillet cut side down, cover, and cook until almost tender (a fork inserted into center of peach meets slight resistance), 3 to 5 minutes.

2 Uncover and continue to cook until liquid is nearly evaporated and cut sides of peaches are beginning to brown, 5 to 8 minutes. Add jelly and butter and cook, shaking skillet occasionally, until glaze is thickened, about 1 minute.

3 Transfer peaches cut side up to serving platter. Spoon glaze over peaches and sprinkle with pistachios. Serve.

VARIATIONS

Raspberry-Glazed Peaches with Walnuts
Substitute ¼ cup raspberry jelly for red currant jelly and ¼ cup toasted and coarsely chopped walnuts for pistachios.

Honey-Glazed Peaches with Hazelnuts
Substitute ¼ cup honey for red currant jelly and ¼ cup toasted, skinned, and coarsely chopped hazelnuts for pistachios.

BANANAS FOSTER

SERVES 4

WHY THIS RECIPE WORKS Although the classic New Orleans dessert bananas Foster is quick and simple, with just a few ingredients (butter, brown sugar, rum, and bananas), things can easily go wrong in the execution. The bananas are frequently overcooked and mushy, and the sauce can be too thin, or overly sweet, or taste too strongly of alcohol. We wanted to develop a foolproof way to make a quick, reliable version of this dessert with tender bananas and a flavorful but not boozy sauce. First, we kept the amounts of butter and brown sugar in check—most recipes use a high ratio of butter to brown sugar, which makes for a thin, greasy sauce. For the rum, we found that a small amount was enough to impart recognizable rum flavor without turning the dessert into a cocktail. We also enhanced the sauce with a little cinnamon and lemon juice, which added some complexity. We made the sauce in our skillet and then cooked the bananas in the sauce until soft, flipping them over halfway through cooking so they turned out tender, not mushy. Traditionally, bananas Foster is flambéed to burn off the raw alcohol flavor and create a rounder, better-tasting dish. But our version of bananas Foster struck the perfect balance of sweetness from the brown sugar, rich depth of flavor from golden rum, toasted notes from one cinnamon stick, and a splash of acidity from lemon juice for a sophisticated dish that made fussy flambéing entirely unnecessary. Look for yellow bananas or those with very few spots; overly ripe bananas will fall apart during cooking. We prefer the flavor of golden rum, but you can substitute white rum if desired.

½ cup packed dark brown sugar

¼ cup plus 2 teaspoons golden rum

2 tablespoons water

1 cinnamon stick

¼ teaspoon salt

3 ripe bananas, peeled, halved crosswise, then halved lengthwise

1 pint vanilla ice cream

4 tablespoons unsalted butter, cut into 4 pieces

1 teaspoon lemon juice

1 Bring sugar, ¼ cup rum, water, cinnamon stick, and salt to simmer in 12-inch cast-iron skillet over medium heat. Cook, whisking frequently, until sugar is completely dissolved, about 2 minutes.

2 Add bananas to skillet cut side down and cook until sauce is glossy and cut sides of bananas are golden brown, 2 to 4 minutes. Flip bananas and continue to cook until soft but not mushy, 2 to 3 minutes. Using tongs, transfer bananas to 4 bowls and top with ice cream.

3 Off heat, discard cinnamon stick. Whisk butter into sauce, 1 piece at a time, until incorporated. Whisk in lemon juice and remaining 2 teaspoons rum. Spoon sauce over bananas and ice cream. Serve.

NECTARINE AND RASPBERRY CRISP

SERVES 6 TO 8

WHY THIS RECIPE WORKS Making a crisp is a perfect, simple way to serve seasonal fruit for dessert. We wanted a version of this classic dish that paired tender nectarines and bright raspberries with a crunchy, sweet topping. Unfortunately, our early tests fell victim to classic fruit crisp shortcomings: They either had thick, sticky fillings or the juicy fruits boiled over the topping, making it soggy and messy. After testing various oven-baking methods, we found that the best technique was actually the easiest one: We used our cast-iron skillet to brown a topping of almonds, sugar, flour, and butter on the stovetop, and then used the same skillet to cook down the filling before combining the two elements for a perfect crisp. To balance the liquid released by the nectarines, we added cornstarch to the fruit filling as a thickener along with sugar, lemon juice, cinnamon, and nutmeg for flavor. Making our topping more like a streusel helped keep it from sinking into the filling. Almonds added to the mix provided deep flavor and extra crispness. You can substitute peaches for the nectarines. A serrated peeler makes easy work of peeling the nectarines. Serve with vanilla ice cream.

TOPPING

¾ cup sliced almonds, toasted

⅔ cup (3⅓ ounces) all-purpose flour

½ cup packed (3½ ounces) light brown sugar

½ teaspoon vanilla extract

¼ teaspoon ground cinnamon

¼ teaspoon salt

6 tablespoons unsalted butter, melted

FILLING

⅓ cup sugar

2 teaspoons cornstarch

3 pounds nectarines, peeled, halved, pitted, and cut into ¾-inch wedges

1 tablespoon lemon juice

Pinch ground cinnamon

Pinch ground nutmeg

10 ounces (2 cups) raspberries

1 FOR THE TOPPING Finely chop ¼ cup almonds. Combine flour, sugar, vanilla, cinnamon, salt, chopped almonds, and remaining sliced almonds in medium bowl. Stir in melted butter until no dry flour remains. Cook almond-flour mixture in 10-inch cast-iron skillet over medium heat, stirring constantly, until lightly browned and fragrant, 8 to 10 minutes. Transfer mixture to large plate and let cool while making filling.

2 FOR THE FILLING Wipe skillet clean with paper towels. Whisk sugar and cornstarch together in large bowl. Add nectarines, lemon juice, cinnamon, and nutmeg and toss gently to combine. Transfer nectarine mixture to now-empty skillet, cover, and cook over medium heat until nectarines are just tender and have released their juice, about 10 minutes.

3 Uncover and continue to cook, stirring occasionally, until nectarines are softened and sauce thickens slightly, 5 to 7 minutes. Stir in raspberries and cook until heated through, about 1 minute. Off heat, sprinkle topping evenly over fruit, breaking up any large chunks. Serve.

CHERRY COBBLER

SERVES 6 TO 8

WHY THIS RECIPE WORKS For an easy, rustic dessert, you really can't beat a cobbler. With a fleet of tender biscuits floating on a sea of sweet fruit, a good cobbler can hold its own against any fancy cake or pastry. For our cast-iron skillet cherry cobbler we looked to jarred, pitted cherries in syrup to deliver maximum cherry flavor with the least amount of prep work. We used a portion of the syrup, thickened with cornstarch and seasoned with allspice, nutmeg, and vanilla, to enrich our fruit filling. For the topping, we wanted fluffy but sturdy biscuits that didn't need to be baked separately from the cherries. To accomplish this, we incorporated a combination of baking powder and baking soda into the biscuit dough. Baking powder encourages baked goods to rise and is activated by heat, so we spaced our biscuits half an inch apart to give them room to grow in the oven. Baking soda, on the other hand, contributes tenderness and is activated by an acidic ingredient, so we added buttermilk, which also lent our biscuits great flavor. The cast-iron skillet went right from the stovetop to the oven for maximum convenience. We prefer the crunchy texture of turbinado sugar sprinkled on the biscuits before baking, but regular granulated sugar can be substituted. For best results, serve within 15 minutes and transfer leftovers to an airtight container.

FILLING

- 6 cups jarred sour cherries in light syrup, drained with 2 cups syrup reserved
- ½ cup granulated sugar
- 3 tablespoons cornstarch
- ½ teaspoon vanilla extract
- ¼ teaspoon ground allspice
  Pinch ground nutmeg
  Pinch salt

TOPPING

- 1½ cups (7½ ounces) all-purpose flour
- 5 tablespoons (2¼ ounces) granulated sugar
- 1½ teaspoons baking powder
- ¼ teaspoon baking soda
- ¼ teaspoon salt
- ¾ cup buttermilk
- 4 tablespoons unsalted butter, melted
- 2 tablespoons turbinado sugar

1 FOR THE FILLING Adjust oven rack to middle position and heat oven to 400 degrees. Whisk cherry syrup, sugar, cornstarch, vanilla, allspice, nutmeg, and salt together in bowl until well combined. Transfer mixture to 12-inch cast-iron skillet and bring to simmer over medium-high heat. Cook, whisking frequently, until thickened slightly, 5 to 7 minutes. Off heat, stir in cherries.

2 FOR THE TOPPING Whisk flour, granulated sugar, baking powder, baking soda, and salt together in medium bowl. Stir in buttermilk and melted butter until just combined. Using spoon, scoop out and drop 1-inch pieces of dough onto filling, spaced about ½ inch apart. Sprinkle biscuits with turbinado sugar.

3 Transfer skillet to oven and bake until biscuits are golden brown and filling is thick and glossy, 30 to 35 minutes, rotating skillet halfway through baking. Serve.

APPLE PIE

SERVES 8

WHY THIS RECIPE WORKS There is nothing quite like a perfect apple pie. However, in the average pie the fruit is unevenly cooked, and its juice turns the crust pale and soggy, making it impossible to slice the pie neatly. Luckily, a cast-iron skillet can solve all of these problems. We started by precooking the apples in the skillet, which drove off some of the extra juice while adding deep caramelized flavor. We enriched our filling with apple cider, maple syrup, lemon zest and juice, and cinnamon. The high sides of the skillet were perfect for a deep-dish pie. Greasing the skillet before lining it with dough ensured a golden-brown crust and made the pie easy to slice and serve. We like a mix of tart and sweet apples; you can also use Empires or Cortlands (tart) and Fuji, Jonagolds, or Braeburns (sweet). If using an enameled skillet, we recommend placing a baking sheet underneath while baking to catch any juices that might bubble over. You can use a double batch of our Foolproof Single-Crust Pie Dough (page 199) or store-bought pie dough in this recipe.

2 tablespoons unsalted butter

2 pounds Golden Delicious apples, peeled, cored, halved, and sliced ½ inch thick

2 pounds Granny Smith apples, peeled, cored, halved, and sliced ½ inch thick

1 recipe double-crust pie dough, top and bottom crusts rolled out into 12-inch rounds

¼ cup apple cider

¼ cup maple syrup

1 tablespoon cornstarch

½ teaspoon salt

½ teaspoon grated lemon zest plus 1 tablespoon juice

⅛ teaspoon ground cinnamon

1 large egg, lightly beaten with 2 tablespoons water

2 teaspoons sugar

1 Heat 10-inch cast-iron skillet over medium heat for 3 minutes. Melt 1 tablespoon butter in skillet. Add half of apples, cover, and cook until apples begin to release their juice, about 4 minutes. Uncover and continue to cook, stirring occasionally, until apples are tender and golden brown, about 5 minutes. Transfer apples and their juice to rimmed baking sheet. Repeat with remaining 1 tablespoon butter and remaining apples; transfer to sheet. Spread apples into even layer and let cool to room temperature, about 30 minutes.

2 Adjust oven rack to lowest position and heat oven to 400 degrees. Grease clean, dry, cooled skillet. Loosely roll 1 crust around rolling pin and gently unroll it onto prepared skillet. Ease crust into skillet by gently lifting and supporting edge of dough with your hand while pressing into skillet bottom and corners with your other hand. Leave any overhanging dough in place.

3 Whisk cider, maple syrup, cornstarch, salt, lemon zest and juice, and cinnamon together in large bowl until smooth. Add cooled apples and any accumulated juices and toss to combine. Transfer apple mixture to dough-lined skillet, mounding apples slightly in middle. Loosely roll remaining crust around rolling pin and gently unroll it onto filling.

4 Trim any overhanging dough to ½ inch beyond lip of skillet, then ease edge of top crust into skillet until flush with bottom crust. Gently press top and bottom crusts together to seal. Roll in edge of crust, then press rolled edge against sides of skillet using index finger to create attractive fluted rim. Using paring knife, cut eight 2-inch vents in top crust in circular pattern. Brush crust liberally with egg wash and sprinkle with sugar.

5 Transfer skillet to oven and bake until crust is deep golden brown and filling is bubbling, 40 to 50 minutes, rotating skillet halfway through baking. Transfer skillet to wire rack and let pie cool until filling is set, about 2 hours. Serve slightly warm or at room temperature.

BLUEBERRY PIE

SERVES 8

WHY THIS RECIPE WORKS Too often, fruit pie appears perfect on the outside while a watery filling and pale, soggy bottom crust hide inside. We wanted our blueberry pie to have a browned, tender crust and a filling full of fresh flavor and plump berries. To thicken the filling, we used tapioca plus a shredded Granny Smith apple, which contains naturally thickening pectin. This combination allowed the bright blueberry flavor to shine through. The heat retention of the cast-iron skillet was crucial in creating a crisp, flaky bottom crust that stood up to a wet fruit filling. To vent the steam from the berries, we cut out circles in the top dough. A well-greased skillet made it easy to get perfect slices out of the pan. This recipe was developed using fresh blueberries, but unthawed frozen blueberries will work. In step 1, cook half the frozen blueberries, without mashing, for 12 to 15 minutes, until reduced to 1¼ cups. Grind the tapioca to a powder in a spice grinder or a mini food processor. Use a coarse grater to shred the apple. If using an enameled skillet, we recommend placing a baking sheet underneath while baking to catch any juices that might bubble over. You can use a double batch of our Foolproof Single-Crust Pie Dough (page 199) or store-bought pie dough in this recipe.

---

30 ounces (6 cups) fresh or frozen blueberries

1 Granny Smith apple, peeled, cored, and shredded

¾ cup (5¼ ounces) sugar

2 tablespoons instant tapioca, ground

2 teaspoons grated lemon zest plus 2 teaspoons juice
Pinch salt

2 tablespoons unsalted butter, cut into ¼-inch pieces

1 recipe double-crust pie dough, top and bottom crusts rolled out into 12-inch rounds

1 large egg, lightly beaten with 2 tablespoons water

1 Adjust oven rack to lowest position and heat oven to 400 degrees. Cook 3 cups blueberries in 10-inch cast-iron skillet over medium heat, mashing occasionally with potato masher, until blueberries are broken down and mixture is thickened and measures about 1½ cups, 6 to 8 minutes; transfer to large bowl and let cool slightly.

2 Place shredded apple in clean dish towel and wring tightly to squeeze out as much liquid as possible; transfer apple to bowl with cooked blueberries. Stir in remaining 3 cups uncooked blueberries, sugar, tapioca, lemon zest and juice, and salt until combined.

3 Grease clean, dry, cooled skillet. Loosely roll 1 crust around rolling pin and gently unroll it onto prepared skillet. Ease crust into skillet by gently lifting and supporting edge of dough with your hand while pressing into skillet bottom and corners with your other hand. Leave any overhanging dough in place.

4 Transfer blueberry mixture to dough-lined skillet and scatter butter on top. Use 1¼-inch round cookie cutter to cut round from center of remaining crust. Cut 6 more rounds from crust, 1½ inches from edge of center hole and equally spaced around center hole. Loosely roll crust around rolling pin and gently unroll it onto filling.

5 Trim any overhanging dough to ½ inch beyond lip of skillet, then ease edge of top crust into skillet until flush with bottom crust. Gently press top and bottom crusts together to seal. Roll in edge of crust, then press rolled edge against sides of skillet using index finger to create attractive fluted rim. Brush crust liberally with egg wash.

6 Transfer skillet to oven and bake until crust is golden brown, about 25 minutes. Reduce oven temperature to 350 degrees, rotate skillet, and continue to bake until crust is deep golden brown and filling is bubbling, 25 to 35 minutes. Transfer skillet to wire rack and let pie cool to room temperature, about 4 hours. Serve.

RUSTIC SUMMER FRUIT TART

SERVES 4 TO 6

WHY THIS RECIPE WORKS Free-form summer fruit tarts are a great way to highlight the best fruit of the season, but ultraripe fruits create the danger of mushy crust and overflowing, sticky messes in the oven. We looked to our cast-iron skillet to solve both of those problems. The skillet captured the fruit juices when they inevitably bubbled up and transformed them into an irresistible caramel-like glaze. The cast iron also did away with the soggy bottom crust by acting like a pizza stone, absorbing heat and creating a crisp crust before the fruit juices had a chance to make it sodden. For the fruit, we kept things simple by tossing a mix of berries and stone fruit with a few tablespoons of sugar for a quick, easy alternative to a more structured pie. Be sure to taste the fruit before adding sugar; use less sugar if the fruit is very sweet, more if it is tart. Do not add the sugar to the fruit until you are ready to fill and form the tart.

1½ cups (7½ ounces) all-purpose flour
½ teaspoon salt
10 tablespoons unsalted butter,
    cut into ½-inch pieces and chilled
4–6 tablespoons ice water
1 pound apricots, nectarines, peaches, or plums,
    halved, pitted, and cut into ½-inch wedges
5 ounces (1 cup) blackberries, blueberries,
    or raspberries
3–5 tablespoons sugar

1 Process flour and salt in food processor until combined, about 5 seconds. Scatter butter over top and pulse until mixture resembles coarse sand and butter pieces are size of small peas, about 10 pulses. Continue to pulse, adding water 1 tablespoon at a time, until dough begins to form small curds that hold together when pinched with fingers, about 10 pulses.

2 Turn mixture onto lightly floured counter and gather into rectangular pile. Starting at farthest end, use heel of hand to smear small amount of dough against counter. Continue to smear dough until all crumbs have been worked. Gather smeared crumbs together in another rectangular pile and repeat process.

3 Press dough into 6-inch disk, wrap tightly in plastic wrap, and refrigerate for 1 hour. Before rolling dough out, let it sit on counter to soften slightly, about

10 minutes. (Dough can be refrigerated for up to 2 days.)

4 Adjust oven rack to middle position and heat oven to 375 degrees. Grease 10-inch cast-iron skillet. Roll dough into 12-inch round between 2 large sheets of parchment paper. Remove top piece of parchment, loosely roll dough around rolling pin, and gently unroll it onto prepared skillet. Ease dough into skillet by gently lifting and supporting edge of dough with your hand while pressing into skillet bottom and corners with your other hand. Leave any overhanging dough in place.

5 Gently toss apricots, blackberries, and 3 tablespoons sugar together in bowl. Transfer fruit to dough-lined skillet, mounding fruit slightly in middle. Fold in sides of dough over fruit, pleating every 2 to 3 inches as needed; gently pinch pleated dough to secure, but do not press dough into fruit.

6 Brush dough with water and sprinkle evenly with remaining 1 tablespoon sugar. Bake until crust is deep golden brown and juices are bubbling, about 1 hour, rotating skillet halfway through baking.

7 Using potholders, transfer skillet to wire rack and let cool for 10 minutes. Being careful of hot skillet handle, gently slide tart onto rack using spatula and let cool until juices have thickened, about 25 minutes. Serve slightly warm or at room temperature.

APPLE FRITTERS

MAKES 10 FRITTERS

WHY THIS RECIPE WORKS Apple fritters should be crisp on the outside and moist within, and their primary flavor should be pure apple. In order to achieve these goals, we had to overcome the problems caused by the amount of liquid in the fruit. We found that the best solution was to dry the apples with paper towels before mixing them with the dry ingredients. This removed the moisture that would otherwise have leached out during frying, ensuring that the final fritters were light and fluffy but still fully cooked. The cast-iron skillet's deep, straight sides were helpful for shallow-frying the fritters. Flattening the fritters as they fried ensured that the insides were cooked through by the time the exteriors had browned. Apple cider in both the batter and the glaze added to the strong apple flavor. We like the tart flavor of Granny Smith apples in these fritters, but you can also use Empires or Cortlands.

2 Granny Smith apples (6½ ounces each), peeled, cored, halved, and cut into ¼-inch pieces

2 cups (10 ounces) all-purpose flour

⅓ cup (2⅓ ounces) granulated sugar

1 tablespoon baking powder

1 teaspoon salt

1½ teaspoons ground cinnamon

½ teaspoon ground nutmeg

1 cup apple cider

2 large eggs

2 tablespoons unsalted butter, melted and cooled

4 cups peanut or vegetable oil

2 cups (8 ounces) confectioners' sugar

1 Adjust oven rack to middle position and heat oven to 200 degrees. Spread apples in single layer on paper towel–lined baking sheet and thoroughly pat dry with paper towels.

2 Whisk flour, granulated sugar, baking powder, salt, 1 teaspoon cinnamon, and ¼ teaspoon nutmeg together in large bowl. In separate bowl, whisk ¾ cup cider, eggs, and melted butter together until smooth.

Add apples to flour mixture and toss to combine, then stir in cider mixture until incorporated.

3 Set wire rack in rimmed baking sheet and line with triple layer of paper towels. Add oil to 12-inch cast-iron skillet until it measures about ½ inch deep and heat over medium heat to 325 degrees.

4 Using greased ⅓ cup dry measuring cup, carefully scoop out and drop 5 heaping mounds of batter into oil. Press batter lightly with back of spoon to flatten. Fry until deep golden brown, 6 to 8 minutes, flipping fritters halfway through frying. Adjust burner, if necessary, to maintain oil temperature between 300 and 325 degrees. Transfer fritters to prepared rack and keep warm in oven. (Fritters can be kept warm in oven for up to 30 minutes.) Return oil to 325 degrees and repeat with remaining batter.

5 Whisk confectioners' sugar, remaining ½ teaspoon cinnamon, remaining ¼ teaspoon nutmeg, and remaining ¼ cup cider together in bowl until smooth. Drizzle 1 heaping tablespoon glaze over each fritter. Let glaze set for 10 minutes before serving.

GERMAN APPLE PANCAKE

SERVES 4 TO 6

WHY THIS RECIPE WORKS A German apple pancake is a crisp, fluffy, skillet-baked treat full of decadent caramelized apples. The pancake puffs and rises as it bakes, then falls in the center a few minutes after it comes out of the oven, creating a creamy, custardlike center. We used our cast-iron skillet to cook the apples until they were golden brown and perfectly tender before adding the thin, crêpelike batter. Half-and-half imparted richness to the batter while keeping the texture nice and light. Pouring the batter into the already hot pan and preheating the oven to a high temperature (then lowering the temperature when the pancake went in) proved the ideal method to create enough steam to get the pancake to puff up without burning or overcooking. Using a cast-iron skillet helps produce the right texture and height in the pancake. Be ready to serve the pancake as soon as it comes out of the oven as its unique puffy shape sinks within just a few minutes. If you prefer sweeter apples, you can use Braeburns in this recipe. Serve with vanilla ice cream.

¾ cup half-and-half

2 large eggs

1 tablespoon granulated sugar

1 teaspoon vanilla extract

½ teaspoon salt

½ cup (2½ ounces) all-purpose flour

1 tablespoon unsalted butter

1¼ pounds Granny Smith apples, peeled, cored, and sliced ¼ inch thick

¼ cup packed (1¾ ounces) light brown sugar
Confectioners' sugar

1 Adjust oven rack to middle position and heat oven to 500 degrees. Process half-and-half, eggs, granulated sugar, vanilla, and salt in food processor until well combined, about 15 seconds. Add flour and process until thoroughly incorporated and no flour pockets remain, about 30 seconds.

2 Heat 10-inch cast-iron skillet over medium heat for 3 minutes. Melt butter in skillet. Add apples and brown sugar and cook, stirring occasionally, until apples are softened and golden brown, 5 to 10 minutes.

3 Spread apples into even layer in skillet. Quickly pour batter over apples and transfer skillet to oven.

Reduce oven temperature to 425 degrees and bake until pancake is lightly browned around edges and puffed, 10 to 12 minutes, rotating skillet halfway through baking.

4 Using potholders, transfer skillet to wire rack. Dust with confectioners' sugar and slice into wedges. Serve immediately.

CORING APPLES

CORING WITH A CORER
Cut small slice from top and bottom of apple. Hold apple steady and push corer through. Peel and cut apple according to recipe.

CORING WITHOUT A CORER
Cut sides of apple squarely away from core. Cut each piece of apple according to recipe.

POUR-OVER PEACH CAKE

SERVES 6 TO 8

WHY THIS RECIPE WORKS Upside-down cakes are a classic skillet dessert, since the pan helps precook and caramelize the fruit, bringing rich, deep flavor to the dish. A pineapple topping on a basic yellow cake is classic, but we looked to almonds and peaches to jazz things up. The key to a great upside-down cake lies in the balance between the cake and the fruit. Ground almonds contributed great flavor to our cake, and they also added structure to help the cake support the fruit. A simple technique turned out to be the best option for the fruit: We made a caramel in the skillet, then nestled sliced peaches in it across the bottom of the pan. We poured the cake batter over the peaches and baked the cake for 25 minutes; after 10 minutes of cooling we inverted the skillet to reveal golden-brown, caramelized edges and juicy peaches above a sturdy but tender cake. If using frozen peaches, be sure to thaw and drain them before using; otherwise they will produce a mushy cake. Serve with whipped cream.

½ cup sliced almonds, toasted

2 tablespoons unsalted butter, plus 6 tablespoons melted and cooled

1 cup (7 ounces) sugar

Salt

1 pound peaches, halved, pitted, and cut into ¾-inch wedges, or 12 ounces frozen sliced peaches, thawed and drained

1 cup (5 ounces) all-purpose flour

1 teaspoon baking powder

⅛ teaspoon baking soda

⅛ teaspoon ground nutmeg

½ cup whole milk

1 large egg plus 1 large yolk

1 teaspoon grated lemon zest

1 teaspoon vanilla extract

1 Adjust oven rack to middle position and heat oven to 350 degrees. Pulse almonds in food processor until finely ground, about 10 pulses; set aside.

2 Melt 2 tablespoons butter in 10-inch cast-iron skillet over medium heat. Add ¼ cup sugar and pinch salt and cook, whisking constantly, until sugar is melted, smooth, and deep golden brown, 2 to 4 minutes. Off heat, carefully arrange peaches cut side down in tight circle around edge of skillet, overlapping as needed. Arrange remaining peaches in center of skillet.

3 Whisk flour, baking powder, baking soda, nutmeg, ¼ teaspoon salt, and ground almonds together in large bowl. In separate bowl, whisk milk, egg and yolk, lemon zest, vanilla, remaining 6 tablespoons melted butter, and remaining ¾ cup sugar together until smooth. Stir milk mixture into flour mixture until just combined.

4 Pour batter over peaches and spread into even layer. Transfer skillet to oven and bake until cake is golden brown and toothpick inserted into center comes out clean, 25 to 30 minutes, rotating skillet halfway through baking.

5 Using potholders, transfer skillet to wire rack and let cake cool for 10 minutes. Being careful of hot skillet handle, run paring knife around edge of cake to loosen. Place wire rack over skillet, and holding rack tightly, invert cake onto rack and let sit until cake releases itself from skillet, about 1 minute. Place rack over baking sheet to catch drips. Remove skillet; gently scrape off any peaches stuck in skillet and arrange on top of cake. Let cake cool completely, about 1 hour. Serve.

CHOCOLATE-HAZELNUT BREAD PUDDING

SERVES 12

WHY THIS RECIPE WORKS Adding rich chocolate flavor to a traditional bread pudding sounds like a winning proposition, but the reality isn't always so great. It's not as simple as just adding cocoa powder or melted chocolate to an existing recipe; that will give you weak, uneven chocolate flavor and can also compromise the texture of the dish. For truly chocolaty bread pudding we turned to a rich custard made with Nutella spread, plus chocolate chips stirred in with the bread to ensure extra chocolate flavor in every bite. The Nutella gave us excellent chocolate presence plus extra depth and dimension from the hazelnut flavor. We used challah (our top choice for its flavor and texture) that we "staled" in the oven to prevent it from turning soggy when combined with the custard. A combination of brown and granulated sugars sprinkled over the top of the dish gave the baked pudding an appealing crunch. Our cast-iron skillet was the perfect vessel for taking this decadent dessert from oven to table while keeping everything warm and melty.

14 ounces challah, cut into ½-inch pieces

½ cup (3 ounces) semisweet chocolate chips

2 cups heavy cream

2 cups whole milk

9 large egg yolks

1 cup Nutella spread

¾ cup (5¼ ounces) plus 1 tablespoon granulated sugar

4 teaspoons vanilla extract

¾ teaspoon salt

2 tablespoons packed brown sugar

1 Adjust oven racks to upper-middle and lower-middle positions and heat oven to 300 degrees. Spread challah evenly in 2 rimmed baking sheets and bake, stirring occasionally, until golden and crisp, about 25 minutes. Transfer bread to 12-inch cast-iron skillet and let cool slightly.

2 Increase oven temperature to 325 degrees. Stir chocolate chips into cooled bread. Whisk cream, milk, egg yolks, Nutella, ¾ cup granulated sugar, vanilla, and salt together until well combined, then pour mixture evenly over bread. Gently press on top of bread to help it soak up cream mixture. Combine brown sugar and remaining 1 tablespoon granulated sugar in bowl, then sprinkle over top of bread mixture.

3 Transfer skillet to oven and bake until pudding is just set and surface is slightly crisp, 45 to 55 minutes, rotating skillet halfway through baking. Using potholders, transfer skillet to wire rack and let cool for 30 minutes. Serve.

MAKING BREAD PUDDING

To prevent challah from turning soggy in custard, spread challah evenly in 2 rimmed baking sheets and bake, stirring occasionally, until golden and crisp, about 25 minutes.

CHOCOLATE CHIP SKILLET COOKIE

SERVES 8

WHY THIS RECIPE WORKS A cookie in a skillet? We admit this Internet phenom made us skeptical . . . until we tried it. Unlike making a traditional batch of cookies, this treatment doesn't require scooping, baking, and cooling multiple sheets of treats; the whole thing bakes at once in a single skillet. Plus, the hot bottom and tall sides of a well-seasoned cast-iron pan create a great crust on the cookie. And this treat can go straight from the oven to the table for a fun, hands-on dessert—or you can slice it and serve it like a tart for a more elegant presentation. What's not to like? We cut back on butter and chocolate chips from our usual cookie dough recipe to ensure that the skillet cookie remained crisp on the edges and baked through in the middle while staying perfectly chewy. We also increased the baking time to accommodate the giant size, but otherwise this recipe was simpler and faster than baking regular cookies. Top with ice cream for an extra-decadent treat.

12 tablespoons unsalted butter

¾ cup packed (5¼ ounces) dark brown sugar

½ cup (3½ ounces) granulated sugar

2 teaspoons vanilla extract

1 teaspoon salt

1 large egg plus 1 large yolk

1¾ cups (8¾ ounces) all-purpose flour

½ teaspoon baking soda

1 cup (6 ounces) semisweet chocolate chips

1 Adjust oven rack to upper-middle position and heat oven to 375 degrees. Melt 9 tablespoons butter in 12-inch cast-iron skillet over medium heat. Continue to cook, stirring constantly, until butter is dark golden brown, has nutty aroma, and bubbling subsides, about 5 minutes; transfer to large bowl. Stir remaining 3 tablespoons butter into hot butter until completely melted.

2 Whisk brown sugar, granulated sugar, vanilla, and salt into melted butter until smooth. Whisk in egg and yolk until smooth, about 30 seconds. Let mixture sit for 3 minutes, then whisk for 30 seconds. Repeat process of resting and whisking 2 more times until mixture is thick, smooth, and shiny.

3 Whisk flour and baking soda together in separate bowl, then stir flour mixture into butter mixture until just combined, about 1 minute. Stir in chocolate chips, making sure no flour pockets remain.

4 Wipe skillet clean with paper towels. Transfer dough to now-empty skillet and press into even layer with spatula. Transfer skillet to oven and bake until cookie is golden brown and edges are set, about 20 minutes, rotating skillet halfway through baking. Using potholders, transfer skillet to wire rack and let cookie cool for 30 minutes. Slice cookie into wedges and serve.

MAKING A SKILLET COOKIE

To ensure a uniformly baked cookie, transfer dough to skillet and press into even layer with spatula.

HOT FUDGE PUDDING CAKE

SERVES 6 TO 8

WHY THIS RECIPE WORKS Hot fudge pudding cake is a magical dessert; what starts out looking like a child's baking experiment gone wrong turns into a two-layered treat that any adult would eagerly tuck into. First, a fairly standard cake batter is topped with a sugar-cocoa layer, then liquid is poured over the top. As the batter bakes, the cake rises to the top, and what's left behind on the bottom turns into a pudding-style chocolate sauce. Most hot fudge pudding cakes end up looking rich and fudgy but have very little chocolate flavor. To make sure ours delivered on flavor as well as on looks, we used a combination of cocoa powder and bittersweet chocolate to add multiple layers of chocolate flavor. For the puddinglike bottom layer, most recipes we found called for water, but we saw an opportunity to take our dessert to the next level. Using 1 cup of coffee in addition to ½ cup of water gave our pudding cake even deeper flavor (without actually making it taste like coffee). Making this treat in a cast-iron skillet was a no-brainer, since hot fudge pudding cake is meant to be served hot; cast iron does a great job of holding onto heat, so there was no worry that the dessert would cool down before it was time to eat. Serve with whipped cream.

6 tablespoons unsalted butter, cut into 6 pieces

2 ounces bittersweet chocolate, chopped coarse

⅔ cup (2 ounces) unsweetened cocoa powder

¾ cup (3¾ ounces) all-purpose flour

2 teaspoons baking powder

¼ teaspoon salt

⅓ cup packed (2⅓ ounces) light brown sugar

1 cup (7 ounces) granulated sugar

1 cup brewed coffee

½ cup water

⅓ cup whole milk

1 tablespoon vanilla extract

1 large egg yolk

1 Adjust oven rack to middle position and heat oven to 325 degrees. Melt butter, chocolate, and ⅓ cup cocoa together in 10-inch cast-iron skillet over low heat, stirring often, until smooth, 2 to 4 minutes. Set aside to cool slightly.

2 Whisk flour, baking powder, and salt together in bowl. In separate bowl, whisk brown sugar, ⅓ cup granulated sugar, and remaining ⅓ cup cocoa together, breaking up any large clumps of brown sugar with fingers. In third bowl, combine coffee and water.

3 Whisk milk, vanilla, egg yolk, and remaining ⅔ cup granulated sugar into cooled chocolate mixture. Whisk in flour mixture until just combined. Sprinkle brown sugar mixture evenly over top, covering entire surface of batter. Pour coffee mixture gently over brown sugar mixture.

4 Transfer skillet to oven and bake until cake is puffed and bubbling and just beginning to pull away from sides of skillet, about 35 minutes, rotating skillet halfway through baking. Using potholders, transfer skillet to wire rack and let cake cool for 15 minutes. Serve.

CONVERSIONS AND EQUIVALENTS

Some say cooking is a science and an art. We would say that geography has a hand in it, too. Flours and sugars manufactured in the United Kingdom and elsewhere will feel and taste different from those manufactured in the United States. So we cannot promise that the pie crust you bake in Canada or England will taste the same as a pie crust baked in the States, but we can offer guidelines for converting weights and measures. We also recommend that you rely on your instincts when making our recipes. Refer to the visual cues provided. If the pie dough hasn't "come together," as described, you may need to add more water—even if the recipe doesn't tell you to. You be the judge.

The recipes in this book were developed using standard U.S. measures following U.S. government guidelines. The charts below offer equivalents for U.S. and metric measures. All conversions are approximate and have been rounded up or down to the nearest whole number.

EXAMPLE

1 teaspoon = 4.9292 milliliters, rounded up to 5 milliliters

1 ounce = 28.3495 grams, rounded down to 28 grams

VOLUME CONVERSIONS

U.S.	METRIC
1 teaspoon	5 milliliters
2 teaspoons	10 milliliters
1 tablespoon	15 milliliters
2 tablespoons	30 milliliters
¼ cup	59 milliliters
⅓ cup	79 milliliters
½ cup	118 milliliters
¾ cup	177 milliliters
1 cup	237 milliliters
1¼ cups	296 milliliters
1½ cups	355 milliliters
2 cups (1 pint)	473 milliliters
2½ cups	591 milliliters
3 cups	710 milliliters
4 cups (1 quart)	0.946 liter
1.06 quarts	1 liter
4 quarts (1 gallon)	3.8 liters

WEIGHT CONVERSIONS

OUNCES	GRAMS
½	14
¾	21
1	28
1½	43
2	57
2½	71
3	85
3½	99
4	113
4½	128
5	142
6	170
7	198
8	227
9	255
10	283
12	340
16 (1 pound)	454

CONVERSION FOR COMMON BAKING INGREDIENTS

Baking is an exacting science. Because measuring by weight is far more accurate than measuring by volume, and thus more likely to produce reliable results, in our recipes we provide ounce measures in addition to cup measures for many ingredients. Refer to the chart below to convert these measures into grams.

INGREDIENT	OUNCES	GRAMS
Flour		
1 cup all-purpose flour*	5	142
1 cup cake flour	4	113
1 cup whole-wheat flour	5½	156
Sugar		
1 cup granulated (white) sugar	7	198
1 cup packed brown sugar (light or dark)	7	198
1 cup confectioners' sugar	4	113
Cocoa Powder		
1 cup cocoa powder	3	85
Butter†		
4 tablespoons (½ stick, or ¼ cup)	2	57
8 tablespoons (1 stick, or ½ cup)	4	113
16 tablespoons (2 sticks, or 1 cup)	8	227

* U.S. all-purpose flour, the most frequently used flour in this book, does not contain leaveners, as some European flours do. These leavened flours are called self-rising or self-raising. If you are using self-rising flour, take this into consideration before adding leavening to a recipe.

† In the United States, butter is sold both salted and unsalted. We generally recommend unsalted butter. If you are using salted butter, take this into consideration before adding salt to a recipe.

OVEN TEMPERATURES

FAHRENHEIT	CELSIUS	GAS MARK
225	105	¼
250	120	½
275	135	1
300	150	2
325	165	3
350	180	4
375	190	5
400	200	6
425	220	7
450	230	8
475	245	9

CONVERTING TEMPERATURES FROM AN INSTANT-READ THERMOMETER

We include doneness temperatures in many of the recipes in this book. We recommend an instant-read thermometer for the job. Refer to the above table to convert Fahrenheit degrees to Celsius. Or, for temperatures not represented in the chart, use this simple formula:

Subtract 32 degrees from the Fahrenheit reading, then divide the result by 1.8 to find the Celsius reading.

EXAMPLE

"Roast chicken until thighs register 175 degrees."

To convert:

$175°F - 32 = 143°$

$143° ÷ 1.8 = 79.44°C$, rounded down to 79°C

Note: Page references in *italics* indicate recipe photographs.

P

Library of Congress Cataloging-in-Publication Data

Names: America's Test Kitchen (Firm)

Title: Cook it in cast iron : kitchen-tested recipes for the one pan that does it all / by the editors at America's Test Kitchen.

Description: Brookline, Massachusetts : America's Test Kitchen, 2016. | Includes bibliographical references and index.

Identifiers: LCCN 2015037708 | ISBN 9781940352480 (alk. paper)

Subjects: LCSH: Skillet cooking. | LCGFT: Cookbooks.

Classification: LCC TX840.S55 C67 2016 | DDC 641.7/7--dc23

LC record available at http://lccn.loc.gov/2015037708

AMERICA'S TEST KITCHEN

21 Drydock Avenue, Boston, MA 02210

Manufactured in the United States of America

10 9 8

Distributed by Penguin Random House Publisher Services

Tel: 800.733.3000

PICTURED ON FRONT COVER: Classic Roast Chicken with Lemon-Thyme Pan Sauce (page 82)

PICTURED ON BACK COVER: Apple Pie (page 257)

EDITORIAL DIRECTOR, BOOKS: Elizabeth Carduff

EXECUTIVE EDITOR: Lori Galvin

SENIOR EDITORS: Stephanie Pixley and Dan Zuccarello

ASSOCIATE EDITORS: Rachel Greenhaus, Sara Mayer, Sebastian Nava, and Russell Selander

TEST COOKS: Leah Colins and Lawman Johnson

DESIGN DIRECTOR: Greg Galvan

ART DIRECTOR: Carole Goodman

ASSOCIATE ART DIRECTOR: Jen Kanavos Hoffman

PHOTOGRAPHY DIRECTOR: Julie Cote

ASSOCIATE ART DIRECTOR, PHOTOGRAPHY: Steve Klise

SENIOR STAFF PHOTOGRAPHER: Daniel J. van Ackere

ADDITIONAL PHOTOGRAPHY: Keller + Keller and Carl Tremblay

FOOD STYLING: Catrine Kelty, Marie Piraino, Maeve Sheridan, and Sally Staub

PHOTOSHOOT KITCHEN TEAM:

　ASSOCIATE EDITOR: Chris O'Connor

　TEST COOK: Daniel Cellucci

　ASSISTANT TEST COOKS: Allison Berkey and Matthew Fairman

PRODUCTION DIRECTOR: Guy Rochford

SENIOR PRODUCTION MANAGER: Jessica Quirk

PRODUCTION MANAGER: Christine Walsh

IMAGING MANAGER: Lauren Robbins

PRODUCTION AND IMAGING SPECIALISTS: Heather Dube, Sean MacDonald, Dennis Noble, and Jessica Voas

PROJECT MANAGER: Britt Dresser

COPY EDITOR: Barbara Wood

PROOFREADER: Elizabeth Wray Emery

INDEXER: Elizabeth Parson

CHIEF CREATIVE OFFICER: Jack Bishop

EXECUTIVE EDITORIAL DIRECTORS: Julia Collin Davison and Bridget Lancaster